Hawaii's Best Hiking Trails

by Robert Smith

A Hawaiian Outdoor Adventures Publication

FIRST Edition 1982
SECOND Edition 1985
  Second Printing April, 1987
THIRD Edition 1991
FOURTH Edition 1994
FIFTH Edition 1999
SIXTH Edition 2004

Copyright ©1982, 1985, 1991, 1994, 1999, 2004
  by Robert Smith
Maps by Kevin G. Chard
Layout by N. Karakawa
Photos by the author and Diane G. Smith
Cover photo by Diane G. Smith

Library of Congress Card Catalog Number 85-040706
International Standard Book Number 0-924308-11-7
Manufactured in the United States
Published by Hawaiian Outdoor Adventures Publications

Dedication

To Sydne & Mason, Aloha ʻO Tutu Kane iā ʻoe

Acknowledgements

Many people made significant contributions to this book. In Hawaii, I am indebted to Ruth Wryn and Vi Saffery of the Wailuku Public Library and to Gail Bartholomew, librarian at Maui Community College, each of whom cheerfully responded to my numerous requests. A number of Hawaii State officials offered information and expertise. Robert Hobdy, Maui forester; Ralph E. Daehler, Kauai District Forester (retired); and Mac Hori, State Park Supervisor on Kauai (retired) were particularly helpful. A very special "mahalo" to Nobuko Yamada on Maui; Roy, Carol, Shari, Frances and Mac Fujioka on Kauai; and Bonnie Harwick on Oahu for their hospitality. On the Mainland, Fred Samia gave his time and professional advice, and he read the manuscript. Mahalo also to Diane, who shared many trails with me. Lastly, many thanks to Norbert Karakawa for his computer skills and and advice in designing this book.

- Robert Smith
Kula, Maui, Hawaii

CAUTION–WARNING–CAUTION

On Sunday, May 9, 1999 tragedy struck at the base of the waterfall in Sacred Falls State Park on Oahu. A landslide from the near-vertical walls of the valley sent tons of boulders, rocks and dirt onto unsuspecting hikers. Eight persons were killed and dozens injured.

Although thousands of people annually hike throughout the Aloha State without mishap or injury, active outdoorspeople should be aware that landslides in Hawaii are common. Hawaii's strata is extremely brittle and unstable and affected by rain and by periods of drought. Rain can undermine the dirt supporting rocks and boulders and drought can cause the dirt to shrink. During periods of heavy rainfall, flash flooding is common.

Be alert and cautious when hiking particularly in narrow valleys, on ridges and along steep, precipitous cliffs.

The State Department of Land and Natural Resources and private landowners may close access to a trail temporarily or permanently so please respect posted warnings. Failure to do so can result in criminal prosecution.

PLEASE respect "KAPU"
("NO TRESPASSING") signs.

Books by Robert Smith

Hawaii's Best Hiking Trails
Hiking Maui, the Valley Isle
Hiking Oahu, the Capital Isle
Hiking Hawaii, the Big Island
Hiking Kauai, the Garden Isle

Video by Robert Smith

Hawaii on Foot

Contents

Aloha!

Introduction

Hawaii - The 50th State

"I'm not going to Hawaii; it's overcommercialized; it's like Los Angeles with coconut trees." These are statements frequently overheard on the Mainland by people who are unknowing. Admittedly, some of the tourist centers on each of the islands have boomed in recent years, and much sand and open space have been replaced with lumber and concrete in the form of shopping centers, condominiums, hotels, bars, souvenir shops, and the like. However, there remains a nearly pristine Hawaii, a wild and free Hawaii, an alluring and enchanting Hawaii, and an exciting and romantic Hawaii. It's still there, only you have to know where to find it! It is the purpose of this book to reveal some of those places in Hawaii which soothe the body and calm the spirit - those special places, which for sometimes unexplainable reasons have an impact on our lives. But with each discovery there is the responsibility to protect and to preserve - "Hi'ipoi i ka 'aina aloha" (cherish the beloved land).

Millions visit Hawaii annually. Some are looking for the dance halls and night clubs along Kalakaua Avenue on Waikiki, some for the slower, more relaxed pace found on the neighbor islands, and some for the beautiful and simple life in Kalalau or Waimanu Valley. Whatever they seek, they probably find it because they keep coming back to what Mark Twain once described as "the loveliest fleet of islands that lies anchored in any ocean." The "fleet" is made up of 132 islands, although only seven are inhabited and only six may be visited (Niihau is privately owned). A little larger than the state of Connecticut in land area, the 50th state joined the Union in 1959 as the only state where no single ethnic group is in the majority, which accounts for a marvelous blend of races and cultures that serves as an example of relatively harmonious living. Recently, Caucasians became the single largest minority group, followed closely by people of Japanese ancestry, with Hawaiian and part Hawaiian a distant third. Then add the Filipinos, Chinese, Koreans, Blacks, Samoans and a dash of European groups and you have Hawaii - almost. The last ingredient is "aloha" - a word that cannot be defined. Some will say it means "hello" or "goodbye" or "love." But "aloha" is a state of mind; it's a feeling of affection and regard that one person has for another be he longtime friend or malihini (newcomer); it's that inner force that causes one person to care for and to share with friends and strangers alike; it's that spiritual quality that binds "brahs" and visitors; in short, it is "aloha." Don't listen to those who say it no longer exists in Hawaii. It's still there. You're likely to find this spirit of brotherhood in meetings with local people in the tourist shops, on the beach, or on the trail. But remember, it has to be reciprocal.

While Hawaiians are justifiably proud of their aloha spirit, there are other unique and distinguishable characteristics in which they take pride. For example, Hawaii is not only the youngest of the 50 states but also the youngest in terms of creation. It is believed that the islands began to be formed about 25 million years ago by eruptions from a 200-mile fault at the bottom of the Pacific. Geologically speaking, Hawaii is still an infant and is still growing, witnessed by Mauna Loa on the "Big Island," the world's largest active volcano, and by Kilauea, also on the "Big Island," the most active volcano in the world. Additionally, the 50th state boasts the wettest place on the earth (Mt. Waialeale, Kauai, average of 460 inches of rain annually).

Hawaiians boast that theirs is the longest state, stretching 1523 miles from the eastern tip of Hawaii, the Big Island, to the tiny speck known as Kure Atoll. But the most alluring characteristic of Hawaii is the climate. Tropical Hawaii has a combination of cooling trade winds and equable temperatures in the vicinity of 75 degrees. For example, in Honolulu, the highest recorded temperature is 88 degrees and the lowest 57 degrees. The highest temperature ever recorded in the state was 100 degrees. In such a setting, outdoor experiences attract thousands each year.

Safe Hiking in Hawaii

Hiking and backpacking have increased in popularity in recent years in Hawaii not only, I suspect, because they are inexpensive ways to travel but also because they are different ways to experience a place. In Hawaii, outdoor experiences are outstanding; however, the outdoorsperson should be aware of a number of problems. For one, violent actions against hikers and campers, while remaining low in percentage considering the numbers who are taking to the trail, have increased. As any community grows and urban centers develop, the ills of city life, including violence and crime, follow. Consequently, hikers, particularly females are cautioned never to hike or camp alone. As a general rule, the farther you hike and camp away from populated areas, the safer your experience is likely to be. NEVER leave valuables unprotected. I always carry a daypack containing those items that I cannot afford to lose - wallet, airline ticket, camera - and I carry it everywhere.

In 1989, the state Department of Health issued a warning to campers and hikers that portable water filters will not protect them from the dangerous bacterium leptospirosis. Health officials say that only boiling or chemical treatment will control this disease that is found in surface water throughout Hawaii. It enters the body through breaks in the skin or through mucous membranes and can cause flu-like symptoms. The disease can also be fatal.

Portable water filters may protect against giardia, salmonella and other bacteria and parasites, but not leptospirosis. The department's release stated that vigorous boiling is the only reliable method of purification. Tablets containing hydroperiodide will work if boiling is not possible, according to health authorities.

Drinking water is available from streams in many areas, but it should be boiled or treated, since cattle, pigs and goats may share the water supply. To avoid the chance of illness, carry one quart of water per person. In many areas, firewood is at a premium. A small, light, reliable backpacking stove is a convenience and a comfort if you plan to cook out.

Another problem facing the hiker in Hawaii is the lack of trailhead signs and trail markers. Most of the trails contained in this book are well-defined, but many are not marked. Consequently, I provide detailed directions to the trailhead and a trail narrative that makes the trail easy to follow. I have included a wide selection of trips from short, easy family walks to long, difficult hikes and backpacks. Most of the hikes are on public lands where well maintained trails await the hiker. Other hikes are on private land - pineapple and sugar cane holdings - and some are on military reservations. In spite of the time and effort required to secure permission from property owners, I have included these worthy hikes. I have not included areas from which hikers are forbidden by law (protected watershed) or where the terrain is dangerous and unsafe even though local people may boast of their adventures in these places. Each year numerous injuries and some fatalities occur where people have hiked in spite of the prohibition. Good judgment and a regard for the time-tested rules of hiking are good protection.

Hikers and campers are always relieved to learn that there are no poisonous snakes, no poison ivy or poison oak in Hawaii. Poisonous centipedes and scorpions are found at low elevations, however. The two biggest pests in Hawaii are the mosquito and the cockroach. Both are very troublesome and they can make an outdoor experience disagreeable unless precautions are taken. You will have to live with the cockroach, but all of the mosquito lotions and sprays seem to provide effective protection. Due to the wet climate, be prepared to make frequent applications.

In order to ensure a safe and enjoyable experience and to protect the environment, *remember:*

1. Do not hike alone.
2. Leave your route and expected time of return with a reliable person.
3. Research your route. Know where you are going and stay on the trail.
4. Check weather conditions and prepare accordingly.

5. Many Hawaiian trails are wet and slippery, and the terrain is loose and brittle. Wear strong shoes or boots.

6. Carry sufficient water (one quart minimum) or purify water from streams. Dehydration is the major cause of fatigue. Drink plenty of water.

7. Wear bright clothing.

8. Carry first-aid items, a mirror, a flashlight, a whistle, a cell phone and medicine.

9. Carry your own food. Contrary to popular belief, it is not possible to live off the land.

10. Although some fruits are available, never eat or taste unfamiliar fruits or plants.

11. A tent with a rain fly ensures comfortable and dry nights.

12. Firewood in most places is not available or is too wet for use. Carry a stove for cooking.

13. Darkness sets in right after sunset.

14. If lost, find an open area and stay put. Don't panic.

15. During heavy rain, go to high ground. Flash flooding is common in Hawaii.

16. Clean boots of dirt & seeds before hiking.

17. Carry your trash out.

18. Bury personal wastes away from streams.

19. Do washing at least 100 feet away from natural water supply.

20. Respect all species. Do not feed wild animals.

Using this Book

In planning a hike, consult the Hiking Chart in order to give due consideration to driving time, hiking time, and the clothing and supplies necessary. I have rated all the hikes and placed them in one of four categories. A "family" rated hike is for those who are looking for short, easy hikes. The "hardy family" classification requires a degree of effort and sound physical condition. Both the "strenuous" and the "difficult" hikes require a measure of endurance, since they are longer and most of them involve a considerable gain in altitude. They also require good footwear and more equipment.

Obviously, hiking time varies from person to person, depending on such things as pace and the extent to which one chooses to linger for lunch and to swim where pools exist. The time noted in the Hiking Chart is based on a leisurely pace. Trail distance is based either on an exact measurement or on an approximation with the aid of a topographic map.

Elevation gain or loss is cited in the Hiking Chart and preceding each trail narrative when the gain or loss is at least 500 feet. The gain or loss in elevation is from the trailhead or starting point cited in the narrative. On the Hiking Chart, preceding the number of feet, "+" means gain and "-" means loss from the trailhead to trail's end. Where the return trip is over the same trail, a like amount of loss or gain will be encountered. Where an alternative return route may be taken from trail's end, you will need to consult the trail narrative to determine the total elevation gain or loss for your entire trip. When the chart indicates both a "+" and a "-" the trail alternately ascends and descends to the trail's end.

Driving time and mileage cited are based on the posted speed limit and are measured from a major point on each island. Specific driving instructions precede each hike description.

Oahu, Kauai and Hawaii have public transportation systems. For each hike on those islands I have included bus directions to the trailhead if applicable. Use the bus; it is both inexpensive and reliable. If you plan to rent a car for transportation, I suggest that you do not volunteer the information to the rental agency that you are going to hike or camp. Most agencies will not rent vehicles to campers because they are concerned about breakdowns in the backcountry and break-ins at the trailhead.

The equipment noted on the Hiking Chart is minimal for hiking enjoyment. As a rule, however, I always carry water, food and a first-aid kit. Although the choice between tennis shoes and hiking boots for some hikes is listed as optional, I prefer hiking boots in most cases. Obviously, your feet are an important consideration in hiking since it is common on an island that has experienced extensive volcanic activity to have volcanic ash or rock underfoot. Usually, the choice of shorts or long pants is optional, except where the brush is thick or when the weather requires warmer clothing.

Before each hike description you will find the hike rating, trail features, hiking distance and time, specific driving instructions, instructions for getting there by bus and introductory notes. On some hikes it is necessary to walk on private property. Information and addresses are provided so that you can secure permission in advance. Permission is usually readily granted either over the telephone or in person when you sign a liability waiver.

In the trail narrative to add to your enjoyment, I usually mention the flora and fauna to be seen along the trail especially the unusual and the unique. But I don't mention everything, You may wish to buy one of several guides to plants and animals of the islands, available at many local stores.

Preceding each trail narrative is a map that will help you find the trailhead and locate trail highlights. The maps show many features of the hikes as well as campsites. The maps are not to scale.

Camping and Cabins

Take a tent to Hawaii and camp out and you will save half the cost of a vacation in paradise and, if living in the out-of-doors is pleasurable to you, you will have the time of your life. What can be better than inexpensive campgrounds (only Honolulu county campgrounds are free), beach camping with an overnight low temperature in the 70's and sunsets and sunrises that stir the senses?

Avoid camping areas in or near population centers, for in them all the ills of urban living are present such as thievery, vandalism, drunkenness, and the chance of personal injury. DO NOT camp alone and do not leave valuables and equipment unattended or unprotected.

For those who do not wish to camp but wish to keep expenses as low as possible, I suggest that you use the national park and state park housekeeping cabins, which are available on all the islands except Lanai and Molokai and which cost only a few dollars per person per night. However, since the cabins are popular with local people, make reservations early.

Beach camping

In the following pages, I have shown all the national park, state park, county and private campgrounds on the maps. As a general rule, I recommend the national park and state park campgrounds.

Detailed camping and cabin information is provided in the "Camping & Cabins" section of each island.

Food and Equipment

For most day hikes your equipment needs are minimal. Although hiking boots are not essential on some hikes, I prefer them because of the rough lava underfooting in many places and because of exposed tree roots on some trails. Drinking water is available from streams in many areas, but should be boiled because cattle, pigs, rats and goats usually share the water supply. To avoid the chance of illness, I suggest you carry sufficient water. One quart per person for short, 2-3 mile hikes and two quarts for longer hikes is recommended. In many areas, firewood is at a premium; so a small, light, reliable backpacking stove is a convenience and a comfort if you plan to cook out. Most hikers find shorts or cutoffs adequate in areas up to 5,000 feet. Even during the summer, heavy sweaters and jackets are necessary when hiking in higher altitudes. Hats and dark glasses are also necessary for protection from the weather and the glaring sun.

Although food is more expensive in Hawaii than on the mainland, it is readily available in the towns. For day hikes you may visit a local delicatessen that prepares box lunches containing local favorites such as tempura, sweet-and-sour spare ribs and sushi. Visit a local market or roadside stand for mango, papaya, pineapple, passion fruit, and local avocado which comes in the large economy size. Hiking and backpacking stores can be found on Maui, Kauai, Oahu and Hawaii where equipment, fuel, and dehydrated food can be purchased. Some stores also offer rental equipment.

The following equipment is recommended for day hikes.

General Equipment:

- Day pack
- Plastic water bottle, quart size (minimum)
- Shorts or longpants
- Sunscreen
- Whistle for each child
- Hat or sun visor
- Towel
- Flashlight
- Cell phone
- *Hawaii's Best Hiking Trails*
- Hiking boots or strong shoes
- Multiple-purpose knife
- Insect repellent
- Bathing suit
- Sun glasses
- Camera and film
- Poncho or raingear
- Waterproof matches
- First-aid
- Medication

Planning and preparation are particularly important for the backpacker. The following equipment is recommended for overnight hikes and for campers.

Backpack Checklist
General Equipment:

- Frame and pack (exterior frame pack recommended)
- Lightweight sleeping bag / blanket (heavy bag above 4,000 ft)
- Backpack tent with rain fly
- Plastic ground cover
- Sleep pad
- Plastic water bottle, quart size
- Multiple-purpose knife

- Flashlight
- 40 feet of nylon cord
- First-aid kit
- Cell phone

Cooking Gear:
- Backpack stove
- Cooking pots
- Plastic bowl
- Waterproof matches
- Fuel
- Fork and spoon
- Sierra cup

Clothing:
- Poncho or raingear
- Shorts and/or bathing suit
- Undershorts
- Socks
- Sweater/warm jacket above 6,000 feet
- Pants
- Hat or bandana
- T-shirts
- Hiking boots

Toilet Articles:
- Soap (biodegradable)
- Toothbrush/powder-paste
- Comb
- Insect repellent
- Mirror
- Part-roll toilet paper
- Chapstick
- Towel
- Sunscreen

Miscellaneous:
- Sun glasses
- Plastic bags
- *Hawaii's Best Hiking Trails*
- Camera and film
- Fishing gear

Hawaiian Made Easy

For your interest, throughout the text wherever a Hawaiian place name is used, I have provided a literal translation if possible. In many instances, Hawaiian names have multiple meanings and even the experts sometimes disagree over literal meanings. The meanings given here are based on the best information available and on the context in which a name is used. As students of the environment, the Hawaiians had a flair for finding the most expressive words to describe their physical surroundings.

Most visitors are reluctant to try to pronounce Hawaiian words. But with a little practice and a knowledge of some simple rules, you can develop some language skill and add to your Hawaiian experience. Linguists regard Hawaiian as one of the most fluid and melodious languages of the world. There are only 12 letters in the Hawaiian alphabet: five vowels, a, e, i, o, u, and seven consonants, h, k, l, m, n, p, w. Hawaiian is spelled phonetically. Correct pronunciation is easy if you do not try to force English pronunciation onto the Hawaiian language. Vowel sounds are simple: a=ah; e=eh; i=ee; o=oh; and u=oo. Consonant sounds are the same as in English with the exception of w. Rules for w are not adhered to with any consistency by local people. Generally, w is pronounced "w" at the beginning of a word and after a. For example, Waimea is pronounced "Wai-may-ah" and walawala is "wah-lah-wah-lah." Hawaiians also usually pronounce w as "w" when it follows o or u: auwaha is "ah-oo-wah-hah," and hoowali is "hoh-oh-wah-lee." When w is next to the final letter of a word, it is variably pronounced "w" or "v"; Wahiawa is "wah-he-ah-wa," but Hawi is "ha-vee." Listen to the locals for their treatment of this letter. Finally, since the Hawaiian language is not strongly accented, the visitor will probably be understood without employing any accent.

Some common Hawaiian words:

'aina ....land

ali'i ....royalty; chief

aloha............................welcome; love; farewell

aloha nui loa................much love

hale ....house

haole............................foreigner; Caucasian

hapa haole ....part Caucasian

heiau............................pre-Christian temple

hukilau ....fish pull

kahili ....feather standard

kahuna ....priest

kai.................................sea

kama'aina.....................native born

kane ....male

kapu ....keep out

kaukau ....food

keiki ....child

kokua ....help

mahalo ....thanks

makai ....toward the sea

malihini ....newcomer
mele ....song
ohana ....family
'ono ....delicious
'opu ....belly
pali ....cliff
paniolo ....cowboy
pau ....finished
puku ....hole
pupus ....snacks
wahine ....female
wikiwiki ....hurry

Some common Pidgin words:

brah ....brother
da kine ....whatchamacallit
hana hou......................encore; again
howzit?.......................what's happening?
pau hana......................quit work
shaka! ....great!
suck 'em up ....drink up
talk stink.....................use profane words
to da max ....all the way

Hiking Chart

	family	hardy family	strenuous	difficult	distance (miles)	time (hours)	gain/loss (feet)	rain gear	boots	tennis shoes	carry water	take food	swimming	waterfalls	views	historical sites	fruits
Hawaii, The Big Island																	
1. Hawaii Volcanoes National Park Trails																	
Mauna Loa Strip Road Area																	
Mauna Loa Summit				X	19.6	4day	+7015	X	X		X	X			X	X	
Kilauea Caldera Area																	
Kilauea Crater Rim			X		(1.6)	day	±500		X	X		X	X			X	X
Halemaumau			X			3.2	2		X	X		X	X			X	X
Byron Ledge			X		2.5	1.5		X	X		X	X			X	X	
Kilauea Iki			X		2.4	2.5		X	X		X	X			X	X	
Thurston Lava Tube	X				(0.6)	.25					X				X		
Devastation	X				0.5	.25					X				X	X	
Sandalwood	X				0.7	.25					X				X	X	
Sulfur Bank	X				.07	.25					X				X		
Kau Desert Area																	
Keauhou				X	6.8	5	-2500	X	X		X	X	X		X	X	
Hilina Pali				X	8.0	day	-2300		X		X	X			X		
Kau Desert				X	18.9	day	-3000		X		X	X			X	X	
Mauna Iki		X			8.8	5			X		X	X			X	X	
Kalapana Area																	
Puu Loa Petroglyphs		X			1.0	.75					X				X	X	
Naulu		X			2.0	1			X			X	X		X		
Napau			X		7.0	4			X			X	X		X	X	
2. Akaka Falls Trail	X				(0.7)	.5					X			X	X		
3. Kalopa State Park Trails																	
Nature	X				(0.7)	1		X		X							
Kalopa Gulch		X			(2.8)	2		X	X		X						X
4. Waipio/Waimanu Trails																	
Waipio Valley			X		3.0	2	∓900	X	X		X	X	X	X	X	X	X
Waimanu Valley				X	9.0	6	±1200	X	X		X	X	X	X	X	X	X
5. Puako Petroglyphs Trail	X				0.7	.5					X	X				X	
6. Kaloko-Honokohau																	
National Historical Park Trail				X	(4.0)	1			X		X			X	X	X	
7. Captain Cook Mnmt. Trail			X		2.5	2	-1400	X	X		X	X	X		X	X	X
Kauai, The Garden Isle																	
8. Kalalau				X	10.8	day	±2000	X	X		X	X	X	X	X	X	X
9. Powerline Trail			X		13.0	day	±2000	X	X		X	X	X	X	X		X
10. Nonou Mountain Trails																	
East-side		X			2.0	1.5	+1250	X	X		X	X			X	X	
Kuamoo-Nonou		X			1.8	1		X	X		X	X			X	X	
West-side		X			1.5	1	+1000	X	X		X	X			X	X	
11. Keahua Trails																	
Keahua Arboretum	X				0.5	.5					X			X			X
Moalepe		X			2.5	1.5	+700	X	X		X	X			X		X
Kuilau Ridge		X			2.1	1.5	+700	X	X		X	X	X		X		X
12. Waimea Canyon Trails																	
Iliau Nature Loop	X				(0.3)	.25					X				X	X	
Kukui			X		2.5	2	-2200	X	X		X	X	X	X	X		X
Waimea Canyon			X		8.0	day		X	X		X	X	X	X	X		
Koaie Canyon				X	3.0	2	+1000	X	X		X	X	X	X	X	X	X

◯ Loop Hike

Hiking Chart

Trail	family	hardy family	strenuous	difficult	distance (miles)	time (hours)	gain/loss (feet)	rain gear	boots	tennis shoes	carry water	take food	swimming	waterfalls	views	historical sites	fruits
Waialae Canyon			X		0.3	.5		X	X		X	X	X		X		
13. Kokee State Park Trails																	
Halemanu-Kokee		X			1.2	1		X	X		X				X		
Waininiunua		X			0.6	.5		X	X		X	X			X		
Kumuwela		X			0.8	1		X	X		X	X			X		
Puu Ka Ohelo/Berry Flat		X			2.0	1		X			X	X	X				X
Ditch			X		3.5	4		X	X		X	X			X		
Alakai Swamp			X		3.5	3	+500	X	X		X	X			X		
Kawaikoi Stream		X			1.75	1.5		X	X		X		X				X
Poomau Canyon		X			0.3	.25		X	X						X		
Kohua Ridge			X		2.5	3	-800		X		X	X			X		
Mohihi-Waialae				X	3.0	3	+800	X	X		X	X			X		
Kaluapuhi	X				1.0	1		X			X	X	X				X
Nature	X				(0.2)	.25				X							
Milolii Ridge			X		5.0	3	-2200	X	X		X	X			X		
Nualolo			X		3.8	3	-1350	X	X		X	X			X		
Nualolo Cliff			X		2.6	1.5		X	X		X	X			X		
Awaawapuhi			X		3.5	2.5	-1600	X	X		X	X			X		
Kaluapuhi	X				1.0	1		X			X	X	X				X
Pihea			X		3.75	3	±500	X	X		X	X			X		
Cliff	X				0.1	.16		X		X					X		
Canyon			X		1.4	.5	-500	X	X		X	X	X	X	X		
Black Pipe			X		0.4	.5		X	X		X	X					
Lanai, The Pineapple Island																	
14. Munro Trail				X	(18.3)	day	±1400	X	X		X	X			X		X
15. Koloiki Ridge Trail			X		2.5	1		X	X		X	X			X		X
16. Shipwreck Beach Trail	X	X	X	X	1-8	.5-4 hrs				X	X	X	X		X	X	
17. Lanai Fisherman's Trail	X				1.5	1				X		X			X		
Maui, The Valley Isle																	
18. Keanae Arboretum			X		2.3	1.5		X		X	X	X	X	X			X
19. Waianapanapa State Park Trails																	
Airport	X				1.0	1			X			X	X		X		
Hana			X		4.0	3			X			X	X		X	X	
Cave Loop	X				(0.5)	.15				X			X		X		
20. Haleakala National Park Trails (Kipahulu Section)																	
Pipiwai		X			1.83	1.5	+900	X	X		X	X	X	X	X	X	X
Kuloa Loop	X				(1.0)	1						X		X	X	X	
21. Haleakala National Park Trails (Volcano)								X	X		X	X			X	X	
Sliding Sands																	
Lauulu																	
Kaupo					Trail Rating: Difficult												
Silversword Loop					see pp. 198-216												
Halemauu																	
Supply			X		2.5	1.5		X	X		X	X			X		
Hosmer Grove Nature	X				(.05)	.5				X							
22. Skyline Trail			X		8.0	4	-3800	X	X		X	X			X	X	
23. Polipoli Park Trails																	
Redwood			X		1.7	1	-900	X	X		X	X			X	X	X
Tie			X		0.5	.5	-500	X	X		X	X			X	X	

○ Loop Hike

Hiking Chart

#	Trail	difficult	strenuous	hardy family	family	distance (miles)	time (hours)	gain/loss (feet)	rain gear	boots	tennis shoes	carry water	take food	swimming	waterfalls	views	historical sites	fruits
	Plum			X		1.7	1.5		X	X		X	X			X	X	X
	Polipoli				X	0.6	.5		X			X	X			X		
	Haleakala Ridge				X	1.6	1	-600	X	X		X	X			X		
	Boundary		X			4.0	2.5		X	X		X	X			X	X	X
	Waiohuli			X		1.4	1.5	-800	X	X		X	X			X		
	Waiakoa		X			7.0	5	±1800	X	X		X	X			X		
	Waiakoa Loop				X	3.0	2	±500	X	X		X	X			X		
	Mamane				X	1.2	3		X	X		X	X			X		
	Kahua Road		X			3.5	3			X		X	X			X		
24.	Waihee Valley Trail				X	2	1.5				X	X	X	X	X	X	X	X
25.	Waihee Ridge Trail		X			3.0	2	+1600	X	X		X	X		X	X		X
26.	Lahaina Pali Trail		X			5.5	3			X		X	X			X	X	

Molokai, The Friendly Isle

#	Trail	difficult	strenuous	hardy family	family	distance (miles)	time (hours)	gain/loss (feet)	rain gear	boots	tennis shoes	carry water	take food	swimming	waterfalls	views	historical sites	fruits
27.	Halawa Valley Trail				X	2.0	1		X		X	X	X	X	X	X	X	X
28.	Kalaupapa Trail		X			3.0	2	-1600		X		X	X	X		X	X	
29.	Hanalilolilo/Pepeopae Trail		X			1.5	1	+500	X	X		X	X		X	X		X

Oahu, The Gathering Place

#	Trail	difficult	strenuous	hardy family	family	distance (miles)	time (hours)	gain/loss (feet)	rain gear	boots	tennis shoes	carry water	take food	swimming	waterfalls	views	historical sites	fruits
30.	Diamond Head Trail				X	0.7	1	+550			X	X				X	X	
31.	Honolulu Mauka Trail System																	
	Makiki Valley Trails																	
	Kanelole				X	0.7	.5	+500	X		X					X		X
	Maunalaha				X	0.7	.5	+555	X		X					X		X
	Makiki Valley				X	1.1	1		X		X					X		
	Nahuina			X		0.75	.5	+600	X		X					X		
	Moleka			X		0.75	.5		X		X					X		X
	Ualakaa				X	0.6	0.5		X		X					X		
	Tantalus Trails																	
	Manoa Cliffs			X		3.4	2	+500	X		X	X	X			X		X
	Puu Ohia				X	0.75	.5	+500	X		X	X	X			X		X
	Pauoa Flats				X	0.75	.5		X		X					X		
	Nuuanu		X			1.5	1	-1000	X	X		X		X	X	X	X	
	Judd				X	.75	.5				X			X		X		
	Aihualama			X		1.3	1.5		X	X		X	X			X		X
	Manoa Falls				X	0.8	1	+500	X		X			X	X	X		
32.	Hanauma Bay Trail				X	2.0	1.5					X	X	X		X		
33.	Kahana Valley Trail				X	8.0	5				X	X	X	X			X	X
34.	Sacred Falls Trail				X	2.2	1.25		X		X	X	X	X	X			
35.	Hauula Valley Trails																	
	Hauula				X	2.5	1.5	±600	X		X					X		
	Maakua Gulch		X			3.0	3	+1100	X			X	X	X	X			
	Papali				X	2.5	2	±800	X			X	X			X		
36.	Aiea Loop Trail				X	8.0	3		X		X	X	X			X		X
37.	Manana Trails																	
	Waimano Pool				X	1.5	1.5		X	X		X	X	X	X			X
	Manana	X				6.0	4	+1700	X	X		X	X			X	X	X
38.	Kuaokala Trail		X			4.5	4	±800	X			X	X			X		X

◯ Loop Hike

Hawaii
The Big Island

The Island

"Here today, gone tomorrow" is applied or misapplied to a variety of situations. It might well be the motto of the Island of Hawaii. Certainly no other island in the Hawaiian chain and perhaps no other place on earth experience such dramatic and spectacular changes in such short periods of time. The "Big Island" - sometimes the "Orchid Island" or the "Volcano Island" - is the site of Mauna Loa, the world's largest active volcano and the largest single mountain on earth. In addition to Mauna Loa's frequent eruptions, another reason for all the change is the active shield volcano, Kilauea, in whose caldera Pele, the legendary and mischievous goddess of volcanoes, is said to reside. Kilauea, the "drive-in volcano," is a place where volcanic eruptions and lava flows can be viewed safely from an automobile or even more closely on foot.

With every eruption, the spewing lava alters the island in some way. Roads are overcome by the flowing lava, hiking trails are covered by ash or pumice, sometimes homes are destroyed, infrequently lives are lost, and, on occasion, new land is added to the state. For example, during an eruption in 1960, lava flowed into the sea and added 500 acres of land to the east side of the island. Thus, Hawaii was now 500 feet closer to California!

Kilauea Volcano has been erupting along its east rift zone since 1983. Between 1987-89, successive eruptions closed the Chain of Craters Road (March, 1987), destroyed the Wahaula Visitor Center (June, 1989), overran and burned 71 homes, and destroyed Kamoamoa campground and beach. Madame Pele is a very busy lady!

The largest (4038 square miles) of the Hawaiian Islands, Hawaii was formed by the building of five volca-

Hawaii, The Big Island

HAWAII—TRAILHEADS, CAMPING

KEOKEA BEACH PK
KAPAA BEACH PK
WAIMANU VALLEY TRAIL
MAHUKONA BEACH PK
WAIPIO VALLEY TRAIL
SPENCER BEACH PK
WAIMEA
HONOKAA
HAPUNA BEACH STATE PK
KALOPA
STATE PK
TRAILS
LAUPAHOEHOE BEACH PK
PUAKO PETROGLYPHS
TRAIL
MAUNA KEA
STATE PK
KOLEKOLE BEACH PK
KALOKO-HONOKOHAU
NATIONAL HISTORIC PK
TRAIL
WAIKOLOA
HILO
AKAKA
FALLS TR
ONEKAHAKAHA BEACH PK
JAMES KEALOHA BEACH PK
KEAAU
KAILUA
NIAULANI
KAPOHO
CAPTAIN COOK
MONUMENT TRAIL
KONA
MAUNA
LOA
ISSAC HALE BEACH PK
CITY OF REFUGE
NATIONAL HISTORIC PK
VOLCANOES
NATIONAL PK
TRAILS
MACKENZIE STATE PK
HOOKENA BEACH PK
PAHALA
KALAPANA
MILOLII BEACH PK
MANUKA
STATE PK
PUNALUU BEACH PK
WHITTINGTON BEACH PK
NAALEHU
SOUTH POINT

CAMPING
CAMPING
(NO DRINKING WATER)
CABINS
TRAILHEADS
HIGHWAYS
(MAP NOT TO SCALE)

noes. In the north, the now-extinct Kohala volcano is the oldest, rising to 5505 feet. Its peaks have been eroded to deep, precipitous valleys. Hualalai volcano (8271 feet) in the west last erupted in 1801 and is considered dormant. Towering, majestic Mauna Kea volcano dominates central Hawaii and at 13,796 feet is the highest peak on the island. Snow and winter sports are popular on its slopes. The remaining two volcanoes command most of the attention because of frequent volcanic activity. Mauna Loa (13,677 feet) is the world's largest active volcano, and Kilauea, while a mere 4077 feet, has been the site of the most recent eruptions on the island.

Madame Pele's artwork!

Hawaii is about the size of Connecticut, and nearly five times the size of any other island in the chain: 93 miles long, 76 miles wide and 318 miles around. One can drive completely around the island on good surfaced roads, a convenience not found on the other "neighbor" islands - Maui, Kauai, Molokai and Lanai.

Historically, Hawaii is believed to be the first island reached by Polynesian settlers, about A.D. 750. It is the birthplace of Kamehameha the Great, who conquered and united the islands in the late 18th century. It is also the place where Captain James Cook was killed after he "discovered" (1778) the islands and introduced Western culture. However, perhaps the most notable resident is Pele, the goddess of volcanoes, who is said to reside in Halemaumau, Kilauea's fire pit.

Hiking and backpacking on the Big Island have increased in popularity in recent years. Backpacks are conspicuous at airline baggage counters as more and more visitors seek to discover a Hawaii different from the standard tourist fare. Trails here take you to enchanting black sand beaches, across the world's most active volcano, and to the highest peaks - Mauna Loa and Mauna Kea - over 13,000 feet in the 50th state.

Camping and Cabins

Camping out on Hawaii will add a dimension to your visit. Campgrounds on Hawaii range from adequate to good and contain most of the amenities. Compared to the Mainland, camping fees are modest. The camping map locates county, state, and national campgrounds as well as camping shelters and cabins.

Hawaii Volcanoes National Park

Campgrounds in Hawaii Volcanoes National Park are on a first-come, first-served basis. Namakani Paio, the only drive-in campground, is located in the shelter of large eucalyptus trees 3.0 miles from the Park's visitor center. Water, a community shelter and cooking pits are provided. There is a seven-day limit per year, and camping is free. Namakani Paio is a convenient and comfortable campground.

All other national park campgrounds, trail cabins and trail shelters are walk-in facilities. Permits are required for backcountry hiking and camping. Two cabins are located on the trail to the summit of Mauna Loa. Red Hill cabin (10,035 feet) contains 8 bunks and mattresses and Mauna Loa cabin (13,250 feet) contains 12 beds and mattresses. Carry all the necessary equipment to ensure a comfortable and safe trip (See "Food and Equipment" section). Check the availability of water at both cabins when securing your permit. Remember to treat or boil the water.

The Park's three-walled trail shelters at Ka'aha, Halape and Keauhou are simple overnight wilderness facilities. Each has a fire ring and drinking water that should be treated or boiled. The cabin at Kipuka Pepeiao has three beds and mattresses and water that should also be treated or boiled. Check at the information desk at the visitor center for current water levels when you pick up your wilderness hiking permit.

Volcano House, the national park concessionaire, offers inexpensive housekeeping A-frame cabins at the Namakani Paio campground, 3 miles from the visitor center. Each cabin contains a double bed and a bunk bed accommodating a total of four persons priced at $40 per night for 2 ($8 each addl.person). Each cabin has mattresses, linen, soap, a picnic table, outdoor barbecue grill, water and a hot shower in a central washroom. Since the cabins are located at 4,000 feet, it is a good idea to bring an extra blanket or sleeping bag with you even during the summer months. Each cabin is a comfortable accommodation in a heavily wooded area. (See Appendix for address).

State of Hawaii

Camping is allowed in three state parks on the Big Island for a fee of $5 per person, per night. McKenzie State Park is a beach park on the east coast, Manuka is a wayside park on the south side and Kolapa is a mountain park on the north east side of the island. Of the three state parks, Kolapa is the only facility with water. Reservations are accepted and permits may be secured from the Division of State Parks (See Appendix for address).

The state also operates three comfortable and inexpensive cabin facilities on the island. Mauna Kea State Park (Pohakuloa cabins) is located on the Saddle Road, 33 miles from Hilo at an elevation of 6,500 feet. Seven cabins accommodating six people each are available at $45 per person and $5 for each additional person. Each cabin contains bedding, towels, cooking and eating utensils, electricity, electric range, refrigerator, showers, and toilets.

The facilities at Kalopa State Park, 42 miles north of Hilo, contain the same amenities, with a central mess/recreation hall. There are two cabins with two units in each accommodating 1-8 persons in each unit. The cost is $55 per night and $5 for each additional person.

The six A-frame shelters at Hapuna Beach State Park, 65 miles from Hilo, are situated above Hawaii's best beach. Wow! What a spot! The wood and screened shelters are simple, containing one table, two wooden platforms for sleeping (a sleep pad or inflatable mattress is a MUST!), electricity, and a central mess hall with refrigerator and electric range that is shared with shelter users. You must bring your own cooking and eating utensils. Cold water showers and flush toilets are provided. Each shelter sleeps four and costs $20 per night.

The state and federal cabins are the best values in Hawaii and are very popular with locals and visitors. You are advised to write early for reservations. (All addresses are in the Appendix).

County of Hawaii

The County of Hawaii has established a system of beach parks which offer amenities from cold-water showers and drinking water to shelters, tables and firepits (see the camping map, p. 23). Camping is permitted at 13 parks. Samuel Spencer Beach Park on the west side of the island is the most popular of the county campgrounds and is frequently full during the summer months. I like Mahukona and Keokea beach campgrounds (see camping map). Permits are required in all parks and may be secured in person or by writing to the Department of Parks and Recreation. Camping is limited to one week per park during the summer months and two weeks per park at other times. Fees at county parks are $5 per day for adults, $2 ages 13-17 and $1 ages 1-12. Drinking water is available only at Spencer and Keokea parks (see camping map). Addresses for all agencies are in the Appendix.

Hiking

Hiking on the Big Island is an exciting and sometimes spectacular experience because of periodic volcanic activity. Few will dispute that the best trails and the most memorable experiences are to be found in Hawaii Volcanoes National Park. However, some prefer the North Kohala Mountains, with its verdant and precipitous valleys. For the backpacker who is looking for that "dream" unspoiled place, Waimanu provides an outstanding hiking experience, while the challenge of hiking to the two highest points in Hawaii - Mauna Kea and Mauna Loa - is irresistible.

Many places of unique and extraordinary beauty are readily accessible to the novice, to the family, and to the elderly who are looking for short, relatively easy hikes or walks. I recommend strong shoes or hiking boots in the Hawaii Volcanoes National Park because of the rough lava surfaces. Most hikers find shorts or cutoffs adequate in areas up to 5000 feet. Even during the summer, however, warm clothing is necessary when hiking to the summit of Mauna Loa or Mauna Kea, both over 13,000 feet. Because snow and ice are not uncommon most of the year on both peaks, heavy sweaters and jackets are recommended. Hats and dark glasses are also necessary for protection from the weather and the glaring sun.

In 1975 the County of Hawaii began daily public transit service from Hilo to Kona, from Hilo to Hawaii Volcanoes National Park and within Hilo and Kona. Call (808) 961-8744 for current fares and routes.

Hitchhiking is legal, but rides are hard to get, especially in outlying areas.

Hawaii Volcanoes National Park Trails

(Hiking Area No. 1)

Rating: See individual hikes.

Features: Most active volcano in the world, lava flows, national park from sea to summit (13,677 feet), wilderness camping, nene (rare state bird of Hawaii), camping, hiking trails.

Permission: Written permits (free) required for hiking and camping in wilderness areas may be secured at the visitor center in person or by mail. Camping is limited to 7 days per campground per year. Write Superintendent, Hawaii Volcanoes National Park, HI 96718. (808) 985-6000. CAUTION: Before hiking check with park officials regarding current volcanic eruptions and trail conditions and closures. Eruption update from (808) 967-7977. Fee to enter Park.

Hiking Distance and Time: See individual hikes.

Driving Instructions:

From Hilo (30 miles, 1 hour) south on Route 11 to Park Entrance.

From Kona (95 miles, 2 1/2 hours) south on Route 11 to Park Entrance.

Bus Instructions:

From Hilo, one bus, M-F.

From Kona, one bus, M-S.

Call (808) 961-8744 for schedule and fares.

Introductory Notes: Hawaii Volcanoes National Park, established in 1916, includes Kilauea, the most active volcano in the world, and Mauna Loa volcano. Kilauea volcano is 4,077 feet in elevation, while the summit caldera of Mauna Loa presides at 13,677. The park's total land area is 344 square miles - at least that is what it was at the time of this writing. It is no exaggeration to note that this is subject to natural change.

Many visitors to Kilauea are amazed that they can walk to within feet of molten lava. Others are excited by being able to hike within the park from sea level to over 13,000 feet. Still others marvel at the fact that natural forces have added over hundreds of acres of land to the park since 1969. As recently as November 29, 1975, about 13 acres of land were lost as land settled into the sea in the Halape region of the park - the site of a wilderness camping area - as a result of a 7.2-magnitude earthquake and a tsunami (seismic sea wave). The once beautiful lagoon at Halape and hundreds of coconut trees were lost. Yet it is typical of Hawaii that simultaneously about 28 acres of land were added as a result of seaward fault movements. The result was a gain of 15 acres!

Change, change, and still more change is the attraction that draws hikers to the black-sand beaches and the lava-strewn slopes of Hawaii. It is the excitement, the anticipation that one can witness the elemental forces of nature at work close up and still survive. Of course, not everyone does survive. The toll of the November 1975 quake was one hiker killed and another missing and presumed dead. Still more change has been taking place at the time of this writing. Kilauea has been erupting along its east rift since 1983. The result to date has been the closing of the Chain of Craters Road (March 1987) when lava flowed over it in several places; the destruction of the Wahaula Visitor Center (June, 1989), the destruction of 71 homes, and the campground at Kamoamoa overwhelmed by lava. Most exciting, visitors have been able to walk as close to the flowing lava as the heat allows - close enough to roast marshmallows!

For convenience, I have divided the park into four hiking areas. The division is somewhat natural, for each area has some unique characteristics. First, the Mauna Loa Strip Road area has the most difficult hike on the island - the 19.6 mile hike to the summit of Mauna Loa. Second, the Kilauea caldera area is the most popular hiking area. Most of the hikes here are short and easy and perhaps the most exciting, for two trails cross the floors

Watch your step!

of active volcanoes. Third, the Kau Desert area is a hot, arid, somewhat barren area where hiking is strenuous and yet rewarding, for most of the trails cross recent lava flows, while others lead to the coastal wilderness areas of the park. Fourth, the Kalapana area is the area where, in 1969, Madame Pele erupted along a line of fissures southeast of the Kilauea caldera and buried three miles of the Chain of Craters Road, thus isolating the Kalapana section of the park. Subsequent eruptions cut off more of the road. In June 1979 a new Chain of Craters Road was opened, thus completing the so-called Golden Triangle, which enabled a visitor to travel from Hilo to Hawaii Volcanoes National Park without doubling back on the same highway. But then in March, 1987, successive eruptions flowed over the road, thus closing it again, and it remains closed to date. Consequently, the only access to the Kalapana area is from the Kilauea Visitor Center. Hiking trails here take you to some of the best examples of petroglyphs on the island.

Because the hiking surface ranges from hard, crusted lava to soft volcanic ash and cinders, sound hiking boots are recommended for protection and comfort. A poncho is suggested in the Kilauea caldera area, which receives 95 inches of rain annually. Sun protection is essential in all areas.

In planning your hiking in the park, consult the Hiking Chart and the maps in this guide. The former will help you select hikes that fit your interests, time schedule, and physical condition. The maps will reveal connecting trails and combinations of trails to return you to your starting point or to a convenient location for transportation.

Park Camping and Rental Cabins

Campgrounds in Hawaii Volcanoes National Park are on a first-come, first-served basis. Namakani Paio, the only drive-in campground, is located in the shelter of large eucalyptus trees 3.0 miles from the Park's visitor center. Water, a community shelter and cooking pits are provided. There is a seven-day limit per year, and camping is free. Namakani Paio is a convenient and comfortable campground.

All other national park campgrounds, trail cabins and trail shelters are walk-in facilities. Permits are required for backcountry hiking and camping. Two cabins are located on the trail to the summit of Mauna Loa. Red Hill cabin (10,035 feet) contains 8 bunks and mattresses and Mauna Loa cabin (13,250 feet) contains 12 beds and mattresses. Carry all the necessary equipment to ensure a comfortable and safe trip (See "Food and Equipment" section). Check the availability of water at both cabins from the Park Ranger when securing your permit. Remember to treat or boil the water.

The Park's three-walled trail shelters at Ka'aha, Halape and Keauhou are simple overnight wilderness facilities. Each has a fireplace and drinking water that should be treated or boiled. The cabin at Kipuka Pepeiao has three beds and mattresses and water that should also be treated or boiled. Check at the information desk at the visitor center for current water levels when you pick up your wilderness hiking permit.

Volcano House, the national park concessionaire, offers inexpensive housekeeping A-frame cabins at the Namakani Paio campground, 3 miles from the visitor center. Each cabin contains a double bed and a bunk bed accommodating a total of four persons priced at $40 per night for 2 ($8 each addl.person). Each cabin has mattresses, linen, soap, a picnic table, outdoor barbecue grill, water and a hot shower in a central washroom. Since the cabins are located at 4,000 feet, it is a good idea to bring an extra blanket or sleeping bag with you even during the summer months. Each cabin is a comfortable accommodation in a heavily wooded area. (See Appendix for address).

Mauna Loa Strip Road Area

The climb to the summit of Mauna Loa is the most difficult and demanding hike on the island because of the hiking distance and the elevation gain. The ascent should be attempted only after considerable planning and preparation. Bear in mind that even if you take 3 or 4 days, there is a considerable altitude change and mountain sickness is a possibility. Another consideration is hypothermia, which sets in when the body is not able to generate enough heat to keep the vital organs warm. Therefore, even during the summer, carry warm clothing and a warm sleeping bag. The cabins at Red Hill and at the summit are free, but you must sign up with the ranger at the visitor center for their use and for hiking permits. The water at each cabin should be boiled or treated.

You should allow at least two days for the ascent: one day to hike to Red Hill (7.5 miles, 3,373 feet gain), and another day to hike to the summit (12.1 miles, 3,642 feet gain). You will probably find that 4 days are necessary for the round trip unless you are a good hiker in good condition.

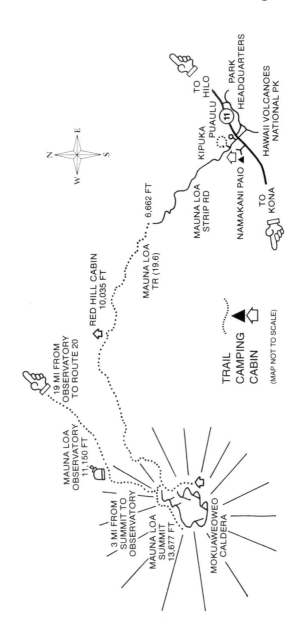

Mauna Loa Summit, 19.6 miles, 3-4 days, 7015-feet gain (trail rating: difficult).

Visitor center to trailhead, 14 miles by car. The Mauna Loa Strip Road, which begins about two miles west of the visitor center off Route 11, though narrow, is paved and well maintained.

Trailhead to Red Hill cabin, 7.5 miles, 3373-feet gain.

Red Hill cabin to summit cabin, 11.6 miles, 3215-feet gain.

Red Hill cabin to summit, 12.1 miles, 3642-feet gain.

On the Trail: The trailhead (6,662 feet) is at the end of the Mauna Loa (lit., "Long Mountain") Strip Road some 14 miles from the Kilauea Visitor Center. There is a parking area and a picnic shelter at road's end. You can hitchhike to this trailhead if you don't have a car.

The excitement of this hike begins immediately. At the trailhead look for the nene (Branta sandvicensis), the state bird of Hawaii. After disappearing, this native goose was reintroduced to Maui in 1962 and has since increased in numbers. It is estimated that about 1,000 nenes survive on Hawaii and Maui. The Park Service has a program to raise goslings and to return them to the wilds in due course. Natural breeding is difficult owing, in part, to a number of introduced predators, such as monogooses, pigs, and feral dogs and cats, for whom the eggs and the young goslings are easy prey. The nene has adapted to its rugged habitat on the rough lava flows far from any standing or running water, and some people suggest that this water fowl is more accurately regarded as a "lava" fowl. The most noticeable anatomical change has been the reduction of webbing between the toes, which better suits its terrestrial life. Its size (22-26") and its variety of muted calls, often resembling the "moo" sound of a cow, make it easy to identify. If you spot a nene, don't be surprised if it walks up to you. It is a very friendly bird, but please do not feed it.

The trail passes through a gate in a fence designed to protect the park from feral goats, whose voracious eating habits tend to destroy the vegetation. Be sure to close the gate. Soon you are above the open ohia (Metrosideros collina) forest at the 8,300-foot level. The bright red blossom of the ohia lehua, the flower of the island of Hawaii, is regarded as sacred to Pele. Legend holds that if a person picks this flower on the way to the mountain, it will rain.

The Red Hill cabin at 10,035 feet is a welcome sight in what is now open country with little growth. It is a comfortable overnight facility and offers a panorama of the island. On a clear day you can see Maui to the north-west and its summit Haleakala - the house of the sun. If you are suffering from altitude sickness - headache and nausea - Red Hill is a good place to lie down with your head lower than your trunk and perhaps take an aspirin. Remember to boil or treat the water.

An early start on the second day will enable you to make a few miles before the hottest part of the day. Your hike to the summit follows the northeast rift of Mauna Loa, where you will find some startling cracks and shapes in the strata caused by recent splatter cones and lava flows. The last eruption along this rift, in 1942, extended over a 2.8-mile area. The lava flowed to within 12 miles of the city of Hilo.

About two miles from the summit, you finally arrive at the North Pit of the great Mokuaweoweo (lit., "fish section" - red part of a fish, which suggests volcanic fires) caldera. The giant Mokuaweoweo caldera is an oval depression 3 miles long, 1 1/2 miles wide, and as deep as 600 feet. The trail to the cabin drops into the caldera and crosses the smooth, flat surface, skirting to the right of Lua Poholo, a deep pit crater formed since 1841. If you haven't fallen into Lua Poholo, the cabin is a short hike up to the rim of Mokuaweoweo. You'll find water at the cabin or ice in a lava crack, a short (1/2 mile) walk southwest of the cabin. Remember to boil or treat the water.

To reach the summit you must return to the junction on the north side of the caldera and follow the ahus (rock cairns) to the 13,680-foot summit. At the summit you are standing on the top of the world's largest active shield volcano and the largest single mountain on earth, when you consider that it rises about 30,000 feet above its base on the ocean floor.

During the eruption of 1949, the floor of Mokuaweoweo caldera was blanketed with new lava. The eruption of Mauna Loa in 1950, the greatest since 1859, was along the southwest rift, with fissures from 11,000 feet down to 8,000 feet. Lava flowed westward and southeastward, and within a day reached the sea. When lava entered the water, it boiled and steam clouds rose 10,000 feet into the air. An estimated billion tons of lava destroyed two dozen buildings and buried a mile of highway. No lives were lost.

The last eruption from the summit caldera occurred on March 25, 1984 and lasted for 21 days. Lava flowed from the summit to 9400 feet along the northeast rift zone. Interestingly, five days later, March 30, 1984, Kilauea Volcano erupted, the first simultaneous eruption of the two in 65 years.

An alternative return off the mountain is via the Observatory Trail. From the s ummit, return along the trail for 1.6 miles to a spur trail that goes northwest (left) for 0.3 mile to the emergency four-wheel-drive road and the Observatory Trail. The trail is on the left side of the road, extending for 3 steep and difficult miles to the Mauna Loa weather observatory at 11,150 feet. Unless you have made arrangements for someone to drive to the observatory to pick you up, it is 19 miles from the observatory to Route 20, and 28 miles on Route 20 to Hilo.

Kilauea Caldera Area

Without question, the Kilauea (lit., "spewing" - referring to eruptions) section of the national park is the most exciting place on the island because dramatic change is so imminent. Like Mauna Loa, Kilauea is a shield volcano with a characteristic broad, gently sloping dome. While the summit is 4,000 feet above sea level, the base of the mountain extends another 16,000 feet to the ocean bottom. The summit caldera, 2 1/2 miles long and 2 miles wide, contains Halemaumau, the "fire pit", which is the legendary home of Pele, the goddess of volcanoes. Halemaumau had an almost continuously active lake of liquid lava throughout the 19th century and the first quarter of the 20th. One commentator in 1826 noted that "the bottom was covered with lava, and the southwest and northern parts of it were one vast flood of burning matter, in a terrific state of ebullition, rolling to and fro its 'fiery surge' and flaming billows....". Today, Kilauea caldera is not as active or quite as romantic, but it continues to provide visitors with some exciting

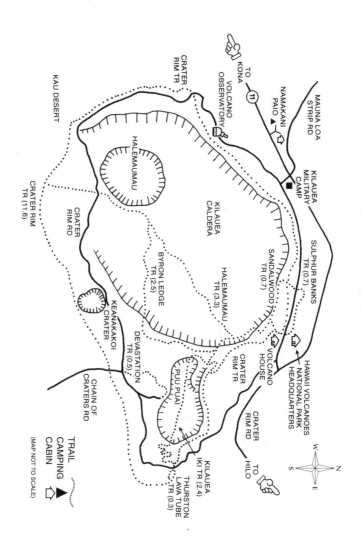

moments and thrilling experiences. Presently, Kilauea has been erupting along its southeast rift about a dozen miles from the caldera since 1983. As a consequence, the Chain of Craters Road was overrun with lava and closed in March, 1987, the Wahaula visitor center was burned in June, 1989, and 71 homes were destroyed over the period. Lava also destroyed several hiking trails and the abandoned Hawaiian village and campground at Kamoamoa.

The Kilauea portion of the park is the most popular hiking area on the island because of the presence of active Kilauea and because of easy access to well-marked hiking trails. In planning your hiking, consult the maps and the text for connecting trails, since most of the trails do not loop. For example, one hike that I would recommend is to take the Halemaumau Trail across Kilauea caldera to the "fire pit," connect with the Byron Ledge Trail to the Kilauea Iki Trail, which ends at the Thurston Lava Tube, and then return to the visitor center via the Crater Rim Trail. This is approximately a 10-mile loop. No special equipment is necessary. However, I recommend a strong, durable pair of boots or shoes, water, sun protection and food.

Crater Rim Trail, 11.6 mile loop, 5-8 hours, 500-feet loss/gain (trail rating: strenuous).

Trailhead at Volcano House.

The best introduction to the Kilauea area is to drive the Crater Rim Road or to hike the Crater Rim Trail, which encircles the caldera. It is a strenuous hike with a 500-feet elevation loss/gain. Plan on the better part of a day to complete the hike. You will want to make some side trips to take in some of the sights and to pause frequently to enjoy the striking panoramas of the volcanic landscape.

On the Trail: Pick up the trail in front of Volcano House and hike counterclockwise (right) in order to pass through the warm Kau Desert in the early morning. The trail initially passes a few steaming vents, which set the mood. At "Steaming Bluff" billowing steam clouds rise from the ground, caused by water getting into the "plumbing" of Kilauea. The steam is accompanied by small amounts of hydrogen sulfide, which smells like rotten eggs. This condition is an eerie introduction to your hike.

The trail continues along the crater rim, passes the Kilauea Military Camp on the opposite side of the road, and climbs slightly up Uwekahuna (lit., "wailing priest") Bluff to the site of the Hawaii Volcano Observatory. From here, scientists have been keeping a watchful eye on Kilauea since 1911, when Dr. Thomas A. Jagger established the observatory. Today, studies continue under the direction of the U.S. Geological Survey. Take time to visit the museum where displays explain the history, culture, and geology of the islands. It is also a good place from which to view Halemaumau and Kilauea and, on a clear day, to admire the striking presence of towering Mauna Loa to the west. This, the highest point on the trail, was once a sacred point for Hawaiians, where offerings were made to the gods.

From the observatory, the trail dips south along the road and then crosses it to the southwest rift of Kilauea and to the trailhead of the Kau Desert region. It was along the southwest rift that an eruption occurred in 1971 which lasted five days and covered an area of 1.3 square miles. A rift is a highly fractured land area on the flank of a volcano along which most of the volcano's eruptions take place.

You might choose to take the Halemaumau Trail to the "fire pit." The fire pit is about a mile off the rim trail across Crater Rim Road to the east side of the caldera (see the Halemaumau Trail , pp. 46-48). If not, you will at least smell the sulfur fumes being emitted by Halemaumau.

The Keanakakoi (lit., "cave of the adzes") Crater marks the beginning of the east rift zone, where in 1974 one of the last major eruptions of Kilauea occurred. During the first part of the year, the Kilauea caldera began to swell, and increased earthquake activity was recorded. Finally in July, rifts opened on the southeastern caldera rim and in the caldera floor, while 200-foot fountains of incandescent lava spurted from fissures. Lava filled Keanakakoi Crater and flowed beyond to cover the Chain of Craters Road.

From here to the fern forest you should find many ohelo (Vaccinium reticulatum) shrubs bearing delectable bright red berries. A small native shrub in the cranberry family, it has many branches with small, rounded, toothed leaves. The berries are edible but sacred to Pele. To avoid Pele's wrath, you should throw half your berries into the fire pit saying,

> *E Pele, here are your ohelos.*
> *I offer some to you.*
> *Some I also eat.*

After crossing the Chain of Craters Road, the trail passes through a sparsely wooded area before entering a thick tree-fern forest. Here you will find some outstanding specimens of Hawaiian tree ferns. The hapuu (Cibotium splendens) is an endemic fern that can reach 16 feet in height. In old Hawaii, hats were made from the stems. The starchy trunk core was used for cooking and for washing. Another endemic tree fern is the amaumau (Sadleria splendens), from which the fire pit Halemaumau (lit., "house of ferns") derives its name. The fronds were used for thatching house frames and for making red dye to color tapa cloth.

Ample rain - about 95 inches annually - sustains this verdant and enchanting forest. The forest is shaded by a canopy of ohia lehua (Metrosideros collina) trees with red powder-puff-like blossoms which were regarded as sacred to Pele. Hawaiians believe that it will rain if the flower is picked.

Crater Rim Trail

The Thurston Lava Tube is a short spur trail off the Crater Rim Trail; it takes you through a 450-foot lava tunnel (see Thurston Lava Tube Trail, pp. 49-50).

Pick up the Crater Rim Trail by crossing the road and the parking lot from the lava tube. The trail follows the edge of Kilauea Iki crater (see the Kilauea Iki Trail description). Kilauea Iki is a pit crater immediately adjacent to the eastern edge of Kilauea caldera. The trail is shaded and cool and offers a number of lookout points with interpretive exhibit cases.

The trail and the road back to Volcano House were closed after the November, 1975 earthquake when some of the ledge fell into the crater and much of the road was severely fractured. The trail and road have since been repaired or rerouted, and it is safe to proceed and to view the power of nature first hand. A short walk will return you to Volcano House.

Halemaumau Trail, 3.3 miles, 2 hours (trail rating: hardy family).

Trailhead at Volcano House.

If your starting point is Volcano House, you might plan a loop trip (consult maps) or arrange to be picked up on the opposite side unless you plan to return across the crater. The hike across the floor is hot and dry, so sun protection and water are important.

On the Trail: The trail begins west (to the right) of the Volcano House and descends through a lush tree-fern forest, passing rocks that have fallen and rolled into the crater. The trail drops about 500 feet, intersecting the Crater Rim Trail, the Sandalwood Trail and the Byron

Ledge Trail before it crosses the floor of the caldera.

Many of the native and introduced plants are identified by markers in the forest, dominated by the ohia lehua tree with its red powder-puff-like blossoms and kahili ginger with its magnificent foot-high yellow blossoms.

As you approach the trail across the lava lake floor of the Kilauea caldera, you may be apprehensive. Knowing that the earth is boiling below your every step can be overwhelming. Consequently, while the hiking is irresistible, you can't wait to finish the hike and to get out of the caldera.

As you approach the rough, brittle, twisted, broken surface, an eerie, somewhat uncomfortable feeling sets in, so that as a piece of lava crumbles underfoot, you swallow hard and breathe a bit more deeply for a moment. The trail is well marked with ahus (rock cairns) and is easy to follow. The shiny black surface of the pahoehoe (smooth and ropy surface) lava sometimes nearly blinds you. The first half mile is fresh lava from a 1974 flow. In fact the trail crosses lava dating from 1885, 1954, 1971 and 1975. See if you can notice the difference.

The caldera has literally had its ups and downs over the years as it has been filled and emptied by successive eruptions. The depth of the caldera changes with almost every eruption as the floor swells and erupts. Some craters fill up and others shrink.

Beyond the junction with the Byron Ledge Trail, the Park Service has constructed a safe viewing overlook into Halemaumau, the "fire pit" and the home of the goddess Pele. Typically, there are steam clouds mixed with hydrogen sulfide, creating an unpleasant "rotten egg" odor. From here you can view the panorama. From left to right, beginning with the summit of Mauna Loa, you'll view the crater rim with the Volcano Observatory, the Steaming Bluffs, Volcano House and Byron Ledge, dividing Kilauea from Kilauea Iki.

The trail continues across the Crater Rim Road to connect with the Crater Rim Trail. However, you may choose to return via the Byron Ledge Trail or the Rim Road.

Byron Ledge Trail, 2.5 miles, 1 1/2 hours (trail rating: strenuous).

Trailhead off Halemaumau Trail.

This is a convenient trail to connect with other trails or to return to the visitor center after hiking the Halemaumau Trail.

On the Trail: From the Halemaumau fire pit, the trail crosses Kilauea caldera eastward and climbs a few hundred feet to Byron Ledge, which separates Kilauea from Kilauea Iki. From the bluff you have views of both craters and of Puu Puai (lit., "gushing hill"), a 400-foot cone of pumice and ash on the south side of Kilauea Iki formed by an eruption in 1959. After the November 1975 earthquake, the ledge trail was closed due to slides on the west wall of Kilauea Iki. In the summer of 1976, Park Service trail crews re-routed the trail, enabling you to hike once again into Kilauea Iki. The fencing here is a project to control wild pigs.

Kilauea Iki Trail, 2.4 miles, 2 1/2 hours (trail rating: strenuous).

Trailhead off Byron Ledge Trail or from Thurston Lava Tube, 3 miles from visitor center to the lava tube by car.

On the Trail: The Kilauea Iki (lit., "little Kilauea") Trail is accessible from Thurston Lava Tube or from Volcano House via the Halemaumau, Byron Ledge, or Crater Rim Trail. From Byron Ledge, the trail descends 400 feet into Kilauea Iki crater. This newly constructed trail was built after slides covered the old trail following the earthquake of November 1975. The trail bisects the crater floor, which is covered with fresh lava from a spectacular 1959 eruption. This eruption, which lasted 36 days, had exploding fountains that reached a record-setting 1,900 feet in height. Cinder, pumice and ash piled up on the crater rim over five feet thick. The devastated area (see Devastation Trail, p. 50) south of the crater was created at this time, while a pool of lava 380 feet deep remained in the crater.

After the trail snakes about 400 feet up the western wall of the crater through an ohia tree-fern forest, it ends in the parking lot at Thurston Lava Tube.

Thurston Lava Tube Trail, 0.3 mile loop, 15 minutes (trail rating: family).

Visitor center to trailhead, 3 miles by car.

This is a short but a "must" trail in the Kilauea section. You can drive to the trailhead via the Crater Rim Road or hike the crater rim clockwise from Volcano House or from the western end of the Kilauea Iki Trail.

On the Trail: The trail to the tube entrance descends through a lush tree-fern rain forest. Many of the plants are identified by marker. Native birds are commonly found here. With luck you may see the small (4 1/2") green and yellow amakihi (Loxops virents) foraging for food, or the vermillion i'iwi (Vestiaria coccinea) with black wings and a long, curved, salmon-colored bill and orange legs.

A metal staircase and bridge allow for an easy entrance and exit from the tube. In addition, electric lights illuminate the tube permitting a safe and comfortable stroll. This prehistoric lava tube was formed when the outer crust of a tongue of flowing lava cooled and solidified while the inner portion continued to flow and eventually emptied the tube, leaving a 450-foot tunnel as high as 20 feet in places.

Devastation Trail, 0.5 miles, 15 minutes (trail rating: family).

Visitor center to trailhead, 4 miles by car.

On the Trail: One of the most photographed and one of the most popular areas in the park, the devastation area was created by a 1959 eruption in Kilauea Iki when 1,900-foot fountains showered the area with ash, pumice and spatter that buried an ohia forest, denuding the trees and leaving their skeletons standing in tribute to the eerie, strangely beautiful effects of Mother Nature. A boardwalk crosses the area to prevent passing feet from creating numerous trails. Today, new growth has altered the landscape so that it is no longer as "devastated" as originally.

Sandalwood Trail, 0.7 miles, 15 minutes (trail rating: family).

Trailhead at Volcano House.

On the Trail: The Sandalwood Trail is one of a number of short, easy trails from the visitor center to scenic overlooks of Kilauea Caldera. The trail begins west (to the right) of Volcano House and gently descends for a hike along the caldera rim to the steam vents at Steaming Bluff. You pass through a rather dense ohia tree-fern forest where many of the plants are identified. A number of steam vents along the trail remind you of the presence of Pele and send off the "rotten egg" smell caused by hydrogen sulfide. You can return to park headquarters via the Crater Rim Trail or loop via the Sulfur Bank Trail.

Sulfur Bank Trail: 0.7 miles, 15 minutes (trail rating: family).

Trailhead at visitors center.

On the Trail: An interesting trail from the visitor center will take you to the sulfur banks, where volcanic fumaroles emit gases that deposit colorful minerals. The glory bush with its pretty, deep-purple blossoms and kahili ginger with its foot-high yellow blossoms flourish along the trail. This is an easy walk and an interesting sight, but the presence of the "rotten egg" smell means you won't linger very long.

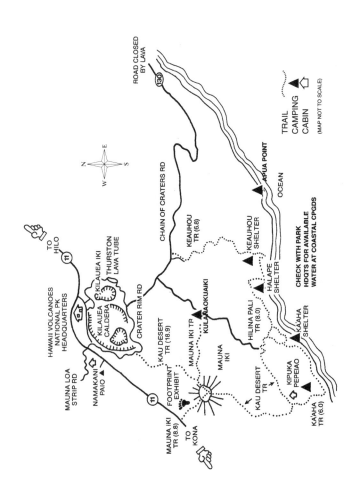

TO
HILO

HAWAII VOLCANOES
NATIONAL PK
HEADQUARTERS

MAUNA LOA
STRIP RD

NAMAKANI
PAIO

KILAUEA IKI
THURSTON
LAVA TUBE

KILAUEA
CALDERA

CRATER RIM RD

ROAD CLOSED
BY LAVA

CHAIN OF CRATERS RD

KEAUHOU
TR (6.8)

APUA POINT

OCEAN

N
W E
S

KAU DESERT
TR (18.9)

MAUNA IKI TR

KULANAOKUAIKI

FOOTPRINT
EXHIBIT

MAUNA IKI (8.8)
TR

TO
KONA

MAUNA
IKI

KAU DESERT
TR

KIPUKA
PEPEIAO

KAAHA
TR (6.0)

HILINA PALI
TR (8.0)

KEAUHOU
SHELTER

HALAPE
SHELTER

KAAHA
SHELTER

**CHECK WITH PARK
HDQTS FOR AVAILABLE
WATER AT COASTAL CPGDS**

TRAIL
CAMPING
CABIN

(MAP NOT TO SCALE)

Kau Desert Area

The Kau (lit., "to place") Desert is indeed just that - a hot, arid, dry, relatively barren and bleak area that composes the southern section of Hawaii Volcanoes National Park. There are no precise boundaries, but the desert region is considered to be all the land south of Kilauea caldera and between Route 11 in the west and the Chain of Craters Road in the east. All the trails here are long and hot, without any guarantee of water. It is an area that tests the hiker and his/her equipment, and perhaps appeals most to those who are seeking solitude. Compared to the other areas of the park, there are no sights to speak of - just a lot of lava, a lot of sun, a lot of stillness, and a lot of sweat!

The Park's three-walled trail shelters at Ka'aha, Halape and Keauhou are simple overnight wilderness facilities with fire rings and drinking water that should be treated or boiled. The cabin at Kipuka Pepeiao has three beds and mattresses and water that should also be treated or boiled. Check at the information desk at the visitor center for current water levels when you pick up your wilderness hiking permit.

Keauhou Trail, 6.8miles, 4 hours, 2500-feet loss (trail rating: difficult).

Visitor center to trailhead, 12 miles by car.

On the Trail: The trailhead is reached by driving south on the Chain of Craters Road past the left turn to Mauna Ulu to a broad expanse of lava from the Mauna Ulu flow to a turnout on the right and the posted trailhead.

This trail is infrequently traveled, which may be a good reason to take it to Keauhou (lit., "new crurrent") Shelter and to the dramatic coastline, an elevation loss of 2,500 feet. It's a long, hot trek, but worth the effort if your looking for solitude. The trail initially traverses open country before reaching low vegetation. Breathtaking views of the coastline and of numerous lava flows along the pali are possible throughout the hike. From the shelter, several trail options are possible to explore the coast or to return to the main road (see map).

Hilina Pali Trail 8 miles to Halape Shelter, 5-7 hours, 2300-feet loss (trail rating: difficult).

Visitor center to trailhead, 17 miles by car.

The Hilina Pali (lit., "struck cliff") Trail begins at the end of the Hilina Pali Road. From the trailhead, the Hilina Pali Trail descends the pali to the Halape Shelter.

On the Trail: The trail southeast from the Hilina Pali Road descends about 2,300 feet to the coast and to the trail shelter at Halape (lit., "crushed missing"). The descent of the pali is a little treacherous, but with some caution it can be negotiated safely. The trail's name is derived from the Hilina Pali Fault, a dramatic example of faulting. A fault is created when a fracture occurs in the earth's crust and the block on one side moves with respect to the block on the other. During the earthquake of November 1975, the south flank of Kilauea slumped seaward along the 15-mile Hilina Pali fault to produce major effects.

After 2.2 miles the trail reaches a junction with the Ka'aha Trail, which goes south 1.6 miles to the Ka'aha Shelter on the coast. From the junction, the Hilina Pali Trail parallals the coast for 4.2 miles before reaching a spur trail to Halape. Remember to treat or boil the water at the shelter. Numerous hiking choices are possible from here (see map).

Kau Desert Trail to Pepeiao Cabin, 9.1 miles, 5 hours, or to Hilina Pali Overlook, 13.9 miles, one day, 3000-feet loss (trail rating: difficult).

Visitor center to trailhead off route 11, 9 miles by car.

To reach the Kau Desert Trail from the trailhead, you must first hike 1.8 miles on the Mauna Iki (lit.,"little mountain") Trail to reach the south branch of the Kau Desert Trail and hike 2.5 on the Mauna Iki Trail to reach the north branch of the Kau Desert trail (see map).

To traverse the entire length of the Kau Desert Trail from Route 11 to the trail cabin at Kipuka Pepeiao requires a stout heart, strong legs and water. This is a long, arid trail that descends about 3,000 feet.

On the Trail: From Route 11, the Mauna Iki Trail passes through a green belt for 1.8 miles before reaching the "Footprints Exhibit" (See Mauna Iki Trail, pp.56-58) and the junction with the south portion of the Kau Desert Trail. At the junction, the Mauna Iki Trail goes 0.7 mile to another junction where the Kau Desert continues for 6.1 miles to join the Chain of Craters Road and the Jaggar Museum. At the junction with the south Kau Desert Trail and the Mauna Iki Trail, you're standing at the foot of Mauna Iki, a lava shield. It's an easy, gradual climb to the summit of Mauna Iki (3,032 feet) from which interesting panoramas of the surrounding area are possible.

The south branch of the Kau Desert Trail descends across relatively barren pahoehoe (smooth and ropy surface) lava. Look in the pukas (holes) for Pele's hair, a thin, golden substance consisting of volcanic glass spun into hairlike strands. It is plentiful on this older lava form, as is Hawaiian "snow", a whitish lichen that is the first thing to grow on new lava. The rest of the trail is an easy descent skirting the Kamakaia (lit., "the fish eye") Hills to Kipuka Pepeiao.

From the cabin, the trail parallels a fault system as it leads to the Hilina Pali Road and Overlook. There are a number of interesting cracks in the earth along the trail which permit you to study a fault system up close. Notice the scars and tears in the pali (cliff) walls where the earth has slipped and has been torn away. From the pali there are dramatic views of the Kau Desert and the coast.

Mauna Iki Trail, 8.8 miles, 5 hours (trail rating: strenuous).

Visitor center to trailhead, 9 miles by car.

Crossing the Kau Desert east-west, the Mauna Iki (lit., "little mountain") Trail connects the Hilina Pali Road and Route 11 and bisects the Kau Desert Trail. The trail also leads to the "footprints exhibit". This convenient trail enables the visitor to cut hiking distance and time to points of interest in the desert.

On the Trial: From Route 11, it is an easy 1.8 mile hike to the junction with the Kau Desert Trail and the footprints exhibit. It is in this locale that armies assembled in 1790 to do battle for control of the island. The armies opposing Kamehameha the Great were overcome by the fumes and dust and overwhelmed by the fast moving lava from Halemaumau. Their footprints were left in the hardening ash. Some believe that Pele interceded to assist Kamehameha.

Some of the footprints were placed under a glass casing several years ago. Since, moisture within the case degraded the footprints to the point that they are not easily identifiable as such.

The trail continues to the top of Mauna Iki (3,032 feet) and to a junction with the Kau Desert Trail. The trail is well-defined by rock cairns. Some of the lava is from the flows of 1971. Indeed, Mauna Iki is geologically an infant, having been formed in 1920. It is a satellite shield volcano built by lava flows from Halemaumau. There are countless cracks in the area that are part of the southwest rift of Kilauea. It is a fascinating place to investigate, but do so with caution.

From Mauna Iki, the trail goes north 0.7-mile to a junction with the Kau Desert Trail. The Mauna Iki Trail goes right (east) from that junction, traversing the desert to the Hilina Pali Road. Along this trail you can find handfuls of Pele's hair: thin, golden, spun volcanic glass in hairlike strands. It is also a good chance to examine and to photograph outstanding examples of pahoehoe feet and toes where the lava has naturally flowed to form footlike shapes. Additionally, you will find lava rivers, numerous pit craters and small cinder cones.

As you approach a low scrub area, the trail is not distinguishable, but if you continue due east you can't miss the road and trail's end. From here, it is about 1 mile to Kipuka Nene, 4 miles to the Chain of Craters Road and 10 1/2 miles to the visitor center.

Kalapana Area

The forces of nature isolated the southern section of Hawaii Volcanoes National Park between 1969 and 1979. Beginning in 1969, a series of eruptions from Kilauea covered miles of the road connecting the Kilauea Visitor Center with the Kalapana area. For 10 years it was a 55-mile drive from the Kilauea center to the Wahaula Visitor Center on Route 13. In 1979, the Chain of Craters road was

Hot foot - Hawaiian style!

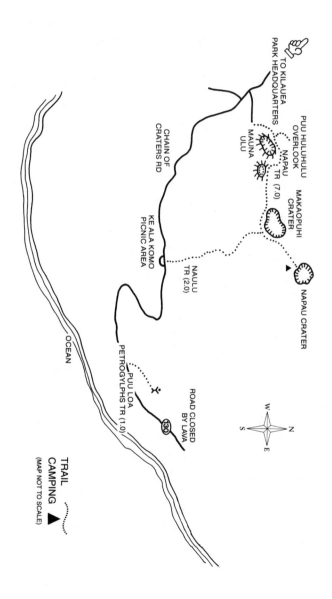

rebuilt and reopened, enabling visitors to drive from the center of the park to the southern section. It was a scenic and pleasant ride of 32 miles. But then in 1983, Kilauea erupted along its east rift causing considerable damage to property and, in 1987, it overran the Chain of Craters Road thus closing it once again. Since 1983, lava has destroyed the Wahaula Visitor Center in Kalapana and destroyed 71 homes. Lava flows in the 90s have destroyed the Kamoamoa Trail and Campground and closed the Kalapana Trail.

Check in at the visitor center for current conditions and volcanic activity.

Puu Loa Petroglyphs Trail, 1.0 mile, 3/4 hour (trail rating: hardy family).

Visitor center to trailhead, 26 miles.

On the Trail: The trailhead is marked by a road sign 26 miles east of the Kilauea Visitor Center. The trail to the Puu Loa (lit., "long-hill") Petroglyphs is marked and well-worn as it crosses pahoehoe lava, which has a smooth and ropy surface, unlike aa lava, which has a rough, clinkery surface. The view upcountry from the trail offers a panorama of the Kilauea eruptions of 1969 through 1972, which flowed to the sea and covered much of the Chain of Craters Road.

You will find the petroglyphs on mounds. There are hundreds, in varying sizes and shapes. There are dots, dashes, lines and bars as well as some figures that are somewhat indistinguishable. Holes in the lava (pukas) were receptacles in which ancient Hawaiians placed the umbilical cords of their children to insure a long life.

Recently, a boardwalk was erected to reduce damage to the petroglyphs. Please protect this interesting and valuable place.

Naulu Trail, 2 miles, 1 hour (trail rating: hardy family).

The trail may be closed by active lava flows. Check at the visitor center.

Visitor center to trailhead, 14 miles by car.

The Naulu (lit., "the groves") trailhead is located on the north side of the Chain of Craters Road 14 miles from the Kilauea Visitor Center. Until the lava flows of 1972 Naulu was a popular forest and picnic area.

On the Trail: The trail begins opposite a turnout along the Chain of Craters Road, Ke Ala Komo (lit., "entrance path"), where there was once a populous village. The first 0.2 mile of the trail, over rough aa lava, parallels the road until it emerges on a 1971 pahoehoe lava flow from Mauna Ulu. Since Naulu is a newly established trail, the lava is not worn, so it is necessary to follow the ahus, or stone piles, as you make your way north. There is no shelter or shade from the hot sun, nor any water. On the right and front right, numerous trees and a variety of scrub have survived successive lava flows. After the first mile the summit of Mauna Ulu comes into view on the front left. Near the end of the trail you reach the remains of the old Chain of Craters Road. Follow the road northwest (left) for a short distance to a junction with the Kalapana Trail, which joins the Napau Trail after 1.2 miles.

Napau Trail, 7 miles, 4 hours
(trail rating: strenuous).

Visitor center to trailhead, 8 miles by car.

(Park maps and a trailhead sign indicate that the first 1.5 miles is known as the Puu Huluhulu Trail).

On the Trail: The first mile of the trail is flat as it crosses over a mix of pahoehoe and a'a lava and through an island of greenery. This phenomenon is called a "kipuka," an area in a forest that has been ringed by successive flows of lava. These island gardens represent the interplay of geological and biological forces. Some believe that Madame Pele, the goddess of volcanoes, spares these places from lava flows so that the birds and other animals can find sanctuary.

Look for some startling shapes formed by the pahoehoe (smooth and ropy surface) lava that are found along the entire length of the trail. These tree-like shapes called "lava trees" were formed when streams of lava engulfed ohia trees. The moisture in the trees caused the lava to cool rapidly, leaving tree-shaped shells. Some are 8-10 feet high. Search the pukas (holes) in the "trees" for "Pele's hair," a golden, hairlike substance consisting of volcanic glass spun in gossamer form.

To the right of the trail, stands a newly built shield volcano, Mauna Ulu (lit., "growing mountain"). Major eruptions broke out along the east rift of Kilauea in 1969, with fountains spewing forth along a fissure that paralleled the Chain of Craters Road. By June 1969 repeated flows and the accumulation of spatter and cinder had built a gently sloping, shield-shaped cone more than a mile across and 400 feet high. Thus was Mauna Ulu born. Subsequent flows filled some nearby craters and covered parts of the road.

After 1.5 miles, the trail passes the gently sloping flanks of Puu Huluhulu (lit., "shaggy hill"), a prehistoric cinder and spatter cone. A spur trail on the left (north) leads to the summit of Puu Huluhulu from which startling views of Mauna Ulu and Puu O'o are possible. The latter is the site of many of the recent eruptions.

From Puu Huluhulu, the Napau (lit., "the endings") Trail continues for 5.5 miles to the Napau Crater. The trail passes north of Alae (lit., "mudhen"), a pit crater created in 1969. In that year, successive eruptions and lava flows from both Alae and Mauna Ulu alternately filled and emptied Alae Crater. It's an exciting and interesting spot.

From near Alae the trail gently descends about 3 miles to a junction with the Kalapana Trail near Makaopuhi (lit., "eye of eel") Crater, which is a crater second in size only to Kilauea. Recent eruptions (1965, 1969) from fissures on the flanks of Makaopuhi (part of the east rift zone of Kilauea) have created havoc and change; the most notable was the destruction of the Chain of Craters Road. From the Napau/Makaopuhi junction, it is two miles to Napau Crater. Not unlike its neighbors, Napau has been active in recent years. Its most dramatic contribution came in 1965 when lava from the crater created a forest of tree molds. This is another interesting place to examine.

Camping is permitted at Napau campground, but be certain to secure a permit and to check conditions at the visitor center.

CAUTION; Remember, even low concentrations of volcanic fumes can irritate your eyes and throat and high amounts can cause heart failure.

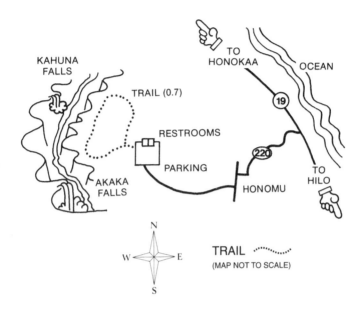

Akaka Falls Trail
(Hiking Area No. 2)

Rating: Family.

Features: 420-foot Akaka Falls, Kahuna Falls, native and introduced flora.

Permission: None.

Hiking Distance and Time: 0.7 mile loop, 1/2 hour.

Driving Instructions:

From Hilo (15 miles, 3/4 hour) north on Route 19, left on Route 220 to end.

From Kona (87 miles, 2 1/2 hours) north on Route 19, right on Route 220 to end.

Introductory Notes: Few dispute that Akaka (lit., "clearness") Falls State Park is everyone's idea of what Hawaii is all about. It is a 66-acre tropical paradise in a canyon park where all of nature's riches seem larger than life. Everything - the ti, the ginger, the bamboo, the tree ferns, the orchids, the azaleas - comes in the large economy size!

On the Trail: A paved trail descends abruptly from the parking lot and thrusts the hiker immediately into the canyon, where a large variety of tropical plants greets one. A guide to Hawaiian flora such as the one by Dorothy and Bob Hargreaves, "*Hawaiian Blossoms*" is a handy booklet to help you identify the many varieties of plants.

Giant bamboo dominates the first part of the trail. Bamboo has long been an important product on the islands, having been used for fuel, furniture, buildings, musical instruments, utensils and paper. Indeed, bamboo sprouts are commonly eaten as a vegetable on the islands.

Your nose will identify the delicately fragrant yellow ginger (Zingiber zerumbet) before you see it. It has a light-yellow blossom that rises at the end of a narrow tube with olive-colored bracts. The leaves are a luxuriant green. You will also find giant torch ginger, red ginger, and shell ginger, with its shell-like flowers. The blossom of the torch ginger (Phaeomeria magnifica) is made up of many bracts shaped like a torch which spring up between 15-foot bamboo-like stalks with large, bright-green leaf blades. Ti (Cordyline terminalis), which is also quite abundant here, is often seen gracing the hips of hula dancers. Although some girls have switched to a plastic material, purists continue to slit ti leaves and fashion them into a skirt. This green leaf plant grows straight and

Kahili ginger

tall (5-8 feet) with very shiny, thick and strong 2-3 foot blades. And there's more: banana, plumeria, ohia lehua, a variety of hibiscus (the Hawaii state flower), bird of paradise, gardenia, heliconia and azalea, to cite a partial list.

At about midpoint on the trail an overlook offers a spectacular view of Kahuna (lit., "the hidden one") Falls across the canyon on the north side. Farther up the canyon, however, is the showpiece of the park. Towering, 420-foot Akaka Falls slips over the ridge and falls lazily into Kolekole (lit., "raw, scarred") Stream, where it nourishes nature's lush gardens. Seeing it across the verdant canyon is a breathless moment in an exciting forest.

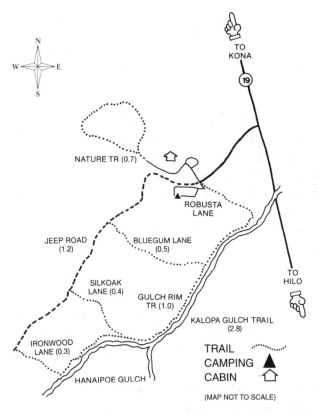

NATURE TR (0.7)

ROBUSTA LANE

JEEP ROAD (1.2)

BLUEGUM LANE (0.5)

SILKOAK LANE (0.4)

GULCH RIM TR (1.0)

KALOPA GULCH TRAIL (2.8)

IRONWOOD LANE (0.3)

HANAIPOE GULCH

TO KONA

TO HILO

TRAIL

CAMPING

CABIN

(MAP NOT TO SCALE)

Kalopa State Park Trails

(Hiking Area No. 3)

Rating: Hardy Family.

Features: Native and introduced flora and fauna, rental cabins and camping.

Permission: None. (Rental cabins and camping permits from Division of State Parks - See Appendix).

Hiking Distance and Time: See individual hikes.
Driving Instructions:
From Hilo (42 miles, 1 hour) north on Route 19, left past 39 mile marker at sign "Kalopa State Park." Follow signs to park.
From Kona (61 miles, 1 1/2 hours) north on Route 19, right at sign "Kalopa State Park." Follow signs to park.
Introductory Notes: Kalopa (lit., "the tenant farmer") State Park offers the visitor not only several enjoyable hiking trails but also comfortable, inexpensive accommodations. Rental cabins (see "Camping" and "Appendix" sections for details) are available for a few persons or for a large group and a campground is located near the cabins. In addition, trail guides are available at the trailheads that detail the flora and fauna. The only shortcoming is the 90 inches of annual rainfall making Kalopa a wet place year round. The state park contains 100 acres of native Hawaiian rain forest and 515 acres of introduced timber species. About 95% of the 2500 native Hawaiian plants are endemic (found no place else in the world).

Nature Trail, 0.7 mile loop, 1 hour (trail rating: family).

The trail guide available at the trailhead provides information and facts about 24 posted stations along the trail. You'll hear and see several native and introduced birds in the forest. If you walk slowly and speak in a low voice, you're more likely to hear them and see them closeup. I recommend *Hawaii's Birds,* published by the Audubon Society, as a companion guide to the park service pamphlet.

Any hike through a true Hawaiian rain forest is a delight. You will find a flat, clear, well-defined trail that is suited for persons of all ages. Many native trees flourish in the forest, but the ohia and kopiko dominate. Ohia (Metrodideros collina) - post #15 - can grow to 80 feet and, when in bloom, its lovely red, pompom-like flowers attract native birds, bees and butterflies. The flowers are a favorite of Madame Pele - the goddess of volcanoes - and it is believed that if they are picked on the way to the mountains she will envelop the visitor in a cloud of mist. However, according to legend, the flowers may be picked on the way out of the forest without danger.

Kopiko (Psychotria hawaiiensis) - also found at post #15 - forms a tall shrub or small tree and bears shiny oblong leaves with white flowers and tiny orange fruit. The kolea (Myrsine lessertiana) is my favorite tree in the forest - a native whose bright pink leaves in young stages gets your attention.

On my last visit here, I saw numerous kalij (Lophura leucomelana) pheasants, hens and chicks, that were introduced to Hawaii from Nepal as a game bird, although they are protected in the park. It is a brown to black bird that has flourished here. You should also see the native elepaio (Chasiempis sandwichensis) a tiny (5 1/2 inches) bird with a loud whistle and chirping voice and a tail in right angle to its body. The body is white and brown with a white rump and dark tail. With luck, you may see the io, or Hawaiian hawk, the only large native bird in the forest. This endangered bird - only a few hundred in the world - with a dark body and streaked underparts, has been sighted in the forest.

Kalopa Gulch Trail, 2.8 mile loop, 2 hours (trail rating: hardy family).

Before hiking, be certain to secure a trail guide found at a display in the parking lot near the cabins. It's an easy, delightful, loop hike for the whole family whose length can be shortened by following one of the tie trails - Bluegum Lane or Silkoak Lane - (see map). The trail is clear, taped and posted.

You can begin your hike from several places, but I prefer starting where Robusta Lane joins the park road near the entrance, because the trail makes a gradual ascent along the gulch and then descends the jeep road at the end of the trek. The initial part of the trail passes through stately groves of eucalyptus and later silk oak, paperbark, ironwood, and tropical ash. Most of the these trees were planted by the Civilian Conservation Corps for erosion control in the 1930's.

Turn right (south) when Robusta Lane meets the Gulch Trail, which follows Kalopa Gulch for one mile. A short distance from the junction you will cross a small gulch and then meet the junction with Bluegum Lane. Along the trail, look for guava and thimbleberries that make a tasty snack. Guava (Psidium guajava) is a yellow, lemon-sized fruit that contains five times the amount of vitamin C than an orange. Thimbleberries (Rubus rosaefolius) are red and grow on a low, thorny bush with white flowers.

There are a few clearings which provide views into Kalopa Gulch from the trail, but the heavy growth prohibits a clear view. Before reaching Silkoak Lane, Kalopa Gulch swings left and the trail turns right and follows Hanaipoe Gulch until it meets Ironwood Lane just inside the park. The latter trail parallels pasture land until it joins the jeep road, which leads to the trailhead completing the hiking loop. Be careful walking the jeep road which can be very slippery when wet.

Waipio / Waimanu Trails
(Hiking Area No. 4)

Rating: See individual hikes.

Features: Ancient Hawaiian settlement, native and introduced flora and fauna, wilderness camping, mountain apple, rose apple, swimming.

Permission: None.

Hiking Distance and Time: See individual hikes.

Driving Instructions:

From Hilo (50 miles, 1 1/2 hours) north on Route 19, right on Route 240, to end of road at Waipio Lookout.

From Kona (65 miles, 2 hours) north on Route 19, left on Route 240 to end of road at Waipio Lookout.

Introductory Notes: When outdoorsmen talk about hiking in Hawaii, they talk about the Kalalau Trail on Kauai, Haleakala Volcano on Maui, and Waipio and Waimanu Valleys on Hawaii. These are the ultimate in wilderness experiences in Hawaii.

Historically, Waipio and Waimanu Valleys were important centers of Hawaiian civilization, particularly Waipio (lit., "curved water"), the larger of the two. Fertile soil and ample water reportedly sustained as many as 50,000 people before the white man arrived. In the past, sugar cane, taro and bananas carpeted this six-mile valley.

In 1823 the first white men visited Waipio and found a thriving community. They were told that Waipio was once a favorite place of Hawaiian royalty; indeed, in 1780, Kamehameha is reported to have received there his war god, who singled him out as the future ruler of the islands. Later, Chinese immigrants came to Waipio, where they cultivated rice until the 1930's.

Today Waipio's population has declined to a few dozen, but taro continues to be an important crop. Most of the farmers now live in towns on the plateau east of the valley, where electricity and other amenities are more readily available. Periodic tsunamis - tidal waves - and seasonal flooding have also discouraged permanent settlement. However, some people are returning to their ancestral homes upon retirement.

Guided tours of the valley are available in four-wheel drive vehicles. (It is impossible for a conventional car to negotiate the 26%-grade jeep road into the valley.) Arrangements can be made at the lookout when you arrive.

Waimanu (lit., "bird water") Valley is not as deep or as wide as Waipio. Nevertheless, this verdant valley once sustained a sizable population, as evidenced by the stone walls and terraces that remain.

Waipio Valley Trail, 3 miles to falls, 2 hours, 900-feet loss/gain (trail rating: strenuous).

The trailhead is at the pavilion, a 900-feet high perch providing a striking panorama of Waipio Valley. Your eye can easily follow the trail to Waimanu, which snakes up the northwest bluff and to numerous waterfalls that drop into Waipio from the Kohala Mountains.

Carry as much water as you can, since safe drinking water is not available. Water in the valley irrigates farms and serves cattle which graze in the Kohala Mountains. To be on the safe side, use purification tablets or boil your water.

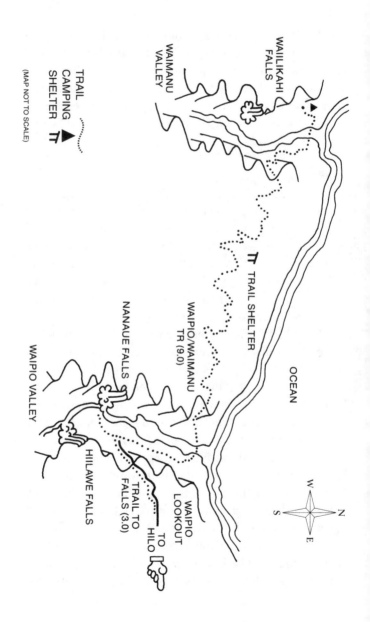

WAIILIKAHI
FALLS

WAIMANU
VALLEY

TRAIL
CAMPING
SHELTER

(MAP NOT TO SCALE)

Π TRAIL SHELTER

NANAUE FALLS

WAIPIO/WAIMANU
TR (9.0)

WAIPIO VALLEY

OCEAN

HIILAWE FALLS

WAIPIO
LOOKOUT

TRAIL TO
FALLS (3.0)

TO
HILO

N
W   E
S

The paved jeep road from the pavillion drops an abrupt mile into the valley to a junction where one road turns toward the beach and another into the valley. Walk cautiously on this narrow, steep, 26% grade road, and be alert to vehicles passing. As you pause in your descent, look for yellow guava (Psidium guajava), some within reach of the road. The yellow, lemon-sized fruit is a tasty treat.

To the Beach: Once on the valley floor, the beach road on the right passes some homesteads along Lalakea (a kind of shark) Fishpond on its way to the gray sand beach. It is common to find locals pushing and dragging their outriggers on Wailoa (lit., "long water") Stream to the open sea for a day of fishing. Note how they use the undulations of the surf to carry them over the rock-laden outlet, and conversely to beach their craft.

The thick, silky, green leaves of beach naupaka (Scaevola frutescens) greet the hiker on the beach. A common sight on most of Hawaii's beaches, the naupaka is a native variety that may grow to ten feet. It has a small, fragrant, white, half flower with small white berries following the flowers. There are several legends surrounding the naupaka flower. One claims that lovers were separated leaving half a flower, the young boy, blooming alone in the mountains, and the other half flower, the girl, blossoming alone on the beach. If a whole flower is found on either the beach naupaka or the mountain naupaka, it means the couple has been united. Another legend, recounts the story of the young prince who wished to marry a commoner. The king interviewed the young woman inquiring as to her family background and her virginity.

The king was skeptical about the latter, so he charged his son and the girl to search the beach and the mountains for a whole flower on the naupaka, since it was the belief that a virgin could find a whole flower. Legend holds that the pair are still looking! Perhaps you can find one!

Ford Wailoa Stream where it enters the ocean and scout the beach for a picnic spot. The ironwood (Casuarina equisetifolia) trees that front the beach provide an umbrella from the hot sun and the rain. Also known as the Australian Pine, the ironwood has long, thin, drooping, dull-green needles whose droppings make a soft mat for a sleeping bag but are a fire danger. Approach ocean swimming with extreme caution: there is a strong surf with riptides.

Into the Valley: To explore Waipio, return to the road junction and follow the road into the valley. You will be walking along the stream and toward Hiilawe (lit., "lift-carry") Falls. The falls may not be "turned on" since the stream that feeds it is used for irrigation and the water is frequently taken out above the falls. The road turns to cut across the valley. You pass the ruins of houses, destroyed by a devastating tidal wave, and some newly constructed homes. The U.S. Peace Corps once trained near here, but flooding in November, 1979 destroyed the abandoned buildings that had served for training recruits destined for Asia. After fording several small streams, you approach Nanaue Falls on the north side of the valley.

When you are about one-fourth mile from the falls, you will reach a stream, a parking area, and a road that goes left. Follow the road until you reach the stream, cross it and follow the road which soon becomes a path leading to the base of the falls.

Please respect "Kapu" (No Trespassing) signs if you try to get to the falls. There is no reliable trail but with a willingness to get wet, you can find your way to this delightful spot to picnic and to swim.

Remember that annual flooding in Waipio destroys roads and changes the flow of streams so that my description may not be applicable. But scout around and find a way to the falls. Nanaue is really a series of falls, some with generous swimming holes at their bases. You have to climb around a bit to find the larger and deeper pools. Use CAUTION if you climb above the lowest fall. It is extremely wet and slippery.

There are numerous cardinals (Richmondena cardinalis) in the valley, which flush from the trees as you make your way. The male, with its all-red body and its pointed crest, and the black-and-red female were introduced from the mainland. Avocado, mountain apple, and yellow guava trees flourish in the valley, but respect the posted "kapu" signs. There are some trees as well as passion fruit vines along the road.

Waimanu Valley Trail, 9 miles, 6 hours, 1200-feet gain/loss (trail rating: difficult).

The most difficult part of the trek to Waimanu is the ascent up the northwest pali (cliff) of Waipio Valley. The trail is easy to find about 100 yards from the beach in the trees at the base of the cliff. Be alert, the switchbacks are steep and may be overgrown. Obviously, this 1,200-foot climb is best approached in the cool of the morning.

From the ridge, the trail crosses 14 gulches to Waimanu; so it's up and down along the pali overlooking the rugged coastline. There are places where some rock slides make the going a bit difficult and slow, so be cautious. The trail is heavily forested and foliated and in some places overgrown. You're more likely to encounter horses than hikers on the trail since Waimanu is a popular pig hunting destination with locals. The trail shelter is nine gulches from Waipio Valley, or about two-thirds of the way to Waimanu. It is a satisfactory place to lunch or camp, although you may have to share it with other hikers.

As you swing out of Pukoa (lit., "coral head") Gulch, you get your first view of Waimanu Valley. The similarity between Waipio and Waimanu will surprise you. Although Waimanu is about half the size of Waipio, it contains a similar verdant valley and is bounded by precipitous cliffs. It's a sight to behold.

Waimanu Stream greets you on the floor of the valley after a steep descent. The best place to ford Waimanu Stream is about 25 feet above the spot where the stream joins the ocean. For drinking water, hike about 1/2 mile along the west side of the pali to an unnamed waterfall. Once again, either treat the water or boil it before drinking. There are numerous beach-front camping sites, so scout around and find one that suits you. As at Waipio, beware of ocean swimming because of the heavy surf with riptides.

There are no trails, since Waimanu, unlike Waipio, has long been abandoned. You will find stone walls and foundations as well as taro terraces remaining from when it was occupied.

The jewel of Waimanu is Waiilikahi (lit., "water with single surface") Falls, about 1 1/2 miles along the northwest pali of the valley. You must make your own trail to the falls. With luck, you'll arrive when the succulent mountain apples (Eugenia malaccensis) are ripe, usually in June. The fruit is a small red and pinkish apple with a thin waxy skin. Its white flesh is crisp and juicy. Interestingly, this was the only fruit on the islands before the Europeans introduced many others. Enjoy your lunch, your apples, and a swim in the large pool below the falls.

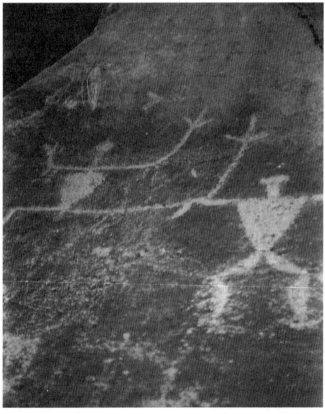

Petroglyphs

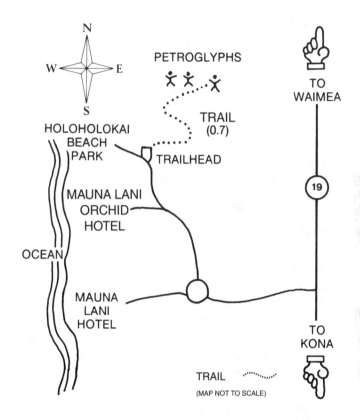

Puako Petroglyphs Trail
(Hiking Area No. 5)

Rating: Family.
Features: Hawaiian petroglyphs.
Permission: None.
Hiking Distance and Time: 0.7 mile, 1/2 hour.

Driving Instructions:

From Hilo (74 miles, 2 hours) north on Route 19, right on road to Mauna Lani Orchid/Hotel and Mauna Lani Hotel. Bear right following signs to Puako Petroglyphs/Holoholokai Beach Park.

From Kona (29 miles, 1 hour) north on Route 19, left on road to Mauna Lani Orchid/Hotel and Mauni Lani Hotel, then as above.

Introductory Notes: Petroglyphs are drawings or carvings on rock made by prehistoric or primitive people. Those at Puako (lit., "sugar cane blossom"), of unknown origin, are some of the finest examples on the islands and probably the most numerous.

On the Trail: Several interpretive signs and displays are found at the trailhead. The trail to the petroglyphs is initially paved, but soon becomes a well-defined dirt path that twists and turns through a kiawe tree forest. The wood of this tree is a source not only of fuel and lumber but also of honey, medicine, tannin and fodder, which is produced from its beanlike yellow pods.

It is a hot and dusty trek through the kiawe forest to the petroglyphs. All the drawings and carvings are on pahoehoe lava, which has a smooth or ropy surface. While the meanings of some of the petroglyphs are obvious, others challenge the imagination. It is almost like browsing in a bookstore or in an antique store. You are irresistibly drawn to look and look and look. To some, petroglyphs are the art of past civilizations and have sophisticated meanings. To others, they are the casual scribbles-just old graffiti. What do you think?

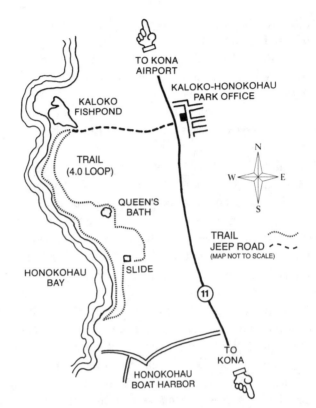

Kaloko-Honokohau
National Historical Park Trail
(Hiking Area No. 6)

Rating: Hardy Family.

Features: Fishpond, queen's bath, holua (ancient slide),
tidepools, swimming.

Permission: None. Park hours are 8 am to 3:30 pm.

Hiking Distance and Time: 4 mile Loop, 2 hours.
Driving Instructions:
   From Hilo (100 miles, 2 1/2 hours) north on Route 19
   (toward Kailua-Kona) right on unpaved jeep road opposite Kona Trade Center to end.
   From Kona (4 miles, 15 minutes) north on Route 19,
   left on unpaved jeep road opposite Kona Trade Center
   to end.
Introductory Notes: Kaloko-Honokohau (Kaloko, lit.,
"the pond" and Honokohau, lit., "adze bay") National Historical Park was established by Congress in 1978 to preserve native Hawaiian activities and culture and to demon-
strate historic land use patterns.A second fishpond, Aim-
akapa, is about one mile south of Kaloko via the coastline
trail. Both ponds are an important home for many water-
birds and an extraordinary biota, including endemic inver-
tebrate species. Early Hawaiian residents built these stone
enclosures with an opening to the sea to allow fish to enter
during high tide and to be closed trapping the fish.
According to Francis Kuailani, Superintendent, the park
includes large Hawaiian fishponds, house sites, a heiau,
petroglyphs, graves, and native and migrant water birds.
Look for the aeo (Hawaiian black-necked stilt) and the
alae keokeo (Hawaiian coot) Both endemic birds and on
Federal List of Endangered Species and are protected by
state and federal laws.To date, more than 200 archeological sites have been recorded in the Kaloko portion.

On the Trail: Facing the ocean, Kaloko Pond is on the
right and the trail (jeep road) goes left from in front of the
ranger's trailer and follows the coastline. After approximately one-fourth mile a spur tail turns away (left) from

the beach and emerges onto a lava field. The trail across the lava field to Queen's Bath is relatively clear to follow as it turns in the direction of the highway and toward ten piles or mounds of lava rock that encircle the bath. It is believed by some residents (not the Park Service) that Queen Kaahumanu, King Kamehameha's favorite wife, bathed here while the king's guards stood atop the lava mounds to ensure her privacy. The bath is quite small, about 30-feet in circumference, is 3-feet deep in the deepest part, and is surprisingly cool. Although it does not appeal to me, you may choose to splash or to sit in the bath.

From Queen's bath the trail goes south, paralleling midway between the beach on the right and the highway on the left and passes between two large lava piles, and turns left in the direction of the main road. The trail becomes obscure as you cross the aa (rough, clinkery type) lava. To reach the holua (sled) loop left around the brush and trees on your right and head for the higher lava flows to the southeast. Don't be discouraged if you cannot find the trail, but be CAUTIOUS walking on the rough underfooting. IT'S HAZARDOUS and razor sharp.

There is no mistaking the holua; it's a large, 15-by-100-foot, long incline that some believe was much longer when first constructed since it probably reached the water or pond enabling fun seekers to end their ride in the water. There are many known slides on the islands since contests were very popular with the royalty and with the people. The surface of the slide was usually covered with mud and pili grass to provide a smooth surface. The papa (sled) was constructed from wood. Some were 8-9 feet long with runners no more than six inches apart. In competition, sledders could reach 30 to 60 miles per hour, and some were known to ride the sled as a surfer rides a board.

Instead of retracing your steps to the trailhead, you could walk south a short distance to a dirt road that turns right to Honolohau Harbor and to the beach where you can find places to cool off. Pick up the coastline trail that goes along the coastline north to return to Kaloko. Morning glory flowers and beach naupaka (Scaevola taccada) dominate the trailside. The latter is a spreading succulent shrub with white berries and small white, half-flowers. One version of a Polynesian legend holds that lovers were separated leaving a half flower of the girl blossoming alone on the beach and her sweetheart blooming alone in the mountains on the mountain naupaka, a relative of the beach variety. If a whole flower is found, it means that the lovers have been reunited.

Captain Cook Monument

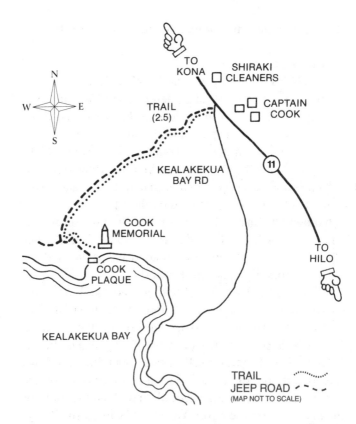

Captain Cook Monument Trail

(Hiking Area No. 7)

Rating: Strenuous.

Features: Site of Captain Cook's death, mango, papaya, avocado, guava, ancient Hawaiian burial caves, swimming, snorkeling.

Permission: None.

Hiking Distance and Time: 2.5 miles, 2 hours, 1400-feet loss.

Driving Instructions:

From Hilo (113 miles, 3 hours) south on Route 11 to the town of Captain Cook, sharp left just past Captain Cook on Bay Road, opposite a cleaning business, and drive one-tenth mile to jeep road (trail) on the right.

From Kona (14 miles, 1/2 hour) south on Route 11 to Captain Cook, right on Kealakekua Bay Road opposite a cleaning business before Captain Cook, and drive one-tenth mile to a jeep road on the right.

Introductory Notes: This is my favorite hike on the island. It is a delightful 1/2-day trek with a generous supply of nature's best fruits to suit anyone's palate, and it's the best snorkeling place in Hawaii!

The trailhead is a bit difficult to find. Look for a dry cleaners on the main road just north of the town of Captain Cook. Almost opposite the store, the road to Kealakekua (lit.,"pathway of the god") Bay drops abruptly to the left. The trail itself begins about 500 feet down this road on the right (bay) side. It is a jeep road, on the corner of which is a large avocado tree. Find the trail, for the hike is worth the effort. You should carry a small daypack to load up on fruits along the first 1/2 mile. Mango (Mangifera indica) is particularly abundant in the fields and along the roadside. Look under the trees for those that have fallen and are not too badly bruised, or find a stick to shake some loose from the trees. If you find a good long stick, leave it near the trail for the next hiker.

One of the favorite fruits of visitors and locals is the papaya (Carica papaya). The ripe yellow fruit varies in size, but can be found growing in clusters at the bases of umbrella-like leaves. In ancient Hawaii, the leaves were used as soap and as a meat tenderizer, and the seeds were used medicinally. You will find numerous papaya trees along the roadside.

As if this weren't enough, there are also some avocado (Persea americana) trees. Their fruit tends to be too watery for some people's taste, but perhaps not for yours.

On The Trail: From the trailhead, the trail/jeep road descends about 50 yards to where the road turns right onto private property. Periodically, the trail is cleared so the trail is distinguishable. Otherwise, the trail may be obsured by tall elephant grass. Either way, the trail goes straight to the coast, paralleling a stone wall on the left. Go slowly and carefully and don't be discouraged. The trail may be heavily overgrown for the first mile, but then opens as you near the coast. Here, the terrain becomes more arid, sustaining only low scrub. You have your first view of the coast, a portion of Kealakekua Bay, and your destination, although the Cook Memorial is not visible. Bear left toward the beach at the first junction in the road. From here, go straight on to the beach. When you reach the beach, follow the coast to the left for a few hundred feet to the memorial. You needn't be concerned about the tourist boats' disturbing your visit, for the passengers usually snorkel around the boat. The boats simply make a pass by the memorial and anchor in the bay for people who wish to snorkel for a short time. You will find that snorkeling is outstanding here.

There are numerous caves beyond the monument and along the walls of the cliff. If you choose to explore, do not disturb any interesting finds. Local people are seeking to preserve what may be ancient Hawaiian burial grounds.

Captain Cook was killed here at water's edge on February 14, 1779 by the Hawaiians. Cook, an English captain in the employ of the Earl of Sandwich, was in search of a northwest passage when he sighted and landed on the Hawaiian Islands (he named them the Sandwich Islands

Where's the trail?

after his benefactor) in 1778 where he supplied his ships. He was thought to be the god Lono who was revered by the natives, so he and his men were treated well. Cook returned a year later, January, 1779, and anchored in Kealakekua Bay where he was warmly greeted again by thousands (estimates range from 30,000 to 50,000 Hawaiians). For a month the haoles (foreigners) were given a bounty of food and supplies to a point that the native people were deprived. This angered some of the people and Cook wisely left on February 4. He was compelled to return a week later since one of his ships was in need of repair and since storms on the north part of the island forced him to seek calmer waters. He again anchored in Kealakekua Bay on February 11. The Hawaiians, who on Cook's previous visit had "borrowed" or "used" or "stolen" items from the ship, "took" a cutter (small boat) from one of the ships. When the captain learned of the matter, he was enraged and with a number of armed marines went ashore to retrieve the boat. Meanwhile, the natives armed themselves and the opposing forces met on the beach. A fight resulted between a few natives and marines, and as Cook turned his back to the Hawaiians (some believe he tried to stop his men), he was struck in the head and he fell. Daggers were drawn and Cook was repeatedly stabbed by numerous natives. The result was that Cook and four marines were killed as well as an indeterminate number of natives. Some historians believe that the Hawaiians engaged in cannibalism, but there is little evidence of this occurring. It does seem certain that the natives stripped his flesh from the bones (a traditional Hawaiian practice reserved for kings) and hid the bones where they could not be found. An unfortunate end for all.

KAUAI—TRAILHEADS, CAMPING

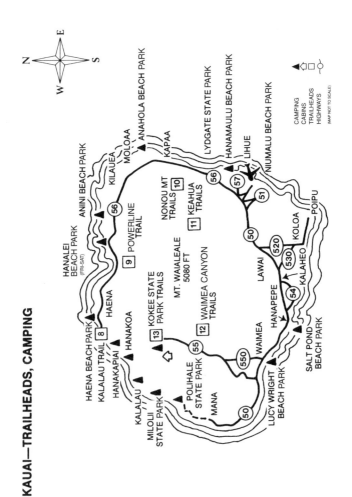

N · E · S · W

ANAHOLA BEACH PARK

LYDGATE STATE PARK

HANAMAULU BEACH PARK

NIUMALU BEACH PARK

CAMPING
CABINS
TRAILHEADS
HIGHWAYS
(MAP NOT TO SCALE)

MOLOAA

KAPAA

LIHUE

56

57

51

KILAUEA

NONOU MT TRAILS [10]

KEAHUA TRAILS

50

[11]

[9] POWERLINE TRAIL

66

ANINI BEACH PARK

HANALEI BEACH PARK (FRI-SAT)

MT. WAIALEALE 5080 FT

520

530

KOLOA

POIPU

HAENA

LAWAI

KALAHEO

54

[13] KOKEE STATE PARK TRAILS

HANAKOA

HANAKAPIAI

[8] KALALAU TRAIL

HAENA BEACH PARK

[12] WAIMEA CANYON TRAILS

55

POLIHALE STATE PARK

HANAPEPE

WAIMEA

550

KALALAU

MILOLII STATE PARK

MANA

50

LUCY WRIGHT BEACH PARK

SALT POND BEACH PARK

Kauai
The Garden Isle

The Island

Some people call it Kauai-a-mano-ka-lani-po - "The fountainhead of many waters from on high and bubbling up from below." Others regard it as "The Grand Canyon of the Pacific" or "The Garden Island" and still others say it is "The land of the Menehune." But even if you just call it "Kauai" - time of plenty, or fruitful season - it is still a land of beauty, grandeur and adventure, and a challenge to the outdoorsperson. There is a lot of hiking pleasure packed into this almost circular little island of 555 square miles.

Kauai lays claim to a number of firsts and unique characteristics. It is the oldest island in the Hawaiian Islands, it is the northern most inhabited island in the chain, and it was the first island visited by Captain Cook - though that is a rather dubious distinction. Still other things of local pride include Mt. Waialeale, the wettest spot on earth; the only place on earth where the iliau, a rare and unique plant is to be found; and the home of the legendary Menehune, a race of pygmies who were short, industrious, strong, and highly skilled workers in stone.

Kauai lies 102 air miles northwest of Honolulu - about a 20-minute flight. Most visitors to Kauai are seeking its solitude and slower pace of life, and many find these in the verdant valleys of the remote Na Pali Coast and in the lush canyonlands of Waimea. Conveniently, the State of Hawaii and the County of Kauai have established miles of trails and jeep roads into remote areas, which will reveal some of the island's secrets.

Kauai offers more natural beauty than most people can absorb. Island trails lead to magnificent waterfalls, to breathtaking vistas into Kauai's canyonlands and to the

Kalalau Valley

wilderness area along the Na Pali Coast. This enchanted land has disappointed no one I have ever known.

It is important to remember, however, that natural and man-made forces have had and continue to have a dramatic impact on Hawaii's topography. Periodic volcanic eruptions, 400-plus inches of rain in several places, earthquakes, the influx of new residents, and the increasing numbers of visitors affect trail conditions. A trail that was cleared and brushed and in good condition can become overgrown after a few weeks of heavy rain, particularly if it is not heavily traveled. For example, the trails in the Kokee/Waimea area were in very good condition in 1999. However, 200-500 inches of rain annually in that area impacts greatly on trail conditions so that the description in this book may differ a bit from what you experience.

In addition to damage to trails caused by natural forces, some people destroy or remove trailhead signs, trail markers and trail mileage posts for some inexplicable reason. Consequently, I have provided clear directions to trailheads and a trail description that does not rely on posted trail markers.

Lihue is the county seat (Kauai is a county). Getting around Kauai has been made easier since 1992, when Kauai inaugurated a public bus system that runs from Hanalei to Kekaha. Call (808) 241-6410 for information and routes. Rental vehicles are available from Lihue Airport. At present, hitchhiking is allowed, although the county council raises the issue from time to time, and may prohibit it in the future. Check with the information booth at the airport regarding the law. If you hitchhike, be patient, for rides are hard to come by in the outlying areas.

Camping and Cabins

Camping out on Kauai will add another dimension to your visit. Campgrounds on Kauai range from adequate to good, contain most of the amenities, and are either free or inexpensive. The accompanying map locates the state and county campgrounds. A third jurisdiction, the Division of Forestry, also provides a number of campgrounds, camping shelters, and camping areas, which are noted on individual maps throughout the book. (See Appendix for addresses). A word about each kind of campground should be helpful.

State Parks

The Division of State Parks regulates camping and hiking along the Na Pali Coast: Hanakapiai, Hanakoa and Kalalau - the three major valleys along the wilderness trail. Campers are charged $10 per person, per night. Camping permits may be obtained from the Division of State Parks (address in Appendix). Camping is limited to five nights total along the Na Pali Coast in any 30-day period. Hanakapiai and Hanakoa are limited to one night each in that period. Hiking permits are required beyond Hanakapiai Valley, even for day hiking.

Polihale State Park offers oceanfront camping, and Kokee State Park offers mountain camping. A camping fee of $5 per person, per night is charged at these two parks (address in Appendix).

The state housekeeping cabins at Kokee are operated by a concessionaire (see p. 141 for details and reservation information).

County Parks

Secondly, the County of Kauai has numerous campgrounds and beach parks around the island. County camping costs $3 per adult per day (no cost to Hawaii residents). Persons under 18 are free if accompanied by an adult. Permits are not issued to persons under 18. Camping permits are issued for up to seven days at each campsite. A total of sixty (60) camping days per year is allowed. For A Reguest for Camping Permit, write to Department of Parks and Recreation, County of Kauai (address in Appendix). An application with detailed information will be forwarded.

State Forestry Parks

Last, the Hawaii State Division of Forestry maintains a number of trailside camping areas in Waimea Canyon, which are identified on the individual maps preceding the text of each hiking area. Camping is free and is limited to three nights within a 30-day period, but this regulation is not regularly enforced. Neither permits nor reservations are necessary. Registration is by sign-in at the trailhead upon entering and leaving a forest-reserve area. All the facilities are primitive and lacking in amenities, but to some people that is their best feature.

Campers are well advised to bring their own equipment because locally it is expensive. For rentals on the island, I recommend Pedal 'n Paddle in Hanalei (address in Appendix). Their store is well stocked with rentals and a complete line of hiking and backpacking needs, and their staff is well informed and helpful.

Camping in Hawaii has always been an enjoyable and inexpensive way to experience the Islands. Recently, however, some campers have been beaten and a few have been killed. Local men, according to the victims, have committed most of the beatings. Most of the assaults have taken place at campgrounds that were close to cities or towns where locals congregate. There has been little or no problem in remote and wilderness areas. The best advice is to avoid camping in areas readily accessible to locals and to avoid contact with groups of people. I recommend Kokee State Park, Haena Beach Park and Salt Pond Beach Park. The latter is one of the best beach camping places in Hawaii.

Addresses for all agencies are in the Appendix.

Hiking

With the exceptions of the Kalalau Trail and some of the trails in the Kokee/Waimea hiking area, hiking on Kauai does not require any special equipment or skill. Many places are readily accessible even to the tenderfoot and to the people not inclined to hike much. Few people dispute that the Kalalau Trail is an outstanding outdoor experience requiring good physical condition and backpacking equipment. However, the first two miles of the trail to Hanakapiai Valley and beach can be hiked by most people of any age who are willing to sweat a bit. Even so, wear good boots or tennis shoes and carry water.

If time allows, spend at least three days at Kokee State Park. The housekeeping cabins and the campground are comfortable, and the hiking experiences include hikes to suit everyone's interest and ability.

Water is available from streams in many areas, but it should be boiled or treated before drinking. Cattle, pigs and goats usually share the stream water with you. I suggest you begin each hike with one quart of water per person. Due to the heavy rainfall on Kauai, dry firewood is rare, so a small, light, reliable backpacking stove is a convenience and a comfort. A hot cup of tea, coffee or soup is invigorating while waiting out a passing storm, and a hot breakfast is desirable after a wet night. Lastly, most hikers find shorts or cutoffs adequate on most trails.

Kalalau Trail
(Hiking Area No. 8)

Rating: See individual hikes.

Features: Wilderness area, camping, coastal views, fruits, waterfalls, swimming, historical sites.

Permission: Access to Kalalau Valley is strictly regulated by the State particularly between May 15 to Labor Day. Sixty (60) permits are issued for each day during that period. Forty (40) permits are issued for each of those days up to one year in advance in person or by mail. Permits for the remaining twenty spots are issued in person for the one week period four (4) weeks in advance. On each Wednesday from May 15 to Labor Day at 8 am numbers will be handed out to those waiting in the line in front of the "LINE FORMS HERE" sign posted on the glass of the front entryway to the State Office Building at 3060 Eiwa Street, Lihue. Reserving space or cutting in line is not permitted. Permits are issued to the applicant in line and one other individual (2 people per permit) until all available spaces are gone. You also must have proper identification (e.g. Drivers License, Passport or Hawaii State ID card) for yourself and the other person named on the permit. Camping is limited to five nights total along the Na Pali Coast in any 30-day period. Hanakapiai and Hanakoa are limited to one night each in that period. A camping fee of $10 per person, per night is expected to be in effect in the summer, 1999.

Only the State of Hawaii could devise such bizarre procedures. Write or call the Division of State Parks in Lihue (see Appendix for address) for the exact dates

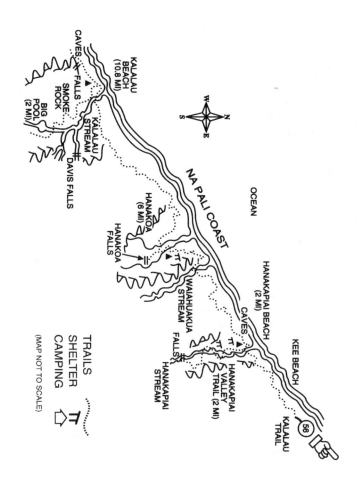

each year of issuing permits in person. You can expect procedures to change from year to year.

Permits to hike and camp are required and are checked regularly. Camping permits are required for Hanakapiai, Hanakoa and Kalalau valleys. Permits are also required to hike beyond Hanakapiai Valley. Permits may be obtained from the Division of State Parks (see Appendix for address).

Hiking Distance & Time: See individual hikes.

Driving Instructions: *From Lihue* (42 miles, 1 1/2 hour), drive north on Route 56 to road's end.

Introductory Notes: When people talk about hiking on Kauai, they talk about visiting the uninhabited valleys of the Na Pali (the cliffs) Coast.The Kalalau ("the straying") Trail from road's end at Kee Beach to Kalalau Valley (10.8 miles) is the most exciting hike on the island and a memorable experience.

Few who have hiked the Kalalau Trail will deny its grandeur and its captivating allure. Cliffs rise precipitously above the blue-green water and the rugged, rocky north shore of Kauai. The valleys of the Na Pali Coast are accessible only by foot or by boat, and only during the summer when the tides expose a generous sandy beach, which is ripped away each year by winter storms.

Hiking the entire trail to Kalalau requires backpacking equipment for a comfortable, safe trip. Sound hiking boots are essential, since a good deal of your hiking is alternately on soft cinders and ash and rocks along the precipitous coast and on rocky trails in the valleys. A strong, waterproof tent is needed to stand up under the wind at Kalalau and the rain at Hanakoa. Although fresh water is available all along the trail, you should boil the water or purify it. People, goats and pigs use the same streams. A light sleeping bag or light blanket is adequate, particularly during the summer months when the nighttime temperature is very comfortable. Little clothing is necessary during the day, and it is still somewhat common to find both sexes hiking without any. A backpacking stove is recommended since dry firewood is difficult to find and tree cutting is not permitted.

The trailhead for the Kalalau Trail is at the end of Route 56, where you will find several parking areas. A word of caution, however, may save some grief: vehicles left overnight in the parking places are occasionally vandalized so do not leave anything in your car. Furthermore, if rental car companies learn that you are backpacking they usually won't rent to you even if you have a reservation. Hitchhiking, which is legal on Kauai, is an alternative to renting a car. Taxi service is available from the Princeville Airport.

Kee Beach to Hanakapiai Beach, 2 miles, 1 hour, 600-feet gain/loss (trail rating: hardy family).

The trek to Hanakapiai (lit., "bay sprinkling food") Beach from Kee (lit.,"avoidance") Beach is one steep mile up and one steep mile down on a wide, maintained trail. This is a much frequented trail because tourist publications promise a verdant valley resplendent with native and introduced flora. No one is disappointed. Particularly abundant is the hala (Pandanus tectorius), an indigenous tree that grows in coastal areas. It is sometimes called "tourist pineapple," since the fruit resembles a pineapple and is jokingly identified as such by locals for tourists. Humor aside, the hala has been a valuable resource, the hollow trunk of the female tree being used as a pipe for drainage between taro patches. The leaves have commercial value being used for weaving many items such as baskets, mats and hats - hats being particularly popular with tourists. In the past, the fruit was eaten in times of famine and was used to make colorful necklaces. When the sections of the fruit were dried, they were used as brushes.

The first half mile up the cliff provides views at a couple of points back to Kee Beach and Haena ("wilderness") reefs. This part of the trail is usually shady because of the large trees and cool because of the trade winds and periodic rain showers. One source of shade is the large kukui (Aleurites moluccana) tree from which a beautiful and popular lei is made. To make a lei, each nut must be sand-

Kee Beach

ed, filed and polished to a brilliant luster that is acquired from its own oil. Until the advent of electricity, kukui-nut oil was burned for light. Nicknamed the "candlenut tree" its trunk was shaped into canoes by early Hawaiians.

The trail leads up and down from the 1/2 to the 1 1/4-mile marker. With any luck you may find some sweet guava (Psidium guajava), a small yellow, lemon-sized fruit that contains five times more vitamin C than an orange. Before eating one break it open and check for worms. They are tiny and are a little hard to see but are common in wild guava.

Near the 1-mile marker, look for a small springlet that flows year round and provides a welcomed face-splashing. At the 1 1/2-mile marker, you'll have your first view of Hanakapiai Beach below, with its generous beach (during the summer months) and its crashing surf. Look for wild orchids, with their delicate purplish flowers, thriving along the banks of the trail.

As you descend to the beach, several warning signs caution visitors not to swim in the ocean because of the heavy surf and of the presence of riptides and strong currents. Several drownings occur here in spite of the posted admonition. From across the stream, you can hike the trail into the valley and to the falls. I suggest a hike to the falls mid-morning when it is more likely to be warm and sunny in the valley.

If you want to stay overnight at Hanakapiai Beach, you have a choice of campsites. There are numerous campsites on the west side of the stream beginning on the bluff overlooking the beach and extending into the valley. Some daring campers sleep in the cave located in the cliff that drops to the beach. It's too close to the ocean for me.

To Hanakapiai Falls, 2 miles, 1 1/2 hours, 800-feet gain/loss (trail rating: strenuous).

The Hanakapiai Valley Trail follows the stream and passes through a rain forest resplendent with native flora. The beginning of the trail on the west side of the valley contains some of the largest mango (Mangifera indica) trees anywhere. One grove surrounding the remains of a coffee mill contains a tree that is 23 feet in circumference. Obviously, it makes a shady sheltered campsite. The mango tree is not native to Hawaii, but its many varieties have done well there, and are popular with locals and tourists. However, the trees in this valley do not bear as well as those in drier areas because of a fungus that kills the blos-

Hanakapiai Beach

soms in wet areas. Many people regard the mango fruit as second to none in appearance and taste.

The hike to the falls is a must not only because the falls are spectacular, but also because much serenity and enchantment are to be found in the valley. The first 1/4-mile is an easy trail that snakes along the stream. "Okole-hau" ("okole" is translated "anus" or "buttocks"; and "hau" can mean "cool.") is the name of a Division of Forestry trail-crew shelter near the coffee mill which you may use when it is not occupied by a trail crew.

You will make several stream crossings depending on the time of year and the amount of rainfall. The trail is always easy to find because the valley is so narrow. However, be alert for unstable places caused by yearly heavy rains and flooding. The last 1/2-mile is the most difficult part, but perhaps the most enchanting, with inviting pools and verdant growth. The trail is cut along the walls of the canyon in a number of places. Caution is well-advised.

Although the pool at the base of the falls is inviting, caution is again advised for there is danger from falling rocks from the cliffs and the ledge above the falls. Hanakapiai Falls cascades and falls about 300 feet in the back of a natural amphitheater. You don't need to be told to swim and enjoy the pools and the surrounding area. You will find safe pools away from falling rocks.

Hanakapiai to Hanakoa, 4 miles, 2 1/2 hours, 800-feet gain/loss (trail rating: strenuous).

Serious hiking on the trail to Kalalau Valley begins at this point as the trail climbs out of Hanakapiai Valley on a series of switchbacks for one mile. This is the most diffi-

cult section of the entire 11-mile trek. Hiking here in the
morning means that the sun will be at your back and, with
the trade wind, it should be relatively cool. The trail does
not drop to sea level again until Kalalau Beach, some
eight miles along the cliffs.

There are two small valleys before Hanakoa. The first
is Hoolulu (lit., "to lie in sheltered waters"), which is first
viewed from a cut in the mountain at the 3 1/4-mile marker. From here you descend to cross the valley and climb
the opposite side. Hoolulu is thickly foliated with native
and introduced plants that are typical of most valleys on
the island. Ti, guava, morning glory, mountain orchids,
and different kinds of ferns can be identified along with
the larger kukui, koa and hala trees. Be careful at points
where the trail narrows along a precipitous slope.

Waiahuakua Valley, at the 4 1/4-mile marker, is
broader than Hoolulu. In June-August, you are likely to
find delicious ohia ai (Eugenia malaccensis), or mountain
apples, growing along the trail. Abundant in Waiahuakua,
these trees have smooth, dark green leaves and some
attain a height of 50 feet. The fruit is a small red or pinkish apple with a thin, waxen skin, while the meat is flesh-
white, crisp and juicy, with a large brown seed in the center - a very tasty repast for those lucky enough to find
some. Additionally, the valley abounds in coffee, ti,
guava, kukui, and mango.

At the 5 3/4-mile marker, you will get your first view
of Hanakoa (lit., "bay of koa trees or of warriors") Valley
which is a broad-terraced valley that was once cultivated
by Hawaiians. Many of the terraced areas provide relatively sheltered camping sites. In addition, "Mango Shelter" has a roof and table, and "Hanakoa Shack," a short

distance away, is a Division of Forestry trail-crew shelter that is open to hikers when not in use by crews. Camping in Hanakoa is quite an experience since it receives frequent rains, and as soon as you dry out, it rains again. So, if you plan to camp in Hanakoa, you should be prepared for a lot of rain, wetness and humidity. To compensate, you will have solitude and a private swimming pool if you camp away from where the trail crosses the stream. The afternoon can be warm and sunny, just perfect for a swim in one of the many pools in the stream and a sunbath on the large, warm rocks along the bank. These are a favorite of nude sun worshippers.

To Hanakoa Falls, 0.4 mile, 1/4 hour

The trail begins between the stream crossing and the 6 1/2-mile marker and passes a wilderness campsite and terraced areas once used by the Hawaiians for growing taro from which the staple food poi is produced. Expect the route to the falls to be overgrown and laden with rocks and boulders as a result of frequent floods in the valley. The falls cascade down the pali in a breathtaking setting.

Hanakoa to Kalalau Beach, 4.8 miles, 3 hours, 800-feet gain/loss (trail rating: strenuous).

Your physical condition and your hiking skill will be tested on the remainder of the trail. Most of the trail traverses switchbacks that pass in and out and up and down through several gulches. At a number of places, the trail narrows along a very precipitous cliff where a misstep can result in a serious mishap. Another hazard is the hot after-

Mangoes trailside

noon sun unless you begin hiking early. However, the views of the northwest coastline are absolutely breathtaking and staggeringly beautiful. It is difficult to think of another view in the world that compares.

At the 6 1/2-mile marker, you enter land that until 1975 was part of the Makaweli (lit., "fearful features") cattle ranch owned by the Robinson Family who also own the island of Niihau off the coast of Kauai. The area becomes increasingly dry as you continue west, and only the smaller more arid types of vegetation survive, like sisal and lantana. Lantana (Lantana camara) is a popular flower that blossoms almost continuously. Its flowers vary in color from yellow to orange to pink to red; infrequently, they are white with a yellow center. If you hike in the early morning or late afternoon you're likely to frighten feral goats foraging near the trail and near some of the small streams along the trail.

Although there are only a few trail-mileage markers over the rest of the route, there is no chance of getting lost. The trail is over open land and visible ahead. There are at least five reliable sources of water between Hanakoa and Kalalau. The admonition to treat, filter or to boil the water applies.

Pohakuao (lit., "day stone") is the last small valley before Kalalau. As you ascend the west side of Pohakuao along a pali with sparse foliage and reddish earth, you reach Red Hill, as it is known to locals, from which you get your first view of Kalalau, a welcome sight after three difficult miles from Hanakoa. There is no mistaking Kalalau, for it is a large, broad valley some two miles wide and three miles long. From the ridge, a precipitous snake-like trail drops abruptly to Kalalau Stream where rushing, cool water and pools await the weary hiker.

Camping is allowed on the beach, in the trees fronting the beach and in the caves at the far end of the beach. Try to find a spot that will shelter you from the strong winds and the hot daytime sun. Some campers find shelter in the low scrub along the beach during the day and then sleep on the beach during the cool and usually wind-free nights. Lantana and common guava are particularly abundant along the trail in the beach area. You should easily find some ripe guava to add to your meals. Don't drink the stream water until you treat or boil the water. The falls at the end of the beach by the caves is the most convenient source of water. Be certain to treat or boil the water. The water from the falls also serves the feral goats that you will undoubtedly see in the morning and at dusk when they visit to refresh themselves. Most campers take a daily shower under the falls.

Kalalau abounds in a variety of life. Beach naupaka (Scaevola frutescens), with small, fragrant, white flowers, can be found near the beach, mixed with the low sisal and lantana. Hala, ti, ferns, bamboo, bananas, mango, kukui, monkeypod and many other species of flora can be identified. Rock terraces where Hawaiians planted taro as late as the 1920s are also common.

Kalalau Beach to Big Pool, 2 miles, 1 1/2 hour, 1000-feet gain/loss (trail rating, hardy family).

The trail into the valley begins on the west side of Kalalau Stream at the marked trailhead. Before heading into the valley, hike to the top of the knoll above the beach, also on the west side of the stream. The remains of a heiau - a pre-Christian place of worship - lie between the knoll and the beach and are clearly identifiable from this vantage point. Little is known about this nameless heiau. Remember that such places are still revered by many people and should be respected.

From the trailhead, the trail parallels the stream for a short distance and then ascends an eroded rise. From here the trail alternately passes open and forested areas. In the wooded areas look for oranges, mango, common guava and rose apple. Each can be found in the valley and can supplement a backpacker's diet. At the one-mile point, Smoke Rock is a convenient place to pause in an open area from which the entire valley can be viewed. This is the place where the valley marijuana growers and residents used to meet to smoke and to talk story. The rest of the trail to Big Pool is under the shade of giant mango and rose apple trees. The latter bears a small,edible, pale-yellow fruit. Before reaching Big Pool, a side stream crossing must be made. Heading into the valley, the next stream crossing is Kalalau Stream. Big Pool, a short distance from this crossing, is easily identified. Two room-sized pools are separated by a natural water slide which is a joy to slip down into the cool water below. It's a delightful place to enjoy the sights and smells of Kalalau, Kauai's most precious treasure.

The Folk Hero of Kalalau

Locals and visitors enjoy speculating about the exploits and the hideouts of Kalalau's most famous citizen, Koolau. Commonly called "Koolau the Leper," this native Hawaiian was born in Kekaha in 1862. Three years after showing signs of leprosy, at the age of 27, Koolau and the other lepers of Kauai were ordered to the leper colony on Molokai, and were promised that their wives and children could accompany them. When the ship sailed without his wife and child, Koolau, realizing he had been tricked, dove overboard and swam ashore. Together with his wife and child he made the perilous descent into Kalalau Valley to join other lepers who sought to escape deportation. A year later, local authorities decided to round up the lepers, all of whom agreed to go to Molokai except Koolau. A sheriff's posse exchanged fire with Koolau, who shot and killed a deputy. Martial law was declared, and a detachment of the national guard was sent from Honolulu with orders to get their man dead or alive. A small cannon was mounted near the site where Koolau was thought to be hiding. In the ensuing "battle" Koolau shot two guardsmen and one accidentally shot and killed himself fleeing the leper. The remaining guardsmen fled from the valley to the beach. In the morning they blasted Koolau's hideout with their cannon. Believing him dead, the guardsmen left the valley. But Koolau had moved his family the night before the cannonading, and they lived in the valley for about five more years, always fearful that the guard was still looking for him. They hid during the day and hunted for food at night. Tragically, their son developed signs of leprosy and soon died; a year later, the dread disease claimed Koolau. Piilani, his wife, buried her husband in the valley that had become their home along with his gun which had enabled them to be together to the end.

To some, Koolau is a folk hero who received unfair treatment by the government. Indeed, locals claim that Koolau frequently left his valley hideout to visit friends and relatives on Kauai. Whatever the facts, it makes for an interesting story and campfire conversation.

No one that I have met has ever been disappointed by their Kalalau experience.

Powerline Trail
(Hiking Area No. 9)

Rating: Strenuous.

Features: Fruit, views, native and introduced flora and fauna.

Permission: None.

Hiking Distance & Time: 13 miles, 6-7 hours, 2,000-feet gain/loss.

Driving Instructions:

To Hanalei Trailhead (32 miles, 1 hour) Drive north on Route 56 past Princeville Airport, turn left onto Pooku Road and drive 1.7 miles to end of pavement. Park off the road.

To Lihue Trailhead (12 miles, 1/2 hour) From Lihue, drive north on Route 56, turn left on Route 580 to University of Hawaii Agriculture Experiment Station and turn left and drive to Keahua Stream and Arboretum. Drive through the stream for 0.2 mile to dirt road and hunter's check station on the right. Park off the road.

Introductory Notes: The powerline trail is exactly what the name implies. The road was built to facilitate the construction of power transmission lines between Lihue and Hanalei. Some evidence suggests, however, that the route was originally an early Hawaiian trail link between the two communities.

Both the Hanalei and Lihue trailheads are readily accessible (see map and Driving Instructions above). Typically, this is a solitary hike over a deeply rutted dirt road where you will need to negotiate mud and water-filled mud holes. This full day hike requires sound footwear, two quarts of water per person, food and essential equip-

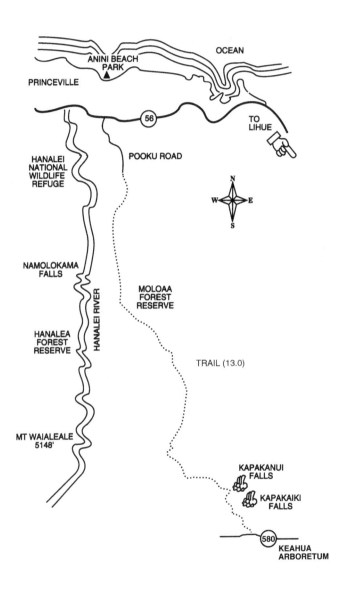

ment noted in the Introduction. For personal safety, wear bright clothing while hiking, particularly during hunting season. Hunting is generally open only on weekends and state holidays, but all hunters may not respect the rules.

You will be richly rewarded if you choose to hike just a few miles or an hour or so from either trailhead. Families with small children will find the first few miles from the Hanalei Trailhead easy going.

On the Trail from Hanalei: From the off-road parking area at pavement's end, a water tank is visible about 100 yards up the trail. The telephone poles and lines are the only unsightly things to intrude on the lushly foliated surroundings. Initially, the trail makes a gentle ascent, levels out and then dips and rises throughout. Yellow, lemon-sized common guava and strawberry guava - red, golf-ball sized fruit - are plentiful throughout the hike. DO NOT,

Strawberry Guava

however, pursue fruit off the trail for the underfooting is
uncertain and can be dangerous.

A break in the trees near the 1/2-mile point affords a
view to the west (right) of Hanalei, the Hanalei River and
the Hanalei National Wildlife Refuge. The latter is home
to several rare, endemic birds such as the Koloa, a Hawaiian duck, (Anas wyvilliana), the Common Moorhen
(Gallinula chloropus sandvicensis) and the Black-necked
Stilt (Himantopus mexicanus knudseni) each of which is
on the federal endangered species list. Trailside, hau (Hibiscus tiliaceus) with its dense tangle of limbs and yellow-
flowered hibiscus and the native ohia lehua (Metrosideros
collina) with its tufted red stamens are readily identifiable.

At the one-mile point and from several vistas thereafter numerous waterfalls come into view, the highest of
which is Namolokama (Lit., "the interweaving bound
fast") Falls plunging several hundred feet from the west
pali from Namolokama Mountain. Indeed, depending on
rainfall, several other falls may be visible. The falling
water rushes to the valley floor and is carried via the
Hanalei River to the sea. Verdant Hanalei Valley at your
feet is a sight beyond description. The trail bisects the
Hanalea Forest Reserve to the west (right) and the
Moloaa Forest Reserve to the east (left).

As you proceed into the interior, the trail follows the
eastern edge of the hunting area so that the likelihood of
coming across feral pigs or goats on the trail increases.
Both are timid and more than likely will rush off into the
brush when you approach. Goats pose little or no threat to
humans and pigs usually will only attack if they feel threatened. I have found that noise and hand clapping frightens
them. You are more likely to come across hunter's dogs
who are working well ahead of their master or are heading

home. I know of no hiker who has been attacked by these dogs. Recently, mountain bike riders have discovered the powerline trail so that bikers, invariably covered with red dirt and mud, may be encountered on the hike.

Throughout the hike, numerous trails/roads branch off your trail. Most lead to power poles and lines while others are used as turnouts for heavy equipment. You'll find pipes, poles and line scattered indiscriminately trailside.

At about midpoint, you'll come across a dilapidated shack that was once used by workers, hunters and hikers.

Beyond the shack the trail ascends to the highest point at Kualapa (2128 feet) from which it seems possible to reach out and touch Mt Waialeale (5148 feet) to the southeast. However, cloud cover may prohibit a view. Waialeale (lit., "overflowing water") is the wettest place on earth receiving and average of 465 inches of rain annually. Kawaikini (Lit., "multitudinous water"), just south of Waialeale is the highest point on the island at 5,243 feet. You have probably donned your poncho while enjoying countless waterfalls that seemingly drop hundreds of feet to the base of the valley and the headwaters of the Hanalei River. It's an awesome sight.

Shortly, the trail jogs southeast on a ridge with Keahua (lit., "the mound") Stream below on your left and Uhauiole (Lit., "rat-hitting") Stream on your right. I have found the remaining 2-3 miles to trail's end to be very wet with countless deep, muddy pools. Be alert for a break in the vegetation to the northeast (left side) of the trail for a view of Kapakanui (Lit., "large raindrop") Falls (left) and Kapakaiki (Lit., "small raindrop") Falls (right).

The last 100 yards is a steep descent to the Lihue trailhead. At the trailhead, turn left and walk 0.2 mile to Keahua Arboretum for a refreshing swim in the stream.

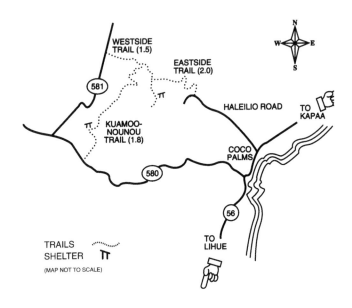

TRAILS
SHELTER
(MAP NOT TO SCALE)

Nonou Mountain Trails (Sleeping Giant)
(Hiking Area No. 10)

Rating: Hardy Family.
Features: Views of Kauai, fruits.
Permission: None.
Hiking Distance & Time: Consult individual hikes.
Driving Instructions: (see instructions preceding each hike below).
Introductory Notes: It is told that the giant Puni lived among the legendary small folk, the Menehune, but was

so clumsy that he continually knocked down their homes and their stone walls. Nevertheless, he was so friendly that the Menehune could not help liking him. One day the little people were faced with an invasion, and they went to the giant in the hope that he would destroy their enemies. However, they found him asleep on a ridge near Kapaa (lit., "the solid or the closing"). In an effort to awaken him, they threw large rocks on his stomach, which rebounded toward the ocean, destroying some of the invading canoes and causing the others to flee. In the morning they tried to awaken Puni again, only to discover that some of the rocks they had thrown at him had landed in his mouth. Tragically, he had swallowed them and died in his sleep.

There are three routes to the summit of Nonou (lit., "throwing") Mountain which are good, well-maintained trails that will take you to the giant's chin and to his forehead. Nonou is truly one of the best hikes on Kauai. Be sure to carry at least one quart of water, since it is a hot hike in spite of frequent trade winds.

If you have a second vehicle, I recommend hiking the East-side Trail to the summit and then return via the West-side Trail to the junction with the Kuamoo-Nounou Trail and follow it to highway 580 - 5.3 miles - (see map).

East-side Trail, 2 miles, 1 1/2 hours, 1,250-feet gain/loss (trail rating: hardy family).

Driving Instructions: *From Lihue* (7 miles, 1/2 hour), drive north on Route 56 past Coco Palms Hotel, turn left on Haleilio Road and drive 1.2 miles to a parking area off the road on the right by the sign "Nonou Trail."

Puni - The "Friendly Giant"

On the Trail: The trailhead is to the right as you drive into the parking area. The trail is a series of well-defined switchbacks along the northeast side of the mountain. Pause frequently and enjoy the vistas overlooking the east side of Kauai. Below you lie the Wailua Houselots, while the Wailua River and the world famous Coco Palms resort are to your front right. There are   1/4-mile trail markers along the entire route.

The large trees that flourish in the area not only offer a relatively shady trail but also provide some shelter from showers. You will find strawberry guava, passion fruit, ti, tree ferns, a variety of eucalyptus, and other flora that deserve special note.

The hau (Hibiscus tiliaceus) tree is of particular interest not only because of its pretty bright-yellow blossom but also because of its long, sinuous branches that interlock to form an impenetrable barrier. Locals jokingly note that the tree is appropriately named (hau, pronounced how) because where they are plentiful, no one knows "hau" to pass through!

On a spacious overlook at about the one-mile point, you can rest in the shade of the ironwood (Casuarina equisetifolia) tree, which resembles a pine because of its long, slender, drooping, dull-green "needles", but it is not a conifer. It is an introduced tree that has a long life and is very useful as a windbreak or shade tree.

Just beyond the 1 1/2-mile marker, the west-side trail merges with ours for the ascent to the summit. Alii (lit., "chief") Shelter and table at the 1 3/4-mile marker is a pleasant place to picnic and to enjoy the panorama of the island and the solitude. There are a number of benches near the shelter that provide comfortable places to meditate. You should see white-tailed tropic birds (Phaethon lepturus) soaring along the pali with its conspicuous 16-inch tail streamers.

From the shelter, walk south about 20 yards past monkeypod trees and survey the trail that leads to the giant's "chin," "nose" and "forehead." Be CAUTIOUS, if you choose to continue, because you must walk across a narrow ridge above a nearly vertical 500-foot cliff, scramble up about 50 feet on your hands and knees to the "chin" and walk on a narrow ridge about 150 yards to the "forehead." From all points of the giant's anatomy, the views are outstanding. Look below the giant's chin for a hole through which the wind rushes.

Kuamoo-Nounou Trail,
1.8 miles, 1 hour (trail rating: hardy family).

Driving Instructions: *From Lihue* (8 miles, 1/2 hour), drive north on Route 56 over Wailua River bridge, turn left on Route 580 (Kuamoo Road) to 5750 Kuamoo Road. The trailhead on the right side of the road.

This trail is a pleasant hike even if you don't hike to the summit of Nonou Mountain. Most of the trail passes under a canopy of native and introduced trees and a picnic shelter near the midpoint affords a panoramic view of the valley and the mountains beyond. The trail is wide with 1/4 mile markers to trail's end.

On the Trail: Initially, the trail passes between a residence on the left and pasture on the right before dropping to a wooden bridge over Opaekaa Stream. Look for ripe common (yellow) and strawberry guava along the stream and throughout the hike. Both trees are prolific and, when in season, the aroma from rotting fruit underfoot is intoxicating. From the bridge, the trail swings left and begins a gradual ascent under a canopy of hau trees, a variety of hibiscus bearing bright yellow blossoms.

Valley Vista trail shelter is 0.75-mile from the trailhead on a perch overlooking Wailua Homesteads to the west, Kawaikini (Kauai's highest point at 5,243 feet) beyond and the Makaleha Mountains to the northwest. Generally, numerous waterfalls are visible.

The trail continues an easy rise to the 1-mile marker before beginning a gradual descent to the junction with the West-side trail at the 1.8-mile point. More guava, a patch of bamboo, eucalyptus trees and a grove of giant

Norfolk Island pines (Araucaria excelsa) are here to enjoy. The latter are tall, perfectly symmetrical trees whose trunks have been used for masts on ships and as Christmas trees by island residents.

The Kuamoo-Nounou Trail meets the West-side Trail after 1.8-miles from where it's 1 mile east (right) to the junction with the East-side Trail and then 1/2-mile to the summit. The West-side Trail goes west (left) down the mountain 0.5-mile to Kamalu Road.

Hala - "Tourist pineapple"

West-side Trail, 1.5 miles, 1 hour, 1,000-feet gain (trail rating: hardy family).

Driving Instructions: *From Lihue* (10 miles, 1/2 hour), drive north on Route 56 over Wailua River bridge, turn left on Route 580 and then go right on Route 581 (Kamalu Road) for 1.2 miles to sign "Nonou Trail" on right side opposite 1055 Kamalu Road.

The West-side Trail is a bit shorter and offers more shade than the East-side Trail.

On the Trail: This trail passes by Queen's Acres and across a cattle range before entering the forest reserve. You will hike through a variety of introduced trees much like those found on the east side.

Look for the wild, or Philippine, orchid (Spathoglottis plicata). The wild variety is usually lavender, with what appear to be five starlike petals, but are actually two petals and three sepals.

The trail reaches a junction with the Kuamoo-Nounou Trail after 0.5 mile. Kuamoo-Nounou Trail goes south (right) for 1.8 miles to Route 580 and your trail (West-side Trail) climbs another mile to join with the East-side Trail from which it's a short trek to Alii Shelter and then to the summit (see East-side Trail description for details).

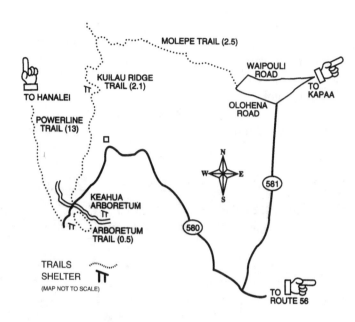

Keahua Trails

(Hiking Area No. 11)

Rating: See individual hikes.

Features: Swimming hole, native and introduced plants, fruits, picnic shelters.

Permission: None.

Hiking Distance & Time: See individual hikes.

Driving Instructions: See instructions preceding each hike below.

Introductory Notes: The three hiking trails in the Keahua area offer some pleasurable experiences. They offer some marvelous views of the eastside coastline and of the Makaleha Mountains. Since the Moalepe Trail intersects the Kuilau Ridge Trail, you have an opportunity to follow the latter trail to Keahua Arboretum where you can hike the Arboretum Trail and enjoy a delightful swimming hole.

I recommend hiking the Moalepe Trail to the Kuilau Ridge Trial and following it to the Arboretum - 4.6 miles (see map).

Keahua Arboretum Trail, 0.5 miles, 1/2 hour, (trail rating: family).

Driving Instructions: To Keahua Arboretum and Kuilau trailheads.

From Lihue (12 miles, 1/2 hour), drive north on Route 56 over Wailua River bridge, turn left on Route 580 and drive to the University of Hawaii Agriculture Experiment Station and go left (1.8 miles) to Keahua Stream. Kuilau Ridge Trailhead is on the right at a small turnout just before the stream and Keahua Arboretum Trailhead is on the left just past the stream opposite a parking area.

Introductory Notes: Keahua (lit., "the mound") Arboretum is a project of the Hawaii State Department of Land and Natural Resources, Division of Forestry. Here is a good chance to view a variety of native and introduced plants and to swim in a cool, fresh-water pool. The arboretum receives an annual average rainfall of 95 inches. The State Forest Reserve area extends west to the top of Mt. Waialeale ("overflowing water"), the wettest place on earth, with an average annual rainfall of 465 inches. It once received a record 628 inches!

Hau trees trailside

On the trail: The trail begins opposite the parking lot under a canopy of painted gum (Eucalyptus deglupta) trees with a colorful bark. This tree species is native to the Philippines and New Guinea. Behind the painted gum trees are rose gum (Eucalyptus grandis), a tree from Australia and less colorful than the painted gum. Several other trees are easy to identify here. Two of them are kukui (Aleurites moluccana) and milo (Thespesia populnea). Kukui trees, also called candlenut trees, had several uses. The most noteworthy use was the burning of its oily nuts for a light source. Kukui is Hawaii's State Tree and identifiable by its pale green leaf and its walnut-sized nuts. Today, as in old Hawaii, the wood of the milo tree is prized for its use in making beautiful umekes, or calabashes.

The trail passes several picnic shelters and parallels the stream and several good swimming holes. The Makaleha Mountains to the west are the source watershed for the domestic water supply. Rain falling on the mountains percolates into the soil and is collected in tunnels for distribution into the county water system. Good forest cover increases infiltration of water into the soil. This not only helps to increase the ground water supply but it also helps prevent soil erosion and floods caused by surface run-off.

One of the most conspicuous trees along the trail is the hau (Hibiscus tiliaceus) whose dense tangle of limbs prohibits entry. This yellow-flowered hibiscus was an early Hawaiian introduced plant. Here, you will also find the most common native tree species in Hawaii, the ohia lehua (Metrosideros collina). Early Hawaiian uses for the wood of the ohia included house timbers, poi boards, idols and kapa beaters. In the early 1900's, railroad ties hewn from ohia logs were exported for use on the mainland. A favorite of Madame Pele (the goddess of volcanoes) the ohia is easily identifiable by its tufted red stamens that remind the visitor of the bottlebrush tree.

Streams in this forest reserve provide a home for native and introduced fish. The native Hawaiian oopu lives here as well as smallmouth bass. Fresh-water Tahitian prawns, esteemed as a delicious food, can also be found here.

As you approach the swimming hole, notice the native hala tree commonly called "tourist pineapple." Its stilt-like trunk and its fruit that resembles a pineapple make this tree easy to identify. The trail descends the hill where you can return to your car or, better yet, go to the stream for a swim. There is usually a rope suspended from a mango tree on the bank about 100 yards from the shelter. It's a fun place.

On the Trail

Moalepe Trail, 2.5 miles, 1 1/2 hours, 700-feet gain (trail rating: hardy family).

Driving Instructions: To Moalepe Trail

From Lihue (12 miles,1/2 hour), drive north on Route 56 over Wailua River bridge, turn left on Route 580, go right for 1.6 miles on Route 581 to Olohena Road and turn left for 1.7 miles to where the road makes a sharp right turn onto Waipouli Road. Trailhead is posted at this junction.

On the trail: Do not attempt to drive beyond the Olohena-Waipouli Road intersection because the road is deeply rutted and, when wet, very slippery. The first part of the trail is on a right-of-way dirt road over pasture land. The usually cloud-enshrouded Makaleha (lit., "eyes looking about as in wonder and admiration") Mountains rise majestically to the northwest. In fact, the State of Hawaii, Division of Forestry, which is in charge of the area, has plans to extend the trail to the top of the Makalehas. Be sure to pause to enjoy the panorama of the coastline, from Moloaa on the north to Lihue on the south. There are some guavas along the fence and even more in the pasture, which is private land. The trail is a popular equestrian route with riders who rent horses from the ranches in the area: evidence of this fact can be found on the trail!

The first mile is a gentle ascent in open country. Then the trail enters the forest reserve. Hereafter, the trail is bordered with a variety of plants and trees, including the wild, or Philippine, orchid, different types of ferns, eucalyptus trees and the popular ohia lehua, with its pretty red blossoms. In the forest reserve the road-trail narrows and begins to twist and turn along the ridge, with many small and heavily foliated gulches to the left and Moalepe (lit., "chick with comb") Valley to the right. You can expect rain and therefore a muddy trail to the end of the hike. The trail reaches a junction with the Kuilau Ridge trail on a flat, open area at the 2-mile point. The Ridge Trail to the south (left) descends to a trail shelter and eventually ends at Keahua Arboretum, 2.1 miles from the junction. From the junction, the Moalepe Trail is a footpath that snakes north-westward a short distance to a lookout point from which an enchanting panorama awaits the hiker.

Kuilau Ridge Trail, 2.1 miles, 1 1/2 hours, 700-feet gain (trail rating: hardy family).

Driving Instructions: See Keahua Arboretum, page 126, for instructions.

On the Trail: One of the most scenic hiking trails on the island, the Kuilau ("to string together leaves or grass") Ridge Trail climbs the ridge from Keahua Arboretum. From the trailhead to trail's end, an abundance of native and introduced plants greets the hiker. The ascent of the ridge is on a well-maintained foot and horse trail lined with hala, ti plants, from which hula skirts are fashioned, and the very pretty lavender wild, or Philippine orchid. But the best prize is a couple of mountain apple trees on the left side of the trail a short distance up from the trailhead. Perhaps you'll find some apples, which are red or pink when ripe.

At the 1 1/4-mile point the trail reaches a large flat area and a trail shelter and a picnic site. It is a delightful place to pause to enjoy views of the many heavily foliated gulches and the Makaleha Mountains beyond. The trail beyond the shelter passes through one of the most beautiful places on the whole island. The Kuilau Ridge Trail twists and turns on a razorback ridge past a number of small waterfalls. It is a treasure to savor. Before reaching the shelter, the trail crosses a footbridge at the bottom of a verdant gulch and then ascends the ridge to a large flat area. From here, the trail continues 0.2 mile to its junction with the Moalepe Trail.

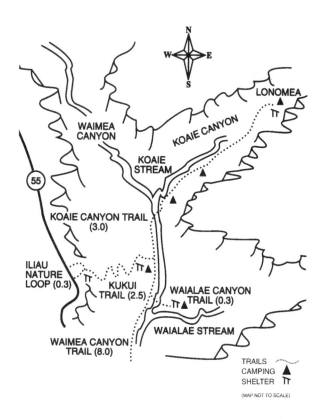

Waimea Canyon Trails

(Hiking Area No. 12)

Rating: See individual hikes.

Features: Views of Waimea Canyon, wilderness hiking and camping, swimming, native and introduced flora and fauna.

Permssion: None, but sign-in and out at the trailhead registry.

Playtime

Hiking Distance & Time: See individual hikes.

Driving Instructions: *From Lihue* (32 miles, 1 1/2 hours), drive south on Route 50, turn right on Route 550 to the Kukui Trailhead on right side just past the 8-mile marker.

Introductory Notes: Waimea (lit., "reddish water") Canyon for obvious reasons is a popular hiking area for locals and visitors. It has been called the "Grand Canyon of the Pacific." Everyone is quite taken by the beauty and grandeur of Waimea Canyon. It is about one mile wide, 3600 feet deep, and 10 miles long. While it does not match the magnificence of the Grand Canyon in Arizona, it has its own unique magic, with verdant valleys, lush tropical forest and rare birds and flora.

Iliau Nature Loop, 0.3 mile, 1/4 hour (trail rating: family).

The nature loop is a good place to see some 20 endemic plants including the rare iliau (Wilkesia gymnoxiphium). A relative to the equally rare Maui silversword, the iliau is endemic to Kauai. It grows 4-12 feet high, it is unbranched, and the stems end in clumps of long, narrow leaves 6-16 inches long. Once in its life, the plant flowers in a flourish of hundreds of tiny yellow blossoms.

At one time, most of the plants found here were identified by name plates, but they have all been destroyed because of weather damage. However, there is no missing the iliau since hundreds flourish in a small area.

The trail provides a number of vistas for viewing the canyon and Waialae (lit., "mudhen water") Falls on the opposite, west wall of the canyon.

Rare Iliau Blossom

Kukui Trail, 2.5 miles, 2 hours, 2,200-feet loss (trail rating: strenuous).

The Kukui (candlenut lamp) Trail is really the only trail into Waimea Canyon (I DO NOT recommend the Waimea Canyon Trail - see below). A Division of Forestry sign marks the trailhead both at the state highway and at the departure point off the Iliau Trail. Sign in and out on the trail registry located near the trail's beginning. Forestry rules limit hiking and camping in the canyon to three days.

The trail drops over 2000 feet into the canyon. The first half is open so that sun protection and a hat are advisable. If you hike during the heat of the day, I am certain you would rather be standing under Waialae Falls which can be seen tumbling from the pali across the canyon. About 0.3-mile down the trail, look for a wooded gulch on the left where several hibiscus (Hibiscus waimeae) trees are growing. This variety is an endemic tree that bears large white flowers that are so fragrant you can smell them from a distance.

You'll probably find numerous half-gallon plastic jugs along the trail. They are left by pig and goat hunters as they descend so they will have fresh water on their return. For safety reasons you should stay out of the brush and wear bright clothing so that you won't be mistaken for a goat or pig by hunters.

The first part of the hike offers some spectacular views of Waimea Canyon and the second part passes through heavy growth until it emerges at Wiliwili (a native tree

Kukui trailhead

bearing red seeds that make pretty necklaces) Camp along the boulder-laden banks of Waimea River. It is a delightful spot to camp in shade with ample water. Many hikers make a base camp at Wiliwili and then hike on the canyon trails and in the side canyons. If you are in good hiking condition, it is possible to make the hike in and out in one day.

There is ample water in the canyon, but it should be treated or boiled before drinking.

Waimea Canyon Trail, 8 miles, 5-6 hours (trail rating: strenuous).

Trailhead is in Waimea Canyon.

I do not recommend the Waimea Canyon Trail. It passes through the hot, dry lower portion of Waimea Canyon. Neither the terrain nor the vegetation is interesting.

You reach the trail by hiking down the Kukui Trail to the river, or by hiking eight miles upriver from Waimea town. The latter not only requires permission from a number of private parties but is a hot, exhausting trek.

The Waimea Canyon Trail travels south from the end of the Kukui Trail through the canyon to Makua Powerhouse, making several crossings of the Waimea River enroute. The trail is easy to follow, but it's a very hot, dusty trek.

There is ample water in the canyon, but it should be treated or boiled before drinking.

Koaie Canyon Trail, 3 miles, 2 hours, 1,000-feet gain (trail rating: strenuous).

Trailhead is in Waimea Canyon.

Koaie Canyon is a favorite of hikers and backpackers for it's a pleasant, foliated trail that leads to a secluded wilderness shelter. The canyon's name comes from the koaie (Acacia koaia) tree, which is endemic to the islands and is much like the koa tree. The wood, however, is harder than koa wood, and was once used to make spears and fancy paddles.

If the water is high in the river, DO NOT CROSS. Flash flooding is an ever-present danger. It is necessary to cross the river to the east side to continue on the Koaie Canyon Trail. You cross the river about a half mile up river just below Poo Kaeha, a prominent hill about 500 feet above the river, pick up Koaie Stream a short distance later, and follow the south side of the stream into Koaie Canyon.

The canyon is a fertile area that was once extensively farmed as is evidenced by the many terraced areas you'll observe and the rock walls and the remains of house sites. You can usually find ample pools in the stream to swim in or at least to cool off in. During the summer months, the water is usually low, but sufficient for some relief from the hot canyon. The Division of Forestry has a number of wildland campsites here; one site at Hipalau and another at Lonomea Camp, an open shelter with a table alongside the stream near a generous pool for swimming at trail's end. The Lonomea (Sapindus cahuensis) is a native tree with ovate leaves which reaches heights of up to 30 feet. They grow only on Kauai and Oahu.

There is ample water in the canyon, but it should be treated or boiled before drinking.

Don't forget to pack out your trash.

Waialae Canyon Trail, 0.3 mile, 1/2 hour (trail rating: strenuous).

Trailhead in Waimea Canyon.

Walk south about one-half mile along the Waimea River from the campground at the terminus of the Kukui Trail to a marker that identifies the point where you can ford the river and enter lower Waialae Canyon. CAUTION; DO NOT CROSS the river when the water level is high.

This short, undeveloped trail takes you east into Waialae Canyon. The trail follows the north side of Waialae Stream for a short distance to "Poachers Camp," where a shelter, table and pit toilets are located. You're likely to meet hunters in Waialae Canyon and you're likely to see evidence of their success by the bones and the carcasses of animals left along the trail.

There is ample water in the canyon, but it should be treated or boiled before drinking.

Breadfruit

Kokee State Park Trails
(Hiking Area No. 13)

Rating: See individual hikes.

Features: Views of Waimea Canyon, Na Pali Coast and Kalalau Valley; swimming, camping, waterfalls, iliau plant, rain forest, wilderness hiking, fruit and native and introduced flora and fauna.

Permission: Camping permits from State Parks and cabin reservations from Kokee Lodge (addresses in Appendix). Fee to camp.

Hiking Distance & Time: See individual hikes.

Driving Instructions: (38 miles, 1 3/4 hours) From Lihue, drive south on Route 50, turn right on Route 550 (Waimea Canyon Drive) to Kokee State Park Headquarters.

Introductory Notes: Kokee (lit., "to bend or to wind") State Park is the most popular hiking and camping place on the island. It ranks in my top five list of favorite hiking places in the 50th State. Kokee has numerous hiking trails and untold hunting trails that snake along the pali (cliff) to otherwise remote and inaccessible places. Technically, this northwest corner of the island is under two state agencies, the Division of State Parks and the Division of Forestry, both of which are under the Hawaii State Department of Land and Natural Resources; and Kokee Lodge is operated by a private concessionaire. While the lodge's cabins are not luxurious, they are very comfortable and in keeping with the surroundings.

Kokee Housekeeping Cabins

The state cabins at Kokee, very popular with locals and tourists, require reservations. Kokee Lodge is not really a lodge but rather 12 rustic cabins completely furnished with refrigerator, water heater, range, cooking utensils, shower, linens, blankets, beds and fireplace. All you need is food, which is not available in the park, but 20 miles away in Waimea. There is, however, a restaurant a short walk from the cabins, open for a light breakfast from 9 a.m. to 11 p.m.and for lunch from 11 a.m. to 3:30 p.m.

Each cabin will accommodate 3-7 persons at a very modest cost from $35-45 per day. The units vary in size from one large room, which sleeps six persons, to two-bedroom cabins that will accommodate seven. State park rules limit a stay to five days and prohibit pets.

The cabins are very popular with locals, so make reservations early - even one year in advance is not too soon. Forward the number in your group as well as the dates you wish to reserve. Payment is refundable, less a $15 service charge, if cancellation is received at least one week prior to the reservation date.Full payment is required for confirmation. Business hours at the lodge are from 9 a.m. to 4 p.m. daily. Write to the lodge for complete information and reservations (address in Appendix).

Kokee Camping

At the north end of a shady, picturesque meadow, tent and trailer camping are available in the shade of tall eucalyptus trees. Camping is limited to five days and a permit is required (see Appendix). Water, tables, barbecues, restrooms and cold-water showers are available. There are a number of wilderness camping areas and shelters in the

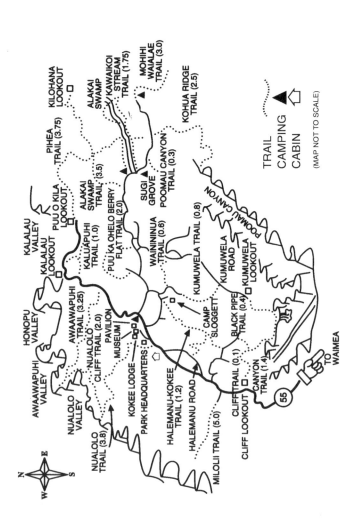

KILOHANA LOOKOUT

KAWAIKOI STREAM TRAIL (1.75)

MOHIHI WAIALAE TRAIL (3.0)

ALAKAI SWAMP

PIHEA TRAIL (3.75)

KOHUA RIDGE TRAIL (2.5)

TRAIL
CAMPING
CABIN

(MAP NOT TO SCALE)

PUU O KILA LOOKOUT

ALAKAI SWAMP TRAIL (3.5)

SUGI GROVE

POOMAU CANYON TRAIL (0.3)

KALALAU VALLEY

KALALAU LOOKOUT

KALUAPUHI TRAIL (1.0)

PUU KA OHELO BERRY FLAT TRAIL (2.0)

WAININIHUA TRAIL (0.6)

KUMUWELA TRAIL (0.8)

POOMAU CANYON

HONOPU VALLEY

AWAAWAPUHI TRAIL (3.25)

NUALOLO CLIFF TRAIL (2.0)

PAVILION

MUSEUM

CAMP SLOGGETT

KUMUWELA ROAD

KUMUWELA LOOKOUT

AWAAWAPUHI VALLEY

KOKEE LODGE

PARK HEADQUARTERS

BLACK PIPE TRAIL (0.4)

NUALOLO VALLEY

HALEMANU-KOKEE TRAIL (1.2)

HALEMANU ROAD

CLIFF TRAIL (0.1)

CANYON TRAIL (1.4)

TO WAIMEA

NUALOLO TRAIL (3.8)

MILOLII TRAIL (5.0)

CLIFF LOOKOUT

55

N E S W

back country available (see the map and the trail descriptions) under the jurisdiction of the Division of Forestry.

In recent years a controversy has existed over the future of the Kokee-Waimea area. Conservationists have sought Federal legislation to establish a national park so that the wilderness can be preserved in relatively pristine condition. Opponents of this proposal seek to retain the present status, because a national park would probably prohibit hunting, land leases for vacation cabins and taking plants.

Whatever the future, whether your interest is hiking, hunting or sightseeing, no trip to Kauai is complete without a visit to Kokee and Waimea Canyon. Kokee is the home of the rare mokihana berry (see pp. 149-150), and the even rarer and beautiful iliau plant (see p.134) and the delicious Methley plum, which is ready for picking throughout the park in late May or early June. The picking season is short because local people flock to the park and carry off buckets full of this delectable fruit. In recent years, pickings have been poor because so many trees have been damaged by hurricanes and harvesters while others have been overwhelmed by other vegetation.

On the Trail: Although it is not required, for safety reasons you should sign in and out in the registry at the Kokee State Park Headquarters when hiking. Your interests, physical condition, and length of stay at Kokee will determine which hike you take. On the whole, trails in the general vicinity of park headquarters are relatively short and easy, while trails into Waimea Canyon, to the valley overlooks or into the Alakai Swamp are full-day or overnight trips. Access to most of the trails is from jeep roads that radiate off the main highway - Route 55. You should not travel these roads in a passenger car even when dry, because many are steep and deeply rutted. The ranger at park headquarters and the museum personnel are the best sources of information about road and trail conditions.

The trails in the Kokee State Park/Waimea Canyon area have been worked, brushed, posted, and taped so that most are in good condition. Trail improvement programs have involved hundreds of student workers, unpaid volunteers, the Hawaii Sierra Club, and the State National Guard, 227th Engineer Company.

The mileage from Park Headquarters to the trailhead via the most direct road is noted preceding each trail description.

Halemanu-Kokee Trail, 1.2 miles, 1 hour (trail rating: hardy family).

Park HQ to trailhead 0.6 mile.

This trail starts just before entering Camp Slogget near the old ranger station and ends on Halemanu Road. It's a hike for those who are interested in a short, pleasant, easy walk with the prospect of seeing some native birds and plants. The trail, linking Mohihi and Halemanu Roads, is an enjoyable hike in itself and also a route to hiking areas on Kokee's west side.

Tall trees dominate the area, such as lehua and the majestic koa. There are three red birds that you can expect to see along the trail. The cardinal has a pronounced crest, which is the most prominent feature distinguishing it from the apapane (Himatione sanguinea), a deep-crimson bird with black wings and tail and a slightly curved black bill, and the iiwi (Vestiaria coccinea), a vermilion bird with black wings and tail and orange legs. The latter also has a rather pronounced curved salmon bill. Unless you get a good look at these birds, it is difficult to identify them, but they can be enjoyed without being identified. One other bird that is common throughout the forest is the elepaio (Chasiempis sanwichensis), an endemic bird that is gray-backed with a rather long, blackish tail and white rump. It is a somewhat noisy bird, giving forth with what is best described as a sort of "wolf-whistle."

Waininiua Trail, 0.6 mile, 1/2 hour (trail rating: hardy family).

Park HQ to trailhead 2.2 miles.

Mostly a short, flat, scenic forest walk, the Waininiua Trail with the Kumuwela Trail completes a loop off Kumuwela Road. There are a variety of native and introduced plants, the most notable being aromatic ginger with its lovely, light-yellow blossoms. Many local girls like to put a fresh ginger blossom in their hair, not only for its beauty but also for its fragrance.

Kumuwela Trail, 0.8 mile, 1 hour, (trail rating: hardy family).

Park HQ to trailhead 1.0 mile.

At the end of the short spur road off Mohihi Road (see map) turn left into the forest for the beginning of the Kumuwela Trail. The trailhead is marked and the trail is well-maintained. The trail dips abruptly into a luxuriant, fern-lined gulch where kahili ginger (Hedychium coronarium) flourishes. The size, fragrance and light-yellow blossoms overwhelm most visitors. You should find many places on and off the trail where feral pigs have been digging to get at roots.

Along this verdant trail there are also specimens of lantana, lilikoi (passion fruit) as well as handsome kukui and koa trees. The last 0.3 mile requires a 300-foot elevation gain to Kumuwela Road, where you can connect with the Canyon Trail.

Puu Ka Ohelo/Berry Flat Trail, 2 miles, 1 hour (trail rating: hardy family).

Park HQ to trailhead 0.9 mile.

An easy, pleasant loop trail off Mohihi (a variety of sweet potato) Road combines the Berry Flat and the Puu Ka Ohelo (Ohelo hill) trails. The trailhead is posted and the trail is clear, broad and easy to follow. You will cross a couple of small streams along this verdant trail. The banana passion fruit (Passiflora mollissima) is found here draping from the trees. It is a wild vine that produces a pretty, light-pink blossom and a small, yellow, banana-shaped fruit. The Park Service regards the vine as a pest because it smothers native trees.

Both trails pass through scenic forest containing mostly introduced trees that should be easy to identify. Particularly noteworthy is a stand of California redwoods (Sequoia simpervirens) that will excite the senses. These wondrous giants tower over the other trees adding a certain majesty to the grove and their droppings provide a luxuriant carpet on which to walk. They are found as you begin the Berry Flat Trail.

In addition, there are stands of Australian eucalyptus, Japanese Sugi pines and the native koa (Acacia koa), which grows to a height of more that 50 feet. The koa has a light gray bark that is smooth on young trees and considerably furrowed on mature trees. The leaves are smooth, stiff and crescent-shaped. Often called Hawaiian mahogany, the wood is red with a wavy grain that makes it popular for use in furniture, woodwork and ukuleles. In older times it had nobler purposes, having been used for war canoes, surfboards and calabashes.

The prize to be sought here is the popular Methley plum that flourishes in the Kokee area. However, plum picking has been poor in recent years because of storm damage to the trees. Look for plum trees whose fruit ripens at the end of May or the first part of June.

There is also a variety of birds along both trails. (All bookstores on the island have small, pocket-sized, inexpensive bird books featuring the most frequently seen birds.) The cardinal (Richmondena cardinalis) is a commonly seen bird on the island which was introduced from the mainland. The male, with his all-red body and pointed crest, has been seen along the trail as well as throughout the park.

Ditch Trail, 3.5 miles, 4 hours (trail rating: strenuous).

Park HQ to trailhead 2.3 miles.

(TRAIL IS CLOSED) Check with Kokee Museum regarding current status.

Shortly after this trail was cleaned and posted in 1988, earth slides in two places damaged the path. Consequently, the Ditch Trail is, what it always has been, an ambitious hike over some very rough terrain. In any event, the trail follows a circuitous route along a cliff and in and out of numerous gulches and small stream canyons. It is best to enter this trail at the trailhead from Mohihi Road.

The trail offers spectacular sights of the interior of Waimea, which is one of the broader and deeper of the canyons. Across the canyon you'll see Kohua Ridge, with its many waterfalls and cascades during rainy periods. Awini ("sharp, bold, forward") Falls is at the southwest tip of the ridge, with Mohihi Falls to the right-rear of the canyon and Moeloa ("to oversleep") Falls to the left-rear of the canyon.

The trail is rich with flora, from the common guava to lehua and a variety of ferns. The variety of tree fern (Cibotium menziesii) seen here is the "monkey's tail" fern, with its wiry black hairs on the frond stems. It has the biggest trunk of all Hawaiian tree ferns, a trunk often used for carving akuas (idols) or tikis.

Alakai Swamp Trail, 3.5 miles, 3 hours, 500-feet gain (trail rating: strenuous).

Park HQ to trailhead 3 miles.

Few will disagree that the Alakai (lit., "to lead") Swamp is the most interesting and exciting place on the island. For interest, there is the beautiful mokihana berry - Kauai's flower - and the native rain forests; and for excitement, there is the swamp with its bogs, where a false step puts you knee-deep in mud and water. I recommend a lightweight, gore-tex or cloth hiking boot for this trail. You can bet on getting very wet and muddy.

The trail begins deceivingly easily off Mohihi (Camp 10) Road, which should be traversed by a four-wheeled vehicle because parts are steep and deeply rutted. (An alternative route is off the Pihea Trail - see below.) A forest-reserve marker identifies the trailhead while the trail follows an old pole line constructed during World War ll for Army communications. After a mile, the trail reaches the Alakai-Pihea Trail junction. From here, our trail follows a newly constructed (1998) boardwalk that makes a steep descent to a small stream, which eventually empties into Kawaikoi Stream. Across the stream, the trail narrows and makes a steep ascent.

Your nose may pickup the fragrance of the mokihana (Pelea anisata) tree, which emits a strong anise odor. It is a small tree whose small berries are strung and worn in leis. Native to the islands, the mokihana berry is frequently twined with the maile vine to make a popular wedding lei. The maile (Alyxia olivaeformis) vine is common along the trail, with its tiny, glossy leaves and tiny, white flow-

Alakai Swamp trailhead

ers. Unlike the Mokihana tree, the maile vine must be cut or its bark stripped before its musky, woodsy scent or anise is noticed.

After ascending and descending a number of small, fern-lined gulches, the broad, flat expanse of the swamp lies before you. The last half-mile of boardwalk was not finished at the end of 1998, but the planking was laid out to direct hikers to trail's end and to portect this environmentally fragile preserve. Be cautious or you'll find yourself ankle or knee deep in mud.

At Kilohana ("lookout point" or "superior") Lookout one has a magnificent view into Wainiha (lit., "unfriendly water") Valley, which extends from the sea to the base of Mt. Waialeale. Beyond Wainiha lies Hanalei (lit., "crescent bay") with its conspicuous wide, deep bay. It's an enchanting place to picnic, rest and reflect. If the cloud cover prevents a view, just wait and it is likely to clear.

Don't linger too long if the cloud cover remains. It can be very wet and very cold in the afternoon hours.

Kawaikoi Stream Trail, 1.75 miles, 1-1/2 hours (trail rating: hardy family).

Park HQ to trailhead 3.8 miles.

Access to the Kawaikoi (lit., "the flowing water") Stream Trail is off Mohihi (Camp 10) Road, which is passable only in a four-wheel-drive vehicle. The trail was made possible in 1975 when the Forest Service and the Hawaii Chapter of the Sierra Club connected the Kawaikoi Trail with the Pihea Trail.

The route begins opposite a planted forest of Japanese sugi pines and follows the south side of Kawaikoi Stream along an easy, well-defined trail in heavy vegetation.

During rainy periods, this is a muddy trail. A short distance past the 0.5-mile point, a trail sign indicates a place to cross the stream to join the Pihea Trail on the north side of the stream. If rocks are not visible, then the water is too high for safe crossing. The Kawaikoi Trail itself continues east on the south side of the stream to a point 100 yards past the 3/4-mile marker, where a trail sign marks the loop portion of the trail. During the 1-mile loop it is necessary to cross the stream twice.

In recent years, there has been a good deal of grass planting and herbicide work in the area in an effort to control blackberry, which is threatening to take over not only this area but also a number of other areas in the park.

There are many swimming holes in this generous stream and places along the bank to spend some peaceful moments. You may agree with Ralph Daehler, District Forester, Retired who says, "Kawaikoi is the most beautiful place on Kauai."

Poomau Canyon Trail, 0.3 mile, 15 minutes (trail rating: hardy family).

Park HQ to trailhead 4.5 miles.

About 0.5 mile past the trailhead for the Kawaikoi Stream Trail on the Mohihi (Camp 10) Road is a marker identifying the Poomau (lit., "constant source") Canyon Trail. This short, easy trail passes through a small stand of Japanese sugi trees, enters a native rain forest, and ends overlooking Poomau Canyon, the largest and northernmost side canyon in Waimea Canyon. Across the canyon on the west rim, the high prominence is Puu Ka Pele (lit., "Pele's Hill") and Highway 55. Legend records that Pele, the fire goddess, left Kauai unable to find a suitable home.

The caldera was created when Pele brought down her foot for the leap across the channel to Oahu. The caldera has since been filled with small stones some say by visitors as an offering to the goddess. The lookout is an excellent place for pictures of the canyon and for picnicking.

Kohua Ridge Trail, 2.5 miles, 3 hours, 800-feet loss (trail rating: strenuous).

Park HQ to trailhead 5.5 miles.

The trailhead to the Kohua Ridge Trail (formerly the Maile Flat Trail) is off Mohihi (Camp 10) Road, which is passable only in a four-wheel-drive vehicle. In 1988, the trail was cleaned and extended to Maile Flat for superb views of Waimea Canyon.

Originally constructed by the Civilian Conservation Corps, the Kohua Ridge Trail is a vigorous hike up Kohua Ridge to Maile Flat, which contains a heavy undergrowth of maile (Alyxia olivaeformis). A fragrant vine, maile has glossy leaves, tiny white flowers and a musky, woodsy scent of anise when it is cut or its bark is stripped. Combined with mokihana berries, it is a popular lei for weddings.

From the trailhead, the trail descends to cross Mohihi Ditch and then swings left to cross Mohihi Stream. If the water level in the stream covers the boulders used to hop across, your hike should end here. DO NOT cross if the water is high. From the stream your trail follows a steep and eroded path to the top of the ridge. Be alert to side trails that hunters follow in search of feral goats. The trail alternately ascends and descends the ridge which is mostly heavily foliated with koa and ohia trees. Periodic breaks permit a marvelous view deep

into Koaie Canyon (left) and, weather permitting, a view to the ocean.

The trail continues an up-and-down course for the last mile. Look for pukiawe (Styphelia tameiameiae) with tiny, evergreen-like leaves with reddish-white berries. A sign at the end of the trail means what it states. Beyond the sign, "Kokua Trail Vista End," is a vertical drop into Koaie Canyon. From here, a peaceful spot to lunch, Poomau Canyon is north (right), Wahane Valley is directly below and Koaie Canyon is south (left). Only the view from the Awaawapuhi Trail rivals this spectacular sight.

Mohihi-Waiale Trail, 3 miles, 3 hours, 800-feet gain (trail rating: difficult).

Park HQ to trailhead 6.2 miles.

I DO NOT recommend this trail because rain, a thick understory and side trails obscure your path to Koaie Camp. For me, the Pihea, Alakai Swamp and Kawaikoi Trails are safer and equally beautiful.

The first three miles of this trail were cleared several years ago, but since it receives few hikers, it can become quickly overgrown. If you choose to hike, DO NOT go beyond the cleared portion since the old trail is in disrepair as it cuts a circuitous route through the Alakai Swamp.

The trail begins at the end of Mohihi (Camp 10) Road at a trail registry, crosses Mohihi Stream, skirts the upper part of the Koaie drainage, continues along a ridge top from which you'll have dramatic views and experience the beauty of the swamp.

Originally constructed by the Civilian Conservation Corps in the 1930's, the trail segment connecting the Mo-

hihi-Waialae Trail and the Waialae Canyon Trail was destroyed by a hurricane in 1959. When funds become available, the trail will be repaired according to state officials.

Nature Trail Loop, 0.2 mile, 15 minutes (trail rating: family).

Behind Kokee Museum

This is a short, pleasant walk behind the museum in a
forest of trees and plants common to the park. Before hiking, pickup a free copy of "Pocket Guide to Plants on the
Nature Trail" in the museum.

Milolii Ridge Trail, 5 miles, 3 hours, 2,200-feet loss (trail rating: strenuous).

0.7-mile from Park HQ.

The trailhead is reached by driving south on Route
550 from park headquarters for one-half mile, turn right
just past the 14-mile marker on Makaha Ridge Road and
drive 0.2-mile to a junction. Milolii Ridge Road and the
trailhead are on the right.

If you have hiked all of the trails in Waimea Canyon
and Kokee State Park, then consider the Milolii (Lit., "fine
twist") Ridge Trail. There is little to recommend the trail
used primarily by goat and pig hunters. Indeed, you can
drive the entire length in a four-wheel drive vehicle. At
trail's end, the views do not compare to the Awaawapuhi
or Nualolo Trails.

Shade from tall koa and ohia trees is intermittent
throughout the trail. Otherwise, it's usually a long, hot,
dusty walk. Be alert for small, red strawberry guava trailside. When ripe, they are delicious. The trail, marked by

conspicuous, white PVC pipe, makes a gentle descent before reaching several very steep, heavily rutted parts of the road that require some agility to negotiate, particularly when wet.

Just before the 2 1/2-mile marker, you have a view of the privately owned island of Niihau to the front-left and a trail shelter on the right just past the marker. Niihau was purchased by the Sinclair Family in 1864. Today, about 200 Hawaiians live on the Island. Most work the cattle and sheep ranch much as their descendants did in the last century. Electricity has come to the ranch house and the school, but not to the homes of the residents. It's probably difficult for visitors to imagine life without television, telephones, shops or restaurants.

Located in a turnout under a canopy of trees, the trail shelter contains a picnic table and sufficient space to accommodate a tent. Sit quietly and you may be visited by the amakihi, a tiny, dull green-yellow, endemic forest bird. I watched several apapane, an endemic bird with a bright red crown, crimson breast and black legs and bill, foraging in the koa trees.

From the shelter the trail follows a steep, abrupt descent, one of several before reaching trail's end in a grove of koa and silk oak trees. Roads here go in different directions. Proceed cautiously north (right) a short distance to a view into Milolii Valley and the ocean beyond. A short walk south (left) leads to views of Makaha Valley. The microwave facility and numerous radio towers are in clear view on the ridge across the valley.

Nualolo Trail, 3.8 miles, 3 hours, 1,350-feet loss (trail rating: strenuous).

50 yards west of Park HQ.

The Hawaii State Division of Forestry has completed cleaning the Nualolo Trail and the Nualolo Cliff Trail (see map) so that a marvelous 9-mile hike is possible by following the Nualolo-Cliff-Awaawapuhi trails.

The Nualolo Trail starts between the ranger station and the housekeeping cabins in Kokee, and if you follow the suggested 9-mile hike, you will exit the Awaawapuhi Trail on Highway 55, 1.5 miles from Park Headquarters.

The first part of the trail passes through a native forest of koa trees with their crescent-shaped leaves for a pleasant, cool hike. After an initial ascent of about 300 feet, the trail then descends about 1500 feet to a number of viewpoints overlooking Nualolo Valley. The first 1.5 miles of trail are broad, posted and easy to follow. A variety of ferns, the beautiful kahili ginger, and edible passion fruit, thimbleberries and blackberries are found along the trail.

The trail narrows somewhat at the 1.5-mile marker, but then opens again at the 2.25-mile post. After this point, you're certain to see the rare, endemic iliau plant (see p. 165 for description). You may also find ripe strawberry guava, a small, red golf ball-sized fruit.

There are several steep parts on the trail in the last mile so be cautious. At the 3.4-mile marker, the Cliff Trail goes right for 2.1 miles until it reaches the Awaawapuhi Trail and the Nualolo Trail goes straight to numerous vista points about 2800 feet above the valley. Trail's end is a marvelous place to picnic and to enjoy the solitude. If you walk out to the end of the ridge, you will have a view of the

Na Pali Coast to the north (right) and the beach fronting Kalalau Valley.

Nualolo Cliff Trail, 2 miles, 1 1/2 hours (trail rating: strenuous).

Reached via Nualolo or Awaawapuhi Trail.

If you have reached the Nualolo Cliff Trail junction from the Awaawapuhi or Nualolo Trail, you should hike the Cliff Trail for the views into Awaawapuhi and Nualolo valleys are outstanding. Additionally, you're likely to see feral goats here as well as the rare, delicately beautiful Kauai hibiscus.

From the Nualolo Trail, the Nualolo Cliff Trail is mostly level until just before reaching the Awaawapuhi Trail, where it makes an easy ascent. One-fourth-mile markers identify the way along which you are certain to see goats foraging for food and bounding on the steep slopes in the upper valley. The trail was cut to provide hikers with a crossover trail between two marvelous trails and to offer some of the best views of the Na Pali Coast.

At the 1.5-mile point, the trail emerges on a flat area used by campers. Here, the trail is not clearly marked. Hike up the ridge away from the valley lookout and you will locate the trail and shortly, a white PVC-pipe-marker.

Between the 0.5 and 0.25-mile markers, look for the rare, endemic Kauai hibiscus (Saint johnianus) with its small, delicate, orange blossom. It's a find.

After an easy uphill, the Nualolo Cliff Trail joins the Awaawapuhi Trail where you can go 0.3 miles left to the end of the trail or go 2.8 miles right to Kokee Road.

Awaawapuhi Trail, 3.25 miles, 2 1/2 hrs, 1,600-feet loss (trail rating: strenuous).

Park HQ to trailhead 1.5 miles.

The Hawaii State Division of Forestry has completed cutting, brushing, posting and taping the Nualolo Trail and the Nualolo Cliff Trail (see map) so that a marvelous 9-mile hike is possible by following the Awaawapuhi-Cliff-Nualolo Trails. I would begin such a trek on the Nualolo Trail and end traversing the Awaawapuhi Trail since the latter is a more gradual ascent.

The Division of Forestry has a guide "Awa'awa'puhi Botanical Trail Guide," which is available from the forestry office in Lihue (see Appendix) and from the Kokee Museum. The Division of Forestry has identified and posted with white PVC pipe 58 plants found along the trail. The white pipe with numbers on top identify the plants while the pipes with numbers on the side are mile markers. Learning about these native and introduced plants will add a dimension to your experience.

Of the trails that extend to points high above the Na Pali Coast and the extraordinarily beautiful valleys of the north shore, this is the best. You should be in good condition before attempting this hike and be prepared with water and food. The rewards are great as you pass through tropical forests to view the extremely precipitous and verdant valleys of Awaawapuhi (lit., "ginger valley") and Nualolo.

The trail begins northwest (left) off Highway 55 about halfway between the Kokee Museum and the Kalalau lookout. There is a forestry trail marker at the trailhead. The trail is well-maintained, and mileage markers show the way.

Awaawapuhi Trailhead

The first part of the trail passes through a moist native forest, dominated by koa trees, for a pleasant, cool hike. Koa trees grow to a height of more than 50 feet. The koa has a light gray bark that is smooth on young trees and considerably furrowed on mature trees. The leaves are smooth, stiff and crescent-shaped. Often called Hawaiian mahogany, the wood is red with wavy grain that makes it popular for use in furniture, woodwork and ukuleles. In older times it had nobler purposes, having been used for war canoes, surfboards and calabashes. A variety of ferns, the beautiful kahili ginger, and edible passion fruit, thimbleberries and blackberries are also found along the trail.

The trail then descends gradually through a moist native forest which becomes drier scrub as it reaches the ridges above the valley. You are most likely to see feral goats in the pali area. With binoculars you can watch goats forage while you pause on any one of a number of look-outs about 2500 feet above the valley. Additionally, you will probably sight helicopters flying tourists in, out, and over the pali, since the Na Pali Coast is a favorite for those who are unable or unwilling to make the trip on foot.

Just before reaching the 3-mile marker, a white PVC-pipe post identifies the Cliff Trail that goes south (left) 2.1-miles to the Nualolo Trail, which leads to the main road between the ranger's house and the housekeeping cabins.

The Awaawapuhi Trail continues for 0.3 mile from the junction to a vertical perch above the Na Pali Coast. This is the best place to lunch and to watch for goats while enjoying enchanting views into Nualolo and Awaawapuhi valleys. It's a startling and exciting place.

Kaluapuhi Trail, 1.0 miles, 1 hour (trail rating: family).

Park HQ to trailhead 1.9 miles.

Access to the trail is a few feet off the main road where a trail marker identifies the trailhead.

Even though the Park Service claims that this trail is "2.0+" miles, the last mile is overgrown with berry bushes and may not be passable. The first mile of the trail is wide and flat and easy to follow. At the 0.5-mile point, an equally wide, flat trail goes left and emerges 0.5 miles later, 0.2 miles northeast (right) of the Kalalau Lookout. This is a pleasant hike for the entire family with the prospect of sweet plums along the trail.

Kaluapuhi (lit., "the eel pit") Trail is a favorite during plum season. If it is a good year for the delicious Methley plum, this trail will take you to some of the best trees. The pickings are generally good here because the only access to the trees is on foot.

Plum picking is regulated by the state and is limited to 25 pounds of the fruit per person per day. Pickers must check in and out at the checking station, usually located near park headquarters. Many local people bring the whole family and stay overnight to get an early start on opening day.

Pihea Trail, 3.75 miles, 3 hours, 500-feet gain/loss (trail rating: strenuous).

Park HQ to trailhead 3.8 miles.

Pihea ("din of voices crying, shouting, wailing, lamentation") Trail begins at the end of the Highway 55 at Puu o Kila (lit., "Kila's Hill") overlooking Kalalau Valley. A hiking sign-in trail registry identifies the trailhead. For your safety, sign in and out in the registry.

The first 3/4-mile follows the remains of a county road project which was begun in a cloud of controversy and which terminated literally in the mire when money ran out, along with the willingness to continue. A road through the Alakai Swamp and down the mountain to Hanalei would have been a great tourist attraction and an engineering feat, but an ecological disaster.

From Kalalau lookout, you can usually see the white-tailed tropic bird (Phaethon lepturus) soaring along the cliffs of Kalalau Valley. This bird is white with large black wing patches above and 16-inch tail streamers. A similar bird that is all white except for red tail streamers is the red-tailed tropic bird (Phaethon rubricauda).

After enjoying the breathtaking views into Kalalau, your trail follows the rim of the valley to Pihea, the last overlook into Kalalau before the Alakai Swamp. From

Kalaulau Lookout - What a sight!

here, expect a wet, muddy trail through heavy vegetation. The trail makes an abrupt right turn as it enters the swamp and then drops in and out of a number of gulches to the junction with the Alakai Swamp Trail.

The Pihea Trail can be used as part of a loop trip from Kalalau into the Alakai Swamp, with a return to park head-quarters via the Alakai Swamp Trail or the Kawaikoi Stream Trail and the Camp 10 Road (see map).

Both the maile vine and the mokihana tree (see pp. 149-150 for description) are common along the trail and are favorites of both locals and visitors. The mokihana's powerful anise aroma attracts immediate attention.

Also common in this area is the ohia lehua (Metrosideros polymorpha), with its tufted red stamens that remind the visitor of the bottlebrush tree. A variety of tree ferns abound along the trail, the hapu'u (Cibotium chamissoi) and the amaumau (Sadleria cyatheoides) being most common. The latter grows to 10 feet. Its pinnate fronds were once used for huts and the juice from it for a reddish dye.

From the junction with the Alakai Swamp Trail, our trail continues over the newest portion passing through native forests, crossing small streams, and winding through verdant gulches until it joins the Kawaikoi Stream Trail.

Cliff Trail, 0.1 mile, 10 minutes (trail rating: family).

Park HQ to trailhead 2.1 miles.

The Cliff Trail provides a scenic vista of Waimea Canyon and a convenient departure point for the Canyon Trail. It begins after a short walk or drive down Halemanu Road. Be quiet as you approach the lookout so that you do not frighten any goats that might be browsing there. Feral goats are commonly sighted here or walking along the pali area opposite the lookout.

Canyon Trail, 1.4 miles, 1 1/2 hrs, 500-feet loss (trail rating: hardy family).

Park HQ to trailhead 2.1 miles.

The Canyon Trail is a popular hike. The trail descends into a gulch and snakes along the cliff to Kokee Stream and Waipoo (lit., "head water") Falls, where you can picnic in the shade and swim or splash in the stream. The best swimming hole is at the base of Waipoo Falls #1.

Although the Canyon Trail is steep in parts and requires some stamina, it offers some of the best views of Waimea Canyon. The trail begins at the Halemanu Road and runs south along the east rim of the canyon. It is somewhat precipitous in places, so be careful. At the Cliff Look-out, which is 0.1 mile beyond the end of the Halemanu Road, you get not only a view of the canyon but also a view of the trail as it descends and snakes along the cliff.

A common plant on the high, dry ridges is the lantana (Lantana camara), which blossoms almost continuously. Its flowers vary in color from yellow to orange to pink or red; infrequently they are white with yellow centers. It is a low shrub with a thick, strong wood.

A small, pretty, yellow-green bird, the anianiau (Loxops parva), is common in the high forests of Kauai. In truth it is difficult for the less-than-expert to tell the difference between the anianiau and the amakihi (Loxops virents), which is the same size and yellow. However, if you get a close look, the amakihi has a dark loral (space between the eye and bill) mark that joins the eye and the curved dark bill. No matter, however, for they are both pretty birds.

When the trail reaches the flat, eroded vista point, you'll have marvelous views of the canyon and beyond to the ocean. From here, the trail makes a short, but steep decent to Waipoo Falls #1 on the left and Waipoo Falls #2, 25 yards farther down the trail.

From the falls, the trail makes a steep climb out of the gulch and ascends the pali, from which some of the best vistas of Waimea are had. Once again, be careful for while the trail is broad and easy to follow, at some places steep walls drop to the canyon below. There are numerous places to pause in some shade to enjoy the view through the canyon to the sea on the south side.

After a steep climb, the trail ends at Kumuwela Look-out, from where you can return on the Canyon Trail or connect with Kumuwela Road.

Black Pipe Trail, 0.4 mile, 1/2 hour (trail rating: hardy family).

Park HQ to trailhead 2.5 miles.

This is a short spur trail that connects the Canyon Trail with the middle fork of the Halemanu Road. The trail descends into a small overgrown gulch and then climbs to follow the cliff to the Canyon Trail. It is along the pali that the rare and beautiful iliau (Wilkesia gymnoxiphium) grows. A relative to the rare silversword that grows on Maui, the iliau is endemic to Kauai and found only in the western mountains. It grows 4-12 feet high, it is unbranched, and the stems end in clumps of long, narrow leaves 6-16 inches long. Once in its life, the plant flowers in a flourish of hundreds of tiny yellow blossoms.

Waipoo Falls #2

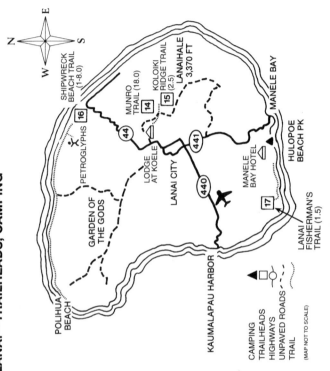

LANAI—TRAILHEADS, CAMPING

N W S E

SHIPWRECK BEACH TRAIL (1-8.0)

MUNRO TRAIL (18.0)

KOLOIKI RIDGE TRAIL (2.5)

LANAIHALE 3,370 FT

MANELE BAY

16

44

14

15

441

PETROGLYPHS

LODGE AT KOELE

LANAI CITY

GARDEN OF THE GODS

POLIHUA BEACH

440

MANELE BAY HOTEL

HULOPOE BEACH PK

17

LANAI FISHERMAN'S TRAIL (1.5)

KAUMALAPAU HARBOR

CAMPING
TRAILHEADS
HIGHWAYS
UNPAVED ROADS
TRAIL

(MAP NOT TO SCALE)

Lanai
The Pineapple Isle

The Island

Lanai is mostly owned by the Dole Pineapple Co. (Castle & Cook, Inc.) which is no longer engaged in large scale production of pineapple on the island. Lanai is small - just 17 miles long and 13 miles wide - with adequate to posh visitor accommodations. It does not have many hiking trails, but it does have one of the best swimming and snorkeling beaches anywhere. Hulopoe Beach is a dream place to "kick back" and a good basecamp from which to explore the island. Camping is permitted on a grassy, shaded area above the beach.

Lanai City is in the center of the island in the foothills of a small mountain range that is topped by Lanaihale (3370 feet), the highest place on the island. Politically, the 2600 residents are part of Maui county. The island has a couple of grocery stores, a few cafes, and the usual assortment of government buildings. Restaurants can be found in the upscale hotels. My favorite eatery is in Hotel Lanai, the island's original accommodation. Since there is no public transportation, it is necessary to rent a vehicle. A four wheel drive car is recommended to travel the pineapple and mountain roads. However, local people are friendly, so that rides are not difficult to get on the main roads.

Although Lanai is known quite properly as the "Pineapple Island" today, its past belies this innocent nickname. Historically, Lanai was a place where kapu (taboo) violators were banished and where life was once difficult on this wild, mostly arid land (42 inches of rainfall in the center of the island). Additionally, the aliis (chiefs) frequently brought their dead to Lanai to be buried. Consequently, legends abound regarding ghosts who inhabit the island today. One legend tells of Kaululaau, who for his evil deeds was exiled by his uncle, the king of Maui. Kaululaau is thought to have made Lanai safe for human habitation by fighting the ghosts and driving off the evil spirits.

Today, this tiny island, which was created by a single crater volcano, Palawai, has entered tourist-oriented Hawaii. Castle and Cook constructed two major resorts complete with professional class golf courses to attract tourists. Lanai is no longer a peaceful stopover for the person who can do without luxury.

However, the small, 11-room Hotel Lanai in Lanai City is still operational and offers moderately priced accommodations and a good restaurant.

Camping

Camping on Hulopoe Beach is a memorable experience. The little used campground is on a grassy, shaded knoll above the beach. Daily, a pod of spinner dolphins visits the bay to entertain campers and the guests at the Menele Bay Hotel. The campground is privately owned by the Lanai Company. There is a $5.00 one-time registration fee and a $5.00 fee per day per person regardless of age. Reservations and applications should be made at least one week in advance by phone or mail. Camping is limited to seven days. There are clean restrooms, fire pits, tables and showers. The latter are "cold water." However, the pipes are so close to the ground surface that the sun heats the water. Be certain to bring snorkeling equipment, for there are few places to compare with Hulopoe.

Address is in the Appendix for Lanai Company.

Hiking

There are four notable hikes on the island -two beach hikes and two in the mountain range above Lanai City. With the exception of the Munro Trial, there is no backpacking experience, although you can hike Shipwreck Beach and camp. However, no water is available. All four trailheads and trails are found on the island map (see p. 166).

Munro Trail

(Hiking Area No. 14)
(See map, p.166)

Rating: Difficult.
Features: Viewpoints, fruits, Lanai's highest point - Lanaihale, 3370 feet.
Permission: None.
Hiking Distance and Time: 18 miles from highway to highway. The trail is posted as 10.5 miles. Full day, 1400-feet gain/loss. (The hike can be reduced by about 2 miles by reaching the Munro Trail from the Koloiki Trail described below).
Driving or Hiking Instructions: From the Post Office on Lanai Avenue drive or walk 2 miles north on Route 430 out to the end of town past The Lodge at Koele. Turn right on a paved-graveled road and go 0.4 mile past a cemetery on the right to the trailhead.

Do not attempt to drive a conventional vehicle on the Munro Trail. It begins innocently, but it soon becomes wet and rutted. It is possible to travel the entire trail in a four-wheel-drive vehicle or to hike it. George C. Munro, after whom the trail is named, was a naturalist who is credited with reforesting this part of Lanai with exotic tropicals in an effort to restore a watershed area.

On the Trail: From the trailhead, the jeep road-trail crosses a flat, grassy place. After 200 yards bear left at a junction with a faint road which bears right. The trail descends into Maunalei (lit., "lei mountain") Gulch, which is shaded for about a mile by large eucalyptus trees. Maunalei was so named because the clouds over the mountain suggest a lei. Edible thimbleberries (Rubus rosaefolius) are plentiful for the entire length of the trail. They grow on a small, thorny bush with white flowers. The trail begins an ascent on the east side of the mountains, from which views of Maui (east) and Molokai (northeast) are possible. At the head of Maunalei Gulch (southeast) is the place where in 1778 the King of Hawaii massacred many Lanai natives who sought shelter in this stronghold. Beyond the gulch, the trail passes alternately through open areas and forested areas in which Norfolk Island pines (Araucaria excelsa) dominate. These tall, perfectly symmetrical trees were chosen by Munro and others to increase Lanai's ground water, since the trees collect moisture from low-hanging clouds. After a steep climb along the east side of the range, the trail reaches some flat areas. At 6.6 miles a spur road turns right onto a small clearing, on which you will find an abandoned rain gauge and a house site.

Along the upper Munro Trail there are numerous flat, grassy places to camp. Legally, you should get a permit to camp from the Department of Land and Natural Resources in Lanai City, but I doubt if anyone does. Lanaihale (lit., "house of Lanai") is reached at 7.7 miles. At 8.3 miles look for a turnout on the right, a good spot to view Lanai City and the west side of the island. It is also a good place to camp, although it can be a bit wet. One-half mile beyond, the Munro trail makes an abrupt descent and from a number of clearings provides views of Maui (east), Kahoolawe (southeast) and Hawaii beyond on a clear day. The trail ends when you reach flat land. Walk north to reach Lanai City or west to the main road.

Koloiki Ridge Trail
(Hiking Area No. 15)
(See map, p.166)

Rating: Hardy Family
Features: Forested, views.
Permission: None.
Hiking Distance and Time: 2.5 miles, 1 hour.
Driving Instructions:
> *From the Post Office on Lanai Avenue* drive north (1.5 miles) on Route 44 to the end of town and bear right to the lodge. Take a right before the entrance to the lodge and drive to the parking lot. A trail guide and map is available from the concierge in the Lodge.

Introductory Notes: The Koloiki (lit.,"little crawling") Ridge Trail is an easy hike for the whole family initially traversing through a heavily wooded area and then over a ridge to viewpoints overlooking the north side of the island. The trail is wide, marked and clearly defined. When first constructed, trail markers were spaced throughout. However, many were vandalize, but the posts on which the markers were fastened remain in the ground.

On the Trail: From the parking lot follow the walkway from the lodge which passes between the reflecting pond and the putting course. Follow the path to the golf clubhouse where a paved road bears right to the golf course and the hiking trail swings left passing over a dirt road which leads to a stand of Norfolk Island pines, nicknamed the "Cathedral of Pines." These majestic, perfectly symmetrical giants are trees, not pines. They have tiny, overlapping leaves that have the appearance of a needle. The strong, straight trunks were once widely used for masts on ships.

The trail/road ascends a slight grade once it emerges from the grove of Norfolk Island pines and shortly reaches a chain linked enclosure.Go right around the fence and continue uphill until reaching the crest and a poleline with transmission lines overhead. The trail then descends into Hulopo'e Gulch passing through a forest of guava trees. At a junction the trail turns left and continues a moderate descent until it meets the Munro Trail (jeep road). Some hikers have sighted deer here and have reported hearing a deer "barking", a warning to other deer of approaching danger.

Turn right on the Munro Trail/road which can be very wet and muddy. Shortly, the road passes Kukui Gulch on the right which gets it name from the large, pale-green kukui (Aleurites moluccana) tree from which a beautiful and popular lei is made. Until the advent of electricity, kukui-nut oil was burned for light. Nicknamed the "candlenut tree" its trunk was shaped into canoes by early Hawaiians.

When you reach a highly eroded clearing on the right side of the road, you'll have your first relatively unobstructed view of the east side of Lanai and the coastline. Just beyond, the road dips slightly. The foot trail, almost the size of the Munro Trail,is posted on the left at the bottom of the dip. Follow this trail which first passes under a low canopy of branches and then onto a flat, open area. Trail's end is in a stand of Norfolk Island pines, a peaceful spot for a picnic and solitude..

Naio (lit., "bastard sandalwood) Gulch to the west (left) was named for the naio tree which like the Hawaiian sandalwood is a pleasantly, scented wood. To the east (right) Maunalei (lit., "lei mountain") Valley is so-named because the low hanging clouds resemble a lei.

Offshore, to the front-left lies Molokai, the "Friendly Island" site of the leprosy colony where Father Damien served in the last century to aid the victims of the disease. Maui, the "Valley Island" is to the front right capped by 10,023-foot Haleakala, the "House of the Sun." Kahoolawe, the "Target Island" is to the right of Maui. The island was used for target practice by the U.S. military from 1942-90.

Shipwreck Beach Trail
(Hiking Area No. 16)
(See map, p.166)

Rating: Family to strenuous.
Features: Shipwrecks, beachcombing for wreckage, shells, glass floats, petroglyphs.
Permission: None.
Hiking Distance and Time: 1 to 8 miles one-way, 1/2 hour per mile.
Driving Instructions:
From the Post Office on Lanai Avenue drive north on Route 44 to the end of town, bear right on Keomuku

Road and drive to the end of the paved road. Just before reaching the beach, turn left on a dirt-sand road and go 1.8 miles, which is as far as even a jeep can travel.

Introductory Notes: The 8 mile hike between Shipwreck Beach and Polihua is long and hot, but not without rewards. The entire length of the beach along the north-northeast shore of Lanai is littered with shipwreckage, sea shells, and a variety of ocean debris. It is certainly a beachcomber's delight; the pickings are good on this little-traveled beach. If you take the entire hike, transportation is a problem unless you retrace you steps. Certainly, the short hike to the petroglyphs and to the largest shipwreck on the coast is worth the hike.

On the Trail: The trail begins on a rocky ledge above the water at Kukui (lit., "candlenut lamp") Point, once the site of a lighthouse. All that remains of the lighthouse is a large concrete slab. The interesting beach house near the point is almost entirely constructed of timbers from ships and an assortment of driftwood. A spur trail goes inland from the concrete pilings for about 100 yards to an interesting but small group of petroglyphs. Painted arrows on the lava show the way. Human and animal shapes can be discerned.

The trail-beachfront is only a few yards wide even at low tide, and the rotting timbers of ships tend to block your passage. It is fun to examine the wreckage and to splash in the shallow water for relief from the heat. There is no good swimming beach, for the surf bottom here is largely rough lava and beach stones. However, it is a good fishing area where locals may be observed pole fishing or throwing a net. One mile from Kukui Point the rusting hulk of a large ship lies 150 yards offshore.

Lanai Fisherman's Trail

(Hiking Area No. 17)
(See map, p.166)

Rating: Family.
Features: Coastal hike, ocean views, dolphins, fishing.
Permission: None.
Hiking Distance and Time: 1.5 miles, 3/4 hour.
Driving Instructions:
> *East side trailhead* at west end of Hulopoe Beach.
> *West side trailhead* at the end of an access road north-west of the golf course. Both trailheads are posted.

Introductory Notes: Volunteers under the direction of Na Ala Hele, the Hawaii Trail & Access System, cleared and cleaned a fisherman's trail along the southwest portion of the island, below the Manele Bay Hotel. Hiking boots or strong shoes are recommended. The underfooting is rough, particularly in places where the trail drops to the shoreline. A hat and sun screen are highly recommended.

On the Trail: The east side trailhead is posted at the far west end of Hulopoe Beach, just below the hotel. The trail is easy to follow as it parallels the perimeter of the hotel. Residents are commonly casting from the shore in the early morning hours. Pause and look seaward for a pod of spinner dolphins who frequent the bay. I have counted 50-100 of these delightful, three-foot long mammals who enjoy emerging from the water to spin on their tails, making several revolutions.

Be cautious in those places where the trail drops to the shoreline. It is necessary to rock-hop on large beach stones , which can be slippery and can roll when touched. Near trail's end, your path turns north (right) and shortly reaches a parking area at the west end trailhead.

Maui

The Valley Isle

The Island

Adventurers come in all shapes, sizes and dispositions. Some enjoy the challenge of trudging through a quagmire in wind and rain in order to stand atop a mountain whose name is unknown to most people. Others find wonder in a crater conformed like the surface of the moon, with no familiar sights or sounds except the sounds made by the wind. Still others prefer a leisurely walk to a fern-rimmed pool and a cool swim beneath a waterfall.

All these options are possible within 729 square miles in a land of contrasts, in a land of unmatched beauty, in a land often equated with paradise by the casual visitor as well as the native-born. It's the Valley Isle - Maui. As the familiar stenciled T-shirt proclaims, "Maui No Ka Oi" - "Maui is the best." Maui has 150 miles of coastline, with 33 miles suitable for swimming. The Valley Isle possesses more beach area than any other Hawaiian island, which probably accounts for its exceptional popularity.

The island of Maui is the result of eruptions of two large volcanoes, which first formed separate land masses that were later joined by succeeding eruptions. Although some debate exists over the origin of the name, many people believe the island was named after Maui, a legendary superman, who lassoed the sun to bring daylight to the island. In spite of this male giant's influence, locals refer to Maui as "our beautiful lady" because of the island's curvaceous physical appearance. Topped by 10,023-foot Haleakala, the lady's shirt fans out in multitudinous pleats in the form of valleys and gulches. Some are usually dry, awaiting the seasonal rains. Others are usually wet and abound with introduced and native flora and fauna.

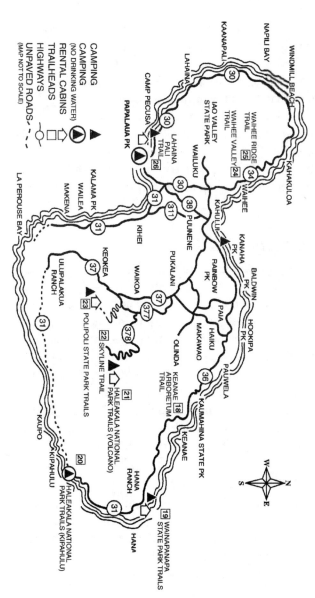

MAUI - TRAILHEADS, CAMPING

Maui is not only the second largest of the Hawaiian Islands in land size (Hawaii is the largest) but also the second most visited. More and more tourists are departing from the tour-bus route and becoming familiar with a Maui previously known only to natives. Campers, bicyclists and hikers are now more numerous and visible. There are hikes on Maui to satisfy the tenderfoot as well as the backpacker: short, easy hikes for the family, which reveal the beauty of the valleys, and more strenuous hikes, which do not necessarily reveal more but which fulfill the spirit of the more adventurous.

Camping and Cabins

Camping on Maui will add a dimension to your visit. Campgrounds range from adequate to good and contain most of the amenities. Fees for county and state campgrounds are modest and camping in the National Parks is free. Consult the camping map for the location of the county, state and national park campgrounds, camping shelters, and rental housekeeping cabins. Campers are advised to bring their own equipment because there are no reliable rental companies on Maui. In addition to the campgrounds, the State of Hawaii and Haleakala National Park operate comfortable and inexpensive rental housekeeping cabins.

County Campground

Kanaha Beach Park and Papalaua Beach Park are the two Maui County campgrounds.The former is located on the coast in Central Maui north of the airport and the latter is on the beach off Route 30 on the south side. Kanaha has outdoor showers, drinking water, tables and restrooms.

Papalaua park has portable toilets, but no water or showers. A permit is required. Camping is limited to three consecutive nights and to 15 days per year. Camping fees are $3.00 for adults and $.50 for persons under 18. For reservations and information, write to the Maui Department of Parks and Recreation. (See Appendix).

State Campgrounds

The State of Hawaii provides two campgrounds, one on the shoreline and the second in a forest high on the slopes of Haleakala Volcano. Waianapanapa State Park, three miles north of Hana, is on a bluff overlooking a black-sand beach. If you are looking for solitude, the other state campground, at Polipoli State Park, will satisfy you. Polipoli is 31 miles from Wailuku in Maui's upcountry at 6,200 feet in a dense forest, which is not frequently visited. The maximum length of stay is 5 nights. A fee of $5 per person, per night is assessed at all state campgrounds. Permits may be obtained from the state parks office (address in Appendix).

Haleakala National Park Campgounds

The National Park Service operates four campgrounds in Haleakala National Park. One campground is located outside the volcano at Hosmer Grove, a short walk from park headquarters at 7,000 feet. No permit is required. Two wilderness campgrounds are located in the volcano - at Paliku Cabin on the east side and at Holua Cabin on the north side. Tenting is limited to three nights (two nights at one site). Tenting is further limited to 50 persons per day, with 25 persons per camping site. Wilderness permits are required and available at park headquarters on a

Crater camping

first-come, first-served basis. Another campground is located at sea level in the Kipahulu Section of the Park. It is a primitive camping area without water. No permit is required at Kipahulu. There is no fee for any of the campgrounds.

Don't pass up hiking and camping in Haleakala National Park. It is one of the best places for both in the islands. (See Appendix).

Private Campgrounds

Camp Pecusa is an Episcopal Church Camp located on the beach near Olowalu, 7 miles southeast of Lahaina and 14 miles southwest of Wailuku. A small sign identifies the highway turnoff. Camping is on a first-come, first-served basis at a rate of $6 per person, per night. The camp has an outdoor, solar heated shower, chemical toilets, picnic tables and campfire pits. Reservations and information are available (See Appendix).

State Rental Cabins

Each of the 12 cabins at Waianapanapa State Park, three miles north of Hana accommodates up to six people and is completely furnished with bedding, towels, cooking and eating utensils, electricity, hot water, showers, electric stoves and refrigerators. The fee schedule at Waianapanapa is $45 for 1-4 persons and $5 for each additional person with a maximum of six in each cabin.

The Polipoli cabin has similar facilities except that it has no electricity and has a gas stove and a cold shower only. The Polipoli cabin accommodates up to 10 persons. Fees for cabin use are $45 for 1-4 persons and $5 for each additional person up to 10. For reservations or permits for cabins, write or contact the Division State Parks. (See Appendix).

Haleakala National Park Rental Cabins

Use of the cabins in Haleakala National Park presents a definite problem because of their popularity with visitors and locals. There are three cabins available in the crater/wilderness — at Paliku, at Holua and at Kapalaoa (see Haleakala map). Each cabin is equipped with water that must be treated, pit toilet, wood-burning cook stove, firewood, cooking and eating utensils, 12 bunks and mattresses (blankets, pillow and sheets are not supplied). You must bring a warm sleeping bag. Use is limited to three nights - two nights at any one site. Rates are $40 per night for 1-6 persons and $80 per night for 7-12 persons. Fees include cabin rental propane and firewood. Cabins have small propane stoves for cooking and firewood for heat.

A lottery is conducted to determine cabin users. To participate, you must write to the Superintendent, Haleakala National Park, at least 90 days prior to the month you're requesting. Forward an outline of your proposed trip, including the number in your group, the exact date(s) and alternative date(s) and the cabin(s) you want to use each night and alternate cabin(s). You will be contacted only if your request is drawn (See Appendix). Occasionally, cabin cancellations are available. To inquire, call (808) 572-9306 between 1-3 pm (Hawaii time). You must have a Visa or Mastercard to accept a cancellation.

Crater cabin

Private Rental Cabins

Cabin facilities are also available at Camp Pecusa for rent by organized groups. Six A-frame cabins with six cots each, a fully equipped kitchen and dining hall, and bathrooms with hot showers are provided at a cost of $9 per person, per night ($240 minimum charge). Users must provide their own bedding (four inch foam mattresses are included), transportation, and food.

Hiking

The island provides a great variety of hiking experiences. The verdant coastline and the valleys on the east side contain some fine hiking trails and places to find solitude. Haleakala National Park, particularly Haleakala Crater, has some outstanding hiking trails which provide the hiker with unique experiences.

The island provides short, easy hikes to suit the short-term visitor, and longer, more ambitious hikes for the visitor with more time and energy to expend. The hiker becomes familiar with a different Maui and views this beautiful lady from a perspective unknown to the ordinary tourist. It is with mixed feelings that I reveal her secrets, for the result may be an intrusion on heretofore pristine areas. Some parts of the island have not yet felt the impact of the visitor, with his frequently careless habits and the resulting pollution and abuse. I proceed under the assumption that the hiker is of a special breed: one who loves and cares for the land, one who tends to minimize his impact on the land, and one who does not violate the earth without feeling he has violated himself. Hike Maui for a week or two and you too will say, "Maui No Ka Oi."

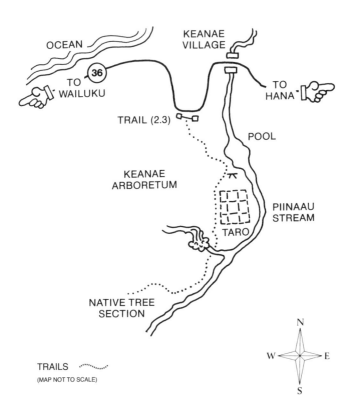

OCEAN

KEANAE
VILLAGE

TO
WAILUKU

36

TO
HANA

TRAIL (2.3)

POOL

KEANAE
ARBORETUM

PIINAAU
STREAM

TARO

NATIVE TREE
SECTION

N

W　　　E

S

TRAILS

(MAP NOT TO SCALE)

Keanae Arboretum Trail

(Hiking Area No. 18)

Rating: Family.
Features: Swimming, fruits and native flora.
Permission: None.
Hiking Distance & Time: 2.3 miles, 1 1/2 hours.

Driving Instructions:

From Lahaina (53 miles, 2 hours) southeast on Route 30, right on Route 38, right on Route 36 to the arboretum.

From Wailuku (34 miles, 1 1/2 hours) east on Route 32, right on Route 36 to the arboretum.

Introductory Notes: Keanae (lit., "the mullet") Arboretum provides an excellent introduction to native and introduced plants in a setting much like old Hawaii. Three distinct sections feature cultivated Hawaiian plants, native forest trees, and introduced tropical trees. You can enjoy all this and a swim in a fresh water pool.

On the Trail: From the turnstile, a short jeep road (0.2 mile) leads to the gated entrance to the arboretum. Continue on the road or wander among the trees and plants, many of which are labeled. Introduced ornamental timber and fruit trees located in this area are all identified for the visitor. The fruit of the pummelo (Citrus maxima) tree is of particular interest and good taste. It is a large, melon-sized fruit that has the aroma and taste of both grapefruit and orange. There are numerous banana and papaya plants. When you reach a section of planted torch (Etlingera elatior) ginger whose blossom feels like plastic, walk directly to Piinaau (lit., "climb, mount") Stream for the best swimming hole in the arboretum and a delightful picnic spot.

From here, the road is bordered by ti whose soft, pliable leaves are commonly used to make a skirt for hulu dancers. The road leads to an area where several patches of irrigated taro are planted. They represent some of the varieties planted by the Hawaiians. Poi, a native staple, is of irrigated taro are planted. They represent some of the varieties planted by the Hawaiians. Poi, a native staple, is produced from the taro root.

At the far end of the domestic-plant section and taro patches, a trail (1 mile) leads to a dense forested flat that is representative of a Hawaiian rain forest. The trail is not maintained so that it may be difficult to follow. It winds through some heavy growth in places and crosses a small stream a dozen times, offering some welcome relief from the heat. Bear left at the first stream crossing and follow the trail, which parallels the stream below. About 100 yards from the first stream crossing, you will find a few pools suitable for a splash.

Arboretum Trailhead

Waianapanapa
State Park Trails
(Hiking Area No. 19)

Rating: Consult individual hikes.

Features: Lava flows and formations, heiaus, burial sites, swimming, camping, blowholes, caves, black-sand beach.

Permission: Camping (fee) and cabin reservations (see State Rental Cabins, page 183) are available from the State Parks Division (address in Appendix).

Hiking Distance & Time: Consult individual hikes.

Driving Instructions:

From Lahaina (70 miles, 3 hours) southeast on Route 30, right on Route 38, right on Route 36, left on road to Waianapanapa State Park.

From Wailuku (51 miles, 2 1/2 hours) east on Route 32, right on Route 36, then as above.

Introductory Notes: A round trip from Wailuku to Hana in one day is exhausting. To enjoy the beauty and serenity of the area, take a couple of days and drive the Hana Highway, camp at Waianapanapa (lit., "glistening water") State Park or secure accommodations in Hana, swim at the black-sand beach, and hike the lava flows to the airport and to Hana.

Cabins situated along the beach are fully furnished and very comfortable. Each has beds, linen, utensils and an electric stove. All you need to bring is food. See "State Rental Cabins" on page 183 for details.

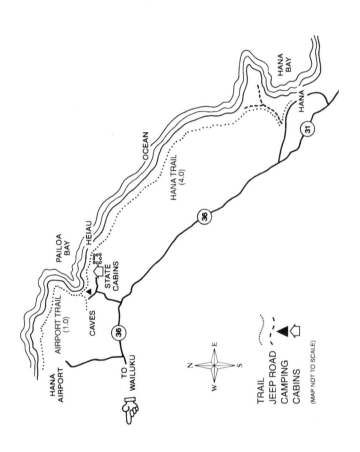

Airport Trail, 1 mile, 1 hour
(trail rating: family).

The trail north from the black-sand beach is particularly rough because of the lava rocks underfoot. After passing two small bays, look for Hawaiian burial grounds and a heiau on your left where the terrain levels somewhat. The gravesites on top of the rough aa rock are rather prominent mounds. As you hike, you will be aware of the pounding surf and the interesting formations in the lava rock. Children enjoy assigning names to these strange forms. Be careful, as the trail is often precariously close to the surf. Pause as you walk and look for turtles who are feeding or playfully riding the surf. You are hiking over an early Hawaiian shoreline trail extending to the Piilanihale Heiau some three miles north of the airport.

You may choose to return to Waianapanapa via the shoreline route or to take the paved road by the airport to the Hana Highway and follow it to Waianapanapa.

Hana Trail, 4 miles, 2 hours
(trail rating: hardy family).

The trail south begins on a cliff above Pailoa (lit., "always splashing") Bay, with its black-sand beach, and follows the coastline - at times coming precariously close to the edge - to the enclosed bay at Hana.

Just below the campground you'll find burial sites decorated with artificial flowers and overlooking a rather fragile lava formation. The lava flow is undoubtedly honeycombed with tunnels and caves, evidenced by the many pits and holes and by the sound of rushing, crashing surf underfoot. Indeed, one blowhole is just a few hundred feet beyond the burial grounds.

The white substance on the lava is called Hawaiian "snow." A lichen, it is the first plant to grow on fresh lava. Other plants along the hike include the hala (Pandanus odoratissimus), which produces a large pineapple-shaped fruit. It is also called "tourist pineapple," since locals jokingly identify it as such to visitors. Beach morning glory (Ipomoea pesca-prae), with its pretty, delicate blue or purple flowers, plays an important role in preventing wind and water erosion of beaches by forming a large carpet. Also, a bush form of sandalwood (Santalum ellipticum) which grows less than three feet high is rather profuse in most areas.

You'll find rental cabins nestled among the hala trees at 0.5-mile, with a number of trails leading from them to the beach. At 0.6-mile a small bridge crosses a natural arch in the lava under which the surf pounds and crashes as small crabs scurry about. Just before the bridge, you may be sprayed by a small blowhole that is particularly active when the surf is up.

Overlooking the sea from its volcanic perch (0.7-mile) is a heiau (a place of worship). Heiaus played an important part in pre-Christian Hawaiian culture. There are hundreds of known heiaus on the islands that served specifically to ensure rain, good crops, or success in war, while others were used for human sacrifice. From the heiau, you pass a generous growth of hala, follow the coastline at its very edge, and reach a point about 50 feet above the surf. From here, about midpoint in the hike, you can see the cross on Mt. Lyons erected in memory of Paul Fagan, founder of the Hana Ranch and Hotel. You can also see tree-covered Kauiki (Lit., "glimmer") Head, an imposing buttress on the south side of Hana Bay.

The trail is no longer clearly identifiable. However, you should not have any problem if you follow the coastline and avoid "ankle twisters" on the broken lava. You will find numerous caves and pits caused by gas that was trapped under the lava as the surface cooled. Later, the brittle surface collapsed, leaving some interesting holes.

When you arrive on a boulder-laden beach, a sign marks the trail's end. From here, you can take any of the roads leading to the Hana Highway for a return trip to Waianapanapa, continue along the beach for 1/2 mile to Hana Bay, or return to the park via the lava flows. It is worth the extra hike to Hana Bay for lunch and a swim at its calm, gray-colored beach. The water at Hana Bay is not dirty but simply discolored by decomposed lava.

Waianapanapa Cave Loop, 100 yards, (trail rating: family).

Before you leave Waianapanapa, be sure to take the short hike to the caves, where it is possible to swim underwater to a chamber with a rock ledge. Legend recounts that a Hawaiian princess hid in the cave from her jealous husband, who, while resting by the cave, saw her reflection in the water. Since the ledge in the cave was a reputed meeting place for lovers, he promptly slew her by smashing her head against the walls of the cave. Consequently, it is said, the water in the pool turns blood-red every April, and her screams can be heard. If you cannot accept this legend, you may choose to believe that the red color of the water is the result of tiny red shrimp that frequent the pool, and the screams are the result of the water and wind sweeping into the lava tube from the ocean.

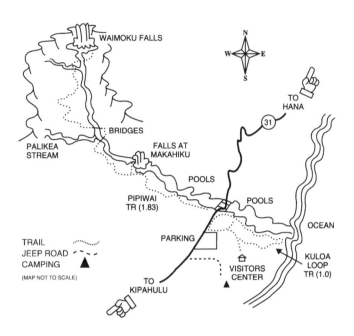

Haleakala National Park Trails

(Kipahulu Section)
(Hiking Area No. 20)

Rating: See individual hikes.

Features: Waimoku Falls, Falls at Makahiku, bamboo forest, ancient Hawaiian agricultural sites, swimming, fruit, Oheo Stream, free camping.

Permission: None to hike or camp.

Hiking Distance & Time: See individual hikes.

Driving Instructions:

From Lahaina (82 miles, 3 hours) southeast on Route 30, right on Route 38, right on Route 36 to Hana. Continue on Route 31 to Haleakala National Park, Kipahulu Section.

From Wailuku (63 miles, 2 1/2 hours) east on 32, right on Route 36, then as above.

Introductory Notes: The Hana Highway and the pools in Oheo Gulch (popularly known as the Seven Sacred Pools) are two of the most popular tourist attractions on the island. To avoid a tiring return trip to Central Maui the same day, you should consider staying at the cabins or campgrounds outside Hana at Waianapanapa State Park or camping in the National Park (see "Maui's Campgrounds" and "Maui's Housekeeping Cabins" in the Introduction for details). The Park Service campground is located on pasture land south of the pools on a bluff overlooking the rugged coastline. NO WATER or amenities are available. Chemical toilets are placed throughout the parking area. Camping is free and no permits are required.

The National Park Service rangers conduct a hike to Waimoku Falls every Saturday, departing from the Ranger Station at 9 :30 a.m. sharp.

Pipiwai Trail, 1.83 miles, 1 1/2 hours, 900-feet gain (trail rating: hardy family).

On the Trail: Begin your hike at the Ranger Station and walk north to the trailhead (posted). The trail goes left and passes through a wooded area to the highway. On the opposite side of the road, the trail ascends under a guava tree forest paralleling the stream below. Sample the yellow, lemon-sized guava while hiking. The fruit contains five times the amount of Vitamin C than an orange. A few hundred yards from the trailhead stands a 10-foot-tall concrete support, which is all that remains of a water-flume system that once spanned Oheo Gulch and carried sugar cane to a now abandoned sugar mill one mile away in Kipahulu. The first highlight along the trail, however, is at the 0.5 mile point, where the 184-foot Falls at Makahiku drops into a stunning gorge below. To the left of the lookout, an abandoned irrigation ditch cut in the cliff allows you to hike to the top of the falls.

At the one-mile point, the trail reaches two newly constructed bridges, one over Pipiwai Stream and the other over Oheo Stream. Here you are likely to find daring young men and women leaping from the pali into the water below. USE EXTREME CAUTION if you choose to follow their practice.

Beyond the bridges, the trail is always wet and muddy. It is well-defined, but expect to hop over slippery rocks, and to carefully avoid the exposed roots on the trail. The Park Service has placed sections of boardwalk in the muddiest places.

The trail takes you through three marvelous bamboo forests. If the wind is up, you'll be serenaded by a discordant symphony of rattling bamboo. Beyond this "musical" forest are the remains of old taro patches, evidenced by walled terraces and shelter sites. Additionally, there are edible thimbleberries, coffee plants and, of course, guavas. With luck you will also find ripe mountain apples (Eugenia malaccensis). Before the falls there are numerous trees that bear a small, deep-crimson fruit with a pure white pulp and a large, round seed.

Shortly, Waimoku Falls comes into view. It's an idyllic spot to picnic after a pleasant hike. USE CAUTION if you opt to shower under the falls,. Remember, most of the rocks in the stream fell from above.

Kuloa Loop,
1 mile,1 hour (trail rating: family).

On the Trail: Everyone loves the pools, and every visitor on the island seems to be there! From the parking lot, follow the trail toward the visitors center that contains several displays and a ranger who can answer questions regarding the Park. Walk north from the center to a junction where the Pipiwai Trail goes left and Kuloa Loop Trail goes right. Picnic tables are stationed in shady places trailside until you reach the pools. Continue on the trail toward the ocean until you reach a bluff overlooking the Pools at Oheo. The pools are usually crowded between the hours of 11 a.m. and 3 p.m. A crudely made staircase leads to the pools below. Here you're likely see young men and women diving and leaping from the bank and even from the bridge high above the water. CAUTION: Enjoy the pools, but be cautious when swimming or diving. Several deaths and serious accidents have occurred here in recent years. The nearest medical facilities are ten miles distant in Hana.

The loop trail ascends the south side of the stream and leads to the highway and the bridge from which marvelous views are possible upstream and downstream to the ocean. The pools upstream are usually less crowded than downstream. CAUTION: DO NOT enter the pools during high or fast moving water. Be alert; Water in the stream can rise quickly.

From the road retrace your steps to the trail junction where one trail continues along the stream and the trail to the parking lot goes right completing the loop.

Haleakala National Park Trails

(Volcano/Wilderness)
(Hiking Area No. 21)

Rating: Strenuous hiking into wilderness.

Features: "Moon" hiking, silversword, nene goose (State bird of Hawaii), lava tubes, lava formations, rental cabins, camping.

Permission: Entrance fee to Park. Hiking and cabin permits from Haleakala National Park (See pp. 181-184 for details).

Hiking Distance & Time: See the mileage tables in the text below.

Driving Instructions:

From Lahaina (59 miles, 2 hours) southeast on Route 30, right on Route 38, right on Route 36, right on Route 37, left on Route 377, left on Route 378 to the summit.

From Wailuku (40 miles, 1 1/2 hours) east on Route 32, right on Route 36, right on Route 37, left on Route 377, then as above.

Introductory Notes: As you drive to the summit of Haleakala look for the large (three-foot) ring-necked pheasant (Phasianus colchicus torquatus) and the smaller chukar (Alectoris graeca) with its brownish black markings and a black band extending through each eye and joining at the lower throat. Both flush along the road and may also be seen in the park.

"Give me my life," pleads the sun after Maui, the demigod, has lassoed it. "I will give you your life," replies Maui, "if you promise to go more slowly across the sky so the women may dry their cloth." To this day, the sun seems to pass more slowly over Haleakala, the House of the Sun. Such legends are still repeated by locals when they speak of nature's cauldron of power and destruction that helped create their island.

Recent evidence, however, credits other forces. Scientists believe that a hot spot exists beneath the earth's crust in the Pacific area and, as a consequence of periodic eruptions of this hot spot, a chain of volcanoes, the Hawaiian Islands, has been created. Centuries of submarine volcanic eruptions piled up successive layers of lava. Finally, this undersea volcano burst through the ocean's churning surface, and eventually reached a height of 15,000 feet above the Pacific Ocean. Nature then began to work her wonders from above, as wind, rain and the sea eroded the new rock, and streams ripped away at its surface, creating valleys. Ultimately, in the Haleakala area two major valleys grew until they met, forming a long depression. Subsequent volcanic activity then filled the depression, while vent eruptions created symmetrical cones. Today, Haleakala stands proudly at 10,023 feet. Nevertheless, Haleakala is not extinct but only dormant, and it can be expected to erupt again some day.

The persistent trade winds, carrying over 300 inches of rain per year, had an equally dramatic effect on Haleakala Volcano. Because these winds blow consistently in one direction, the volcano has eroded unequally, and the vegetation differs correspondingly. Erosion has created two gaps in the volcano: the Kaupo Gap on the south side, and the steeper Koolau Gap on the north side. It is possible to hike down the Kaupo Gap.

Statistically, the "House of the Sun" is a large dormant volcano, covering an area of 19 square miles. It is 7 1/2 miles long, 2 1/2 miles wide, and 21 miles in circumference. Experts do not regard the "crater" as a true volcanic crater since thousands of years of erosion have carved a valley. Park officials no longer refer to the "depression" as a "crater" but as a "valley" which they now refer to as the "wilderness." Some 36 miles of well-marked trails invite the hiker to enjoy the awesome yet delicate beauty, and the unmatched serenity and solitude of the valley/wilderness area.

Hiking into the wilderness is serious business because of the distance involved, the terrain, the altitude and the temperature which commonly ranges between 40-65 degrees Fahrenheit. Below freezing temperatures with a wind-chill factor are not uncommom at any time . Another consideration is hypothermia, which sets in when the

Haleakala Crater

body is not able to generate enough heat to keep the vital organs warm. Hypothermia can be fatal, so that visitors are well-advised to carry warm clothing - shoes, jacket, long pants - even during the summer. Water is available at the cabins in the wilderness, but IT MUST BE TREATED OR BOILED.

If your schedule allows, choose a day with a full moon and hike into the wilderness in the evening. During the summer months, the temperature ranges from 35 to 77 degrees Fahrenheit so that warm clothing is essential, but the experience is marvelous.

Park rules require that wilderness hikers adhere to the following:

1. Hiking off-trail and shortcutting switchbacks is prohibited.
2. Collecting anything is prohibited.
3. To protect the environment and assure solitude, group size is limited to 12 persons for all hiking and camping.
4. No pets allowed in the wilderness or on trails.
5. Firearms, motors, radios, bicycles, wheeled vehicles, and open fires are prohibited in the wilderness.
6. Pack out everything you pack in.
7. Do not feed or harass the nene or any wildlife.
8. Use pit toilets at campgrounds or cabins.

Experienced hikers can plan a trip from the information contained herein. For others, I recommend the following hikes.

Part-day hikes
Sliding Sands Trail to Kaluu o Ka Oo
An enjoyable 3-4 hour, 5-mile round-trip hike can be made by good hikers partway into the wilderness via the Sliding Sands Trail. From the trailhead, you descend 2 miles and 1,400 feet into the wilderness to a posted junction. A 0.5-mile spur trail leads to Kaluu o Ka oo (lit., "the plunge of the digging stick"), which is the only place in Haleakala that you can stand atop a cinder cone and look into the depression on the top. Remember that the return ascent to the summit is demanding at this altitude.

Full-day hikes
Halemauu Trail to Holua Cabin
This is a vigorous, eight-mile-round-trip, 1,400-feet gain hike over a foot and horse trail to the floor of the valley. Food and water are a must on the trail, although water (treat it) is available at Holua Cabin.

Sliding Sands Trail to Holua Cabin, exit by Halemauu Trail
If you only have one day and if you want to hike into the wilderness and if you are a good hiker in good physical condition, then this it the hike for you. It's a difficult 11-mile, 1,400-feet gain, one-day hike, but it will take you down the marvelous Sliding Sands Trail, across the valley floor, and up the Halemauu Trail. Whew!

Better yet, plan an overnight stay at Holua Cabin or campground.

Overnight Hikes

Sliding Sands Trail to Holua Cabin, exit by Halemauu Trail (see previous description)

This is a pleasant hike, and moderately strenuous when it includes an overnight stay in a rustic cabin. Tenting in the campground near the cabin is permitted. Remember, advance reservations are necessary to secure Holua cabin.

Sliding Sands Trail to Kapalaoa Cabin, exit by Halemauu Trail

This hearty, 13.5-mile hike features an overnight visit at Kapalaoa Cabin. In the morning you can traverse the valley floor, visiting Pele's Paint Pot and the Silversword Loop, and then exit via Halemauu Trail.

Sliding Sands Trail to Paliku Cabin to Kaupo Village

Hikers in good condition can take this 17.5-mile hike from the highest point on Maui to sea level. It covers the sparsely vegetated crater and the lush foliage of the Kaupo Gap. An overnight visit at Paliku is particularly rewarding, since the rich flora there is in marked contrast to the rest of the Park.

If you are able to spend more than one night in the wilderness, I recommend staying at Holua or Paliku Cabins. Time permitting, spend a night at each cabin. This will certainly enable you to enjoy the Park at a leisurely pace.

TRAIL MILAGE

Sliding Sands Trail - Summit at 9,745 feet to:

Holua Cabin	7.4
Kapalaoa Cabin	5.8
Paliku Cabin	9.8
Kaupo Village	17.5

Halemauu Trail - Park road at 8,000 feet to:

Holua Cabin	3.9
Silversword Loop	4.8
Kawilinau	6.2
Kapalaoa Cabin	7.7
Paliku Cabin	10.2
Kaupo Village	17.9

On the Trail: The following description of trails and highlights encountered along the way correspond to the numbers on the map. Six interconnected trails in the wilderness are listed on the hiking chart.

1. Sliding Sands Trail

The trail begins just above the visitor center on the south side of Pakaoao at 9,740 feet and descends 2500 feet in four miles to the valley floor. Pause before descending for a broad panorama of the Park. With the map, a number of prominent points can be identified. Koolau (lit., "windward") Gap is to the north and Kaupo Gap is south of Paliku.

Pakaoao has an interesting history as a place used by wayfarers and by robbers who waylaid them. The southwest slope was once covered with stone-walled enclosures used by the Hawaiians as sleeping shelters and for protection from the elements.

As you begin your hike, you will agree that the Sliding Sands Trail is appropriately named. The cinders and ash that make up the area around the trail were expelled from vents during eruptions and were carried by the wind to line the inner volcano. As you descend, the contrasts of the volcano become evident. The lush forest of the Koolau Gap to the north and the usually cloud-enshrouded Kaupo Gap southeast stand in marked contrast to the seemingly barren terrain around you.

After 2 miles and a 1,700-feet descent, you reach a trail marker which identifies a spur trail that leads to Kaluu o Ka oo, a cinder cone. At the end of this short spur trail, you stand atop a cinder cone and examine its design close up.

You will find some common plants in this area. The pukiawe (Styphelia tameiameiae) has tiny, evergreen-like leaves with reddish-white berries. The plant with yellowish flowers on upright stems is the kupaoa (Dubautia menziesii) which, literally translated, means "fragrant." A few isolated silversword plants (see Haleakala Trail Description No. 12) are located just off the trail.

2. Puu O Pele ("Hill of Pele")

Although legend has it that Pele, the Hawaiian goddess of fire, lives in Kilauea Volcano on the island of Hawaii, this hill was named in her honor. With binoculars, you are able to see Paliku Cabin in the distance. The building visible to the north is not Holua Cabin but a horse corral used by maintenance crews.

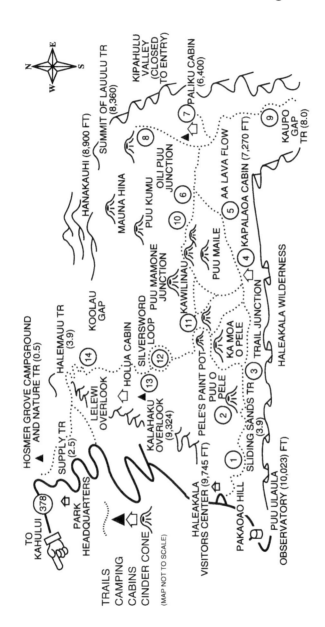

(MAP NOT TO SCALE)

3. Trail Junction

You have hiked 3.9 miles and are now on the valley floor at 7,400 feet. Until recently, you could hear and see goats in the wilderness. The Park Service has since completed a fencing program to keep goats out of the Park, but they are found outside. The goats are descendants of those brought to the islands by Captain George Vancouver in the late 1700s. While they seem to delight and entertain visitors, they create a number of problems, since they would eat the silversword, mamane and other desirable vegetation.

Flora in the area includes a native grass (Trisetum glomeratum) that grows in tufts or bunches and is known locally as mountain pili (lit., "cling, stick"). Mountain pilo (lit., "bad odor") (Coprosma montana) is common and may be identified by its orange berries and handsome bush. A favorite of foraging pigs is the bracken fern (Pteridium aquilinum), a fern found in many lands that may be familiar to you.

TRAIL MILAGE (from the Junction)	
East to:	
Kapalaoa Cabin	1.9
Paliku Cabin	6.0
Kaupo Village	13.7
North via Ka Moa O Pele Trail to:	
Kawilinau	1.7
Holua Cabin	3.5

4. Kapalaoa Cabin (7,270 feet)

Kapalaoa (lit., "the whale or whale tooth") Cabin is one of three comfortable cabins maintained by the Park Service. There is no tent camping permitted in this area.

5. Aa Lava Flow

The hike to Paliku Cabin (3.5 miles) crosses a lava flow composed of aa (lit., "stony") lava, a Hawaiian word that is accepted today by geologists to identify lava whose surface cooled, hardened and fractured into rough pieces. The trail is difficult, with extremely rough under-footing.

Hawaiian "snow," a whitish lichen is very common on the aa lava. About midpoint, Paliku Cabin is visible straight ahead across the lava flow, nestled in a grove of native trees.

6. Oili Puu ("hill to appear") Junction

Get out the poncho, if you have not already, for the rainy portion of your wilderness experience usually begins at this point if you are going on to Paliku Cabin. A different type of lava (pahoehoe) appears in this area. It is a smooth variety that frequently forms lava tubes when the outside chills and hardens and then the still-molten interior flows out of the cool shell.

Very pretty mamane (Sophora chrysophylli) trees are conspicuous with their yellow blossoms. Hikers favor the fruit of the ohelo (Vaccinium reticulatum) bush, which bears a tasty red, edible berry in the late summer. It is rather prolific in this section of the Park.

Although the jet-black berries of the kukaenene (lit., "goose dung") (Coprosma ernodeoides) bush are eaten by

TRAIL MILAGE (from Oili Puu Junction)	
East to:	
Paliku Cabin	1.3
Kaupo Village	9.1
Northwest to:	
Kawilinau	2.7
Holua Cabin	5.0
Park Road via Halemauu Trail.......................	8.9

the nene, the Hawaiian goose, they are used as an emetic by Hawaiians. You are well-advised to avoid them.

7. Paliku Cabin (6,400 feet)

Unless you have cabin reservations or a water-repellent tent and sleeping bag, you won't spend too much time enjoying Paliku (lit., "vertical cliff"). The rain and wind blow for a while, stop, and then start again. It is precisely this yearly 300-plus inches of rain, however, that creates a lush garden of native and introduced plants and makes Paliku the most enchanting spot in the Park. The cabin is located at the base of a pali (lit., "cliff") that towers 1,000 feet above. The campground is in a grassy area to the front-right of the cabin.

Behind the cabin and surrounding the a toilet, the akala (lit., "pink") (Rubus hawaiiensis), a Hawaiian raspberry, grows profusely. It bears a large, dark, edible berry that is rather bitter to eat but makes a delicious jam. In addition to the mamane described above, other native trees include the ohia (Metrosideros polymorpha), the island's most common native tree, with its gray-green leaves and red flowers that look like those of the bottle-brush plant. The kolea (lit., "boast") (Myrsine lessertiana) is conspicuous around Paliku, since it grows to a height of 50 feet and has thick leaves and dark purplish-red or black fruit. Hawaiians used the sap of the bark to produce a red dye for tapa cloth. Several Methley plum trees are mixed in with the foliage. When ripe, usually May-June, these deep purple, ping-pong-sized fruits are a special treat. In recent years, however, the area has become overgrown and some of the branches of the plum trees have been broken so that fruit has been scarce.

Throughout the Park, look for the nene (Branta sand-vicensis), the state bird of Hawaii. After disappearing, this native bird was reintroduced on Maui in 1962 and has

Nene in the crater

since done fairly well. The Park Service has a program to raise goslings and to return them to the wilds in due course. The natural breeding cycle is difficult, owing in part to a number of introduced predators such as mongooses, pigs, and feral dogs and cats, for whom the eggs and the young goslings are easy prey.

The nene has adapted to its rugged habitat on the rough lava flows far from any standing or running water. The most noticeable anatomical change has been a reduction of webbing between the toes, creating a foot that better suits its terrestrial life.

If you are fortunate enough to spot a nene, don't be surprised if it walks up to you. They are very friendly birds. But please, DO NOT FEED them. They are wild animals and they have sufficient food available in the Park.

8. Lauulu Trail

The trail begins behind Paliku Cabin and zigzags 2.3 miles up the north wall. Although the trail is not maintained, a "good" hiker can make it. Kipahulu (lit., "fetch from exhausted gardens") Valley lies beyond the pali and extends to the ocean. It is a wilderness area that has been explored by a few daring souls who have hiked the difficult Lauulu (lit., "lush") Trail to Kalapawili (lit., "twisting") Ridge. From the ridge there are excellent views of the Hana coast, the Kaupo Gap and the Park. THIS IS A DEAD-END TRAIL. HIKING INTO KIPAHULU VALLEY IS PROHIBITED.

9. Kaupo Gap

Kaupo (lit., "night landing") Trail follows Kaupo Gap and is a popular exit from the wilderness portion of the

Park, but one that presents a transportation problem from Kaupo Village to Central Maui or to Lahaina and Hana. Although the road has been improved around the south side of Kaupo Village, it remains rough and bumpy. Hitchhiking from Kaupo is only a remote possibility, since few cars are found on the road. However, if you are up to a nine-mile hike to Kipahulu, a ride from there to your destination is more likely.

The trail is well-defined and initially follows the base of the pali, from which a number of waterfalls and cascades during rainy periods are visible, as well as views of the coastline and the Kaupo area. You are using some muscles you didn't use in the volcano, for your descent is 6,000 feet in eight miles, which means you will be "braking" all the way. You may hear goats and pigs along the trail, although they may not be visible in the heavy brush.

About halfway, the trail becomes a jeep road, used by the Kaupo Ranch, which may be used by four-wheel-drive vehicles with permission. The road continues to the trailhead where another road descends to the main road, a short distance from the Kaupo Store.

10. Aa Lava Flow

On the connecting trail between the east and west sides, you are crossing the ancient divide between the Koolau and Kaupo valleys, in addition to one of the most recent lava flows in the crater, which is 500-1000 years old. Just before the trail junction, on the north side, is a prominent wall constructed of lava rock which was once used to corral cattle being driven into the valley to graze on the lush, rich grasses at Paliku.

At the junction, the vertical, slablike columns of rock protruding from the ridge are volcanic dikes that are remnants of the ancient divide between the valleys. Puu Nole (lit., "weak hill") opposite the dikes is a small cinder cone with a number of silversword plants on its slopes.

11. Kawilinau

In recent years a safety railing has been built around this pit, which is 10 feet in diameter and only 65 feet deep. Some locals claim the pit extends to the sea. The pit was formed by superheated gases that blasted through from beneath.

In an earlier period, Hawaiians threw the umbilical cords of their newborn children into this pit to prevent (they believed) the children from becoming thieves or to ensure them strong bodies later in life. The Hawaiians' motive for this practice varied.

As you continue on the trail northwest about 100 yards beyond the pit, look for Pele's Paint Pot, a colorful area that was created by the many different minerals present in the magma. Some people, however, believe that after painting the volcano, Madame Pele discarded her excess paint here. Many volcanic "bombs," hunks of lava in spherical shapes, are identifiable.

12. Silversword Loop

Don't fail to hike this short (0.4-mile) loop trail to view some of the best examples of silversword in the crater. Silversword (Argyroxiphium sandwicense) is probably the single most popular attraction in the crater. The plant is endemic to the islands and, thanks to protection by the Park Service, it is recovering and thriving. Its enemies are "feral" visitors, who pick the firm, silver-colored leaves for souvenirs.

A relative of the sunflower, the silversword has stiff, stiletto-shaped leaves and a brilliant flower stalk. Typically, the plant will grow from four to twenty years, its age marked by the size and number of silverswords at the base. Then in a brilliant burst, the flower stalk will grow from one to nine feet in height, sometime between May and October, and will produce hundreds of purplish sunflower like blooms. After flowering only once, the entire plant dies and the seeds are left to reproduce. The species does surprisingly well, surviving on 16-50 inches of rain annually. Viewers familiar with the yucca blossom of the Southern California desert will find the silversword familiar, although the two plants are not related. Please stay on the trail when viewing the silversword. The roots are close to the surface and can be easily damaged causing the plant to die.

13. Holua Cabin

A day or two's stay is particularly enjoyable at Holua (lit., "sled"). Behind the cabin, about 25 feet up the cliff, is a cave that Hawaiians once used as a campsite. About 100 yards to the front-right of the cabin is a lava tube through which you may walk with the aid of a flashlight. It is about 150 feet long and exits through a hole in its roof. A recent archeological survey found the remains of an adult male and two young children entombed in the portion of the tube between the entrance and spatter vent known as Na Piko Haua (lit., "the hiding place of the navel cords"). Ancient Hawaiians hid the umbilical cords of their newborn in such pits. It was regarded as unlucky for the child if the cords were found.

At dusk, be certain to listen for the strange call of the dark-rumped petrel (Pterodroma phaeopygia), which sounds like the barking of a small dog. This white-and-black sea bird makes its nest on the volcano's inner slopes, where it produces one white egg annually. For six months afterward, it flies in from the ocean each day to tend the nest, arriving after sundown. It's "bark" seems to assist it in finding the nest after nightfall. This rare creature is now threatened by rats which have invaded the park.

TRAIL MILAGE (from Holua)

East to:

Silverwood Loop	0.9
Pele's Paint Pot	2.2
Kawilinau	2.3
Kapalaoa Cabin	3.8
Paliku Cabin	6.3
Kaupo Village	14.1

North to:

Park Road via Halemauu Trail	3.9

14. Halemauu Trail

Halemauu (lit., "grass hut") Trail, constructed by the Civilian Conservation Corps in the 1930s, remains in good condition. Horse and mule pack trains enter and exit the wilderness via Halemauu on a series of switch-backs for most of the 3.9-mile course, ascending 1,400 feet to the park road at 8,000 feet and 3.5 miles from Park Headquarters.

After a night's rest at Holua Cabin, the hike out offers spectacular views of the Park and the east side when the weather is clear. There are a number of comfortable spots at which to rest in the morning shade. Keep a sharp eye out for the Maui wormwood shrub (Artemisia mauiensis), which is two to three feet high and usually grows on the cliff. It has aromatic silvery leaves and small orange flowers. Hawaiians still pound the leaves to use in treating asthma.

Once on the rim of the volcano, the trail levels somewhat and begins a gradual ascent passing through a gate in a fence constructed to keep goats out of the wilderness. The trail then passes the Supply Trail on the right and continues on to the trailhead and parking lot.

Supply Trail, 2.5 miles, 1 1/2 hours, 1000-feet gain (trail rating: strenuous).

The Supply Trail connects hikers and campers in Hosmer Grove with the Halemauu Trail, which takes you into the wilderness of Haleakala National Park. The trailhead (posted) is located on the southside of the road a short distance before reaching the main park road from Hosmer Grove. From here the mostly rough (underfooting) trail ascends 1000 feet to the Halemauu Trail.

Initially, the trail is wide and easy to follow, but the underfooting is a mixture of lava rock and volcanic ash. A hat and sunscreen offer some protection from the sun's rays. Bright yellow evening primrose (Oenethera stricta) flowers flourish trailside and throughout most of the Park.

Look also for ohia lehua (Metrosideros polymorpha), the island's most common native tree. The bright red blossom is a favorite of Madame Pele, goddess of fire and volcanoes. Legend holds that if the blossom is picked on the way to the mountain, it will rain. However, it may be picked on a return trip without risk.

About midway, your trail reaches an abandoned road. The trail continues on the opposite side and soon passes a rain shed and water tanks. Weather permitting, views of the eastside are possible. At the trail junction, the trail to the right goes to the Halemauu Trailhead and the main road. Follow the trail to the left to several magnificent viewpoints into the volcano.

Hosmer Grove Nature Loop, 0.5-mile, 1/2 hour (trail rating: family).

The grove contains a small campground and picnic area with six tables, fire grills and a tenting area. It is a delight for an overnight visit. It's a good, convenient spot to camp if you wish to see the sunset or the sunrise from the summit of Haleakala. The campground is wheelchair accessible. Camping is free and permits are not required.

A short, 0.5-mile, self-guiding trail is adjacent to the campground, and trail pamphlets are available to assist in identifying the native and introduced plants. Many of the introduced plants were established by Dr. Ralph S. Hosmer, the first Territorial Forester of Hawaii. There are excellent examples of sugi (Japanese cedar), cypress cedar, juniper, Douglas fir, eucalyptus spruce and a number of pines. Native plants include sandalwood, mamane, aalii, mountain pilo, oheo and kupaoa.

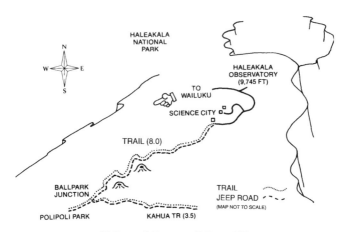

Skyline Trail

(Hiking Area No. 22)

Rating: Strenuous.

Features: Views of Lanai, Kahoolawe and Hawaii, and West Maui Mountains, cinder cones, historical sites, Polipoli Park, and native and imported flora.

Permission: None.

Hiking Distance & Time: 8 miles, 4 hours (to Polipoli Park), 3,800-feet loss.

Driving Instructions:

From Lahaina (59 miles, 2 hours) southeast on Route 30, right on Route 38, right on Route 36, right on Route 37, left on Route 377, left on Route 378 to the summit (Park headquarters is 11 miles before the summit.

From Wailuku (40 miles, 1 1/2 hours) east on Route 32, right on Route 36, then as above.

Introductory Notes: Skyline Trail begins on the south side of Science City. As you approach the summit and Puu Ulaula (lit., "red hill") Observatory, a road on the left leads to Science City, where, a hundred yards farther, another road bears left, marked by a sign indicating the park boundary. Follow this road to a sign which identifies the Skyline Trail. At this point, you are at the 9,750-foot level on the southwest rift of Haleakala Volcano. As noted on the sign, the jeep road is ordinarily closed to vehicles because the instruments used in astronomical research at Science City are sensitive to dust.

On a clear day, the big island of Hawaii can be viewed to the southeast. The island of Kahoolawe (lit., "carrying away by current"), seven miles off the coast, is uninhabited and until 1991 was used by the military for bombing practice. Known locally as the "Cursed Island," Kahoolawe was once used as a base by opium smugglers. The ghost of a poisoned smuggler is said to walk at night. Between Maui and Kahoolawe, tiny, U-shaped Molokini (lit., "many ties") appears. Lanai is to the northwest.

On the Trail: On this trail you will descend a total of 3,800 feet. Be alert for mountain bikers who share the trail. The first 1,000 feet is your "moon walk" over rugged and barren terrain, with several cinder cones and craters along the rift. You are compensated, however, by a spectacular panorama of the island. The eye easily sweeps the offshore islands, the West Maui Mountain range, central Maui and the east side. The Maui "neck" is clearly visible from the trail.

The mamane (lit., "sex appeal") tree line begins at the 8,600-feet level, and the native scrub becomes denser and more varied. A mamane tree (Sophora chrysophylla) in full bloom is a beautiful sight, with its bright yellow flowers. It is a favorite of feral goats, who eat them greedily and quickly exterminate them in an area. The gate across the jeep trail at the 8,200-feet level marks the halfway point to Polipoli. When you reach this point, you will have hiked four miles.

An additional two miles brings you to the Papaanui-Kahikinui (lit., "large, parched-great Tahiti") Junction at 7,000 feet. On the left of the trail is a large open area that was used as a baseball field by members of the Civilian Conservation Corps during the 1930s. The area is referred to as "Ballpark Junction" by locals. From the junction, it is a one-mile trek to a point where a sign identifies the Haleakala Ridge Trail. After 0.3-mile from the sign, take the Polipoli Trail to the camping area some 0.6-mile farther, passing through dense stands of cypress, cedar and pine.

Polipoli Park provides camping facilities, water, flush toilets-and a stand of redwood trees. There are also numerous easy family hiking trails in the vicinity (see Hiking Area No. 23). Between May and July, delicious Methley plums are a favorite of locals, who swarm over the area in search of the fruit. Unhappily, many trees have been damaged by pickers or overwhelmed by vegetation so the pickings are poor. All along the trail, you can expect to be surprised by California quails, with their curved head plume, ring-necked pheasants, and chukars, which are brownish-black ground-dwelling partridges.

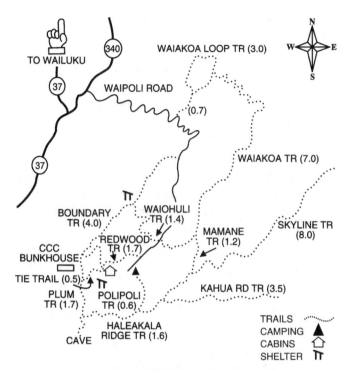

TO WAILUKU

340

37

WAIPOLI ROAD

WAIAKOA LOOP TR (3.0)

(0.7)

WAIAKOA TR (7.0)

37

BOUNDARY
TR (4.0)

WAIOHULI
TR (1.4)

SKYLINE TR
(8.0)

MAMANE
TR (1.2)

REDWOOD
TR (1.7)

CCC
BUNKHOUSE

TIE TRAIL (0.5)

PLUM
TR (1.7)

POLIPOLI
TR (0.6)

KAHUA RD TR (3.5)

HALEAKALA
RIDGE TR (1.6)

CAVE

TRAILS
CAMPING
CABINS
SHELTER

Polipoli Park Trails

(Hiking Area No. 23)

Rating: See individual hikes.

Features: Plums, redwoods, solitude, fresh and crisp air, birds and camping.

Permission: Camping (fee) and cabin reservations (see State Rental Cabins, page 183) are available from the State Parks Division (address in Appendix). Trail shelters are first come, first served. No fee and no permits are required to hike or to use the trail shelters.

Hiking Distance & Time: Consult individual hikes.
Driving Instructions:

From Lahaina (50 miles, 2 hours) southeast on Route 30, right on Route 38, right on Route 36, right on Route 37 past Kula, left on Route 377 for 0.4 mile, right (10.5 miles) on Waipoli Road to end.

From Wailuku (31 miles, 1 1/2 hours) east on Route 32, right on Route 36, then as above.

Introductory Notes: The Waipoli Road to Polipoli (lit., "mounds, bosom") follows a steep, winding, bumpy course. The initial portion of the road is paved, but the last three and one-half miles are not. Four-wheel-drive vehicles are recommended.

Polipoli Park is an enjoyable hiking and camping area for the whole family. Although the road is rough and steep, it is well worth the effort for an overnight visit. On weekends, usually in the early morning hours, you may be treated to some local hang-gliding enthusiasts "doing their thing" on the slopes of Haleakala. These daring people, harnessed to kites that measure about 2 by 20 feet, take off around the 6,000-feet level for a fifteen-minute plus glide to the Forest Reserve entrance below.

Polipoli Park is only a part of 12,000 acres that also comprise the Kula (lit., "open country") and Kahikinui (lit., "great Tahiti") Forest Reserve on the upper west and south slopes of Haleakala Volcano. Native forests of koa, ohia and mamane have been largely destroyed since the 1800s by cattle, goats, fires and lumbering. During the 1920s a major reforestation and conservation project was begun by the state, and it was continued in the 1930s by the Civilian Conservation Corps. The result was the planting of hundreds of redwood, Monterey cypress, ash, sugi, cedar, and numerous types of pine.

Early mornings and evenings are usually clear, with fog, mist and light rain arriving later in the day. Annual rainfall is 20-40 inches, and the nights are generally cold-unexpected by visitors to Hawaii. Indeed, winter nights frequently have below-freezing temperatures. But don't be discouraged: at least those pesky mosquitoes are absent!

A number of birds may be found in the park along the trails. With the aid of a small booklet, *Hawaii's Birds*, published by the Hawaii Audubon Society, I have been able to identify the ring-necked pheasant (Phasianus colchicus torquatus), the chukar (Alectoris graeca), the California quail (Lophortyx californicus) with its distinctive head plume, the skylark (Alauda arvensis), and the ever-present mynah (Acridotheres tristis), which is probably the noisiest bird known to man. Indeed, the mynah, one of the most common birds on the island, is both intelligent and entertaining. One clue to recognizing it is that it walks as well as hops.

Redwood Trail, 1.7 miles, 1 hour, 900-feet loss (trail rating: hardy family).

The trail begins at the camping area at 6,200 feet and follows a circuitous route through stands of redwoods and other conifers to the 5,300-feet level. A State Park cabin is located a couple of hundred yards from the camping area along the Redwood Trail. The view from the cabin is exciting and the sunsets can be very beautiful. Don't miss either. Markers identify many of the trees along the way, such as Mexican pine, tropical ash, Port Oxford cedar, sugi, and some junipers.

Aptly named, this trail is my favorite at Polipoli because of the hundreds of redwoods (Sequoia sempervirens) that were planted as part of the reforestation program in 1927. Since that time, these wondrous giants have grown to a height of about 90 feet, and some measure four feet or more in diameter at the base. The hike is a particular joy for those familiar with the California redwoods. To walk among these majestic trees, to delight in their fragrance, to feel the soft sod from accumulated needles underfoot, and to view the sun trying to force its way through their dense foliage is an overwhelming experience.

At trail's end, you are met by a generous garden of hydrangeas that seem to engulf the ranger's cabin, which is occupied only when the area is being serviced. However, flowers are not the main attraction here. Locals flock to this part of the park yearly to pick the Methley plum, which grow just below the cabin. The plums usually ripen in June, although they may be sweet by the end of May.

Tie Trail, 0.5-mile, 1/2 hour, 500-feet loss (trail rating: family).

A trail shelter located at the junction of the Tie Trail and the Redwood Trail contains four bunks. The Tie Trail does what the name implies: it connects the Redwood Trail with the Plum Trail, descending 500 feet through stands of sugi, cedar and ash. The Tie Trail junction is 0.8-mile down the Redwood Trail. The Tie Trail joins the Plum Trail 0.6-mile south from the ranger's cabin.

Plum Trail, 1.7 miles, 1 1/2 hours
(trail rating: hardy family).

The trail begins at the ranger's cabin and the old Civilian Conservation Corps (CCC) bunkhouse and runs south until it meets the Haleakala Ridge Trail. The trailhead is a favorite spot to pick Methley plums during June and July. Both the ranger's cabin and the old CCC bunkhouse may be used for overnight shelter, but both are rough and weathered and do not provide drinking water or other facilities. Often, during late afternoon, the trail becomes shrouded by fog or mist, which makes for wet, damp, cool hiking. You should be prepared with rain gear.

Although the plums attract hikers, there are stands of ash, redwood and sugi trees as well. The trail terminates on a bluff overlooking the Ulupalakua ranch area of Maui.

Polipoli Trail, 0.6-mile, 1/2 hour
(trail rating: family).

This trail connects the camping area of the park with the Haleakala Ridge Trail. From the park it passes through rather dense stands of Monterey pine, red alder, cedar, pine and cypress, all of which emit delicious fragrances. Many fallen and cut trees provide an abundant supply of firewood for campers.

Haleakala Ridge Trail, 1.6 miles, 1 hour,
600-feet loss (trail rating: family).

For a full panorama of the island, the Ridge Trail provides the best views, since it is not as heavily forested as other portions of the park. It begins at the terminal point of the Skyline Trail, at 6,550 feet, and follows the southwest rift of Haleakala to join with the Plum Trail at 5,950 feet.

Monterey pine, cypress, eucalyptus, blackwood, hybrid cypress and native grasses are identified by markers along the trail. At trail's end, be certain to investigate a small ten-by-twenty-foot dry cave located in a cinder cone and used as a trail shelter. An eight-by-ten-foot ledge in the cave provides a relatively comfortable king-sized bed. A spur trail to the cave is clearly marked and easy to follow.

Boundary Trail, 4.0 miles, 2 1/2 hours (trail rating: hardy family).

The Kula Forest Reserve boundary cattle guard on the Polipoli Road marks the trailhead for the Boundary Trail. This trail descends gradually along switchbacks to follow the northern boundary of the reserve to the ranger's cabin at the Redwood-Plum Trail Junction. Numerous points along the trail provide views of central Maui.

The trail crosses many gulches that abound in native scrub, ferns and grasses as well as stands of eucalyptus, Chinese fir, sugi, cedar and Monterey pine. About 1/2 mile below the cabin, fuchsia bushes proliferate to the point of obscuring the trail. As you pass through this garland of delicate red, lantern like flowers, a clearing encircled by eucalyptus trees appears across the fence.

Waiohuli Trail, 1.4 miles, 1 1/2 hours, 800-feet loss (trail rating: hardy family).

The rough Waiohuli (lit., "churning water") Trail begins on the Polipoli Road at 6,400 feet and goes straight down the mountainside to meet the Boundary Trail at the 5,600-feet level. The trail first passes rough, low, native scrub, young pine plantings and grasslands, and then wanders through older stands of cedar, redwood and ash.

The trail eventually joins the Boundary Trail, which is well-maintained and clearly identifiable. At this junction, another overnight shelter is conveniently located.

Waiakoa Trail, 7.0 miles, 5 hours, 1,800-feet gain/loss (trail rating: strenuous).

The Upper Waiakoa Trailhead is opposite the Waiohuli Trailhead off the Polipoli Road. Carry sufficient water since no source can be found trailside. Initially, the trail ascends along switchbacks to the junction with the Mamane Trail, to a natural cave shelter and then turning northerly (left) and passing over rugged terrain consisting mostly of scrub vegetation. Look for pheasant and chukar partridge throughout the hike.

Outstanding views of central and West Maui are possible as you near the high point of the trail at 7,800 feet. Eucalyptus, mixed pine species, cedar, ash and native scrub dominate throughout interrupted by open places that offer a view of the summit of Haleakala, conspicuous by the white domes containing telescopes. Pukiawe, a common native bush in this forest, has tiny, evergreen leaves with reddish-white berries.

From there, the trail descends about 1,800 feet along a series of switchbacks to connect with the Waiakoa Loop Trail.

Waiakoa Loop Trail, 3 miles, 2 hours, 500-feet gain/loss (trail rating: hardy family).

From the Hunter Checking Station, it's 3/4-mile to the Waiakoa (lit., "waters used by warrior") Loop Trailhead, which is a 3 mile Loop. From the game-checking station on the Polipoli Road follow the dirt road to the posted trailhead.

Once through the gate, the trail contours the hillside and after 100 yards it intersects the loop trail. Bearing right, the trail passes under a variety of trees, mostly black pine and eucalyptus. The latter are introduced trees planted for soil conservation.

When in bloom the native mamane tree offers a brilliant shower of bright yellow blossoms. The Hawaiians once used the hard wood for making spades and sled runners. Mamane trees are sometime mistaken for the wattle found throughout the trail. Wattle is an introduced tree with yellow blossoms, but usually much taller than the mamane.

After a mile or so, the trail emerges onto an area dominated by native and introduced scrub. At the 1 1/2-mile point, the trail begins to loop and descend over open, grassy swales and then forested places before beginning an ascent to complete the loop. fallen trees and large rocks throughout the hike afford places to pause to enjoy a snack, to inhale the fresh, crisp mountain air and to look for birdlife.

Mamane Trail, 1.2 miles, 1 hour (trail rating: hardy family).

The Mamane Trail links the Skyline and Waiakoa trails and is used by hikers and bicyclists so be alert. The trail was reconstructed by volunteers under the direction of Na Ala Hele, the Hawaii State Trail and Access System. The trail passes through sparse native scrub brush and over cinder and rock.

Skyline Trail Junction

Kahua Road Trail, 3.5 miles, 3 hours (trail rating: strenuous).

Used primarily by hunters, this road begins at Ballpark Junction where the Skyline Trail joins the road at 7,100 feet. It leads east on the contour through very rough lava country to the cinder cone called Kahua (lit., "jealousy"). Even a four-wheeled drive vehicle has difficulty traversing this road. An overnight cabin here is maintained by the state, and arrangements can be made in Wailuku for its use. It accommodates four people and has water. The primary attraction is the view of the east side and the rugged coastline. On clear days it is possible to see across Kahukinui to the Kaupo Gap. This is a very hot and difficult hike.

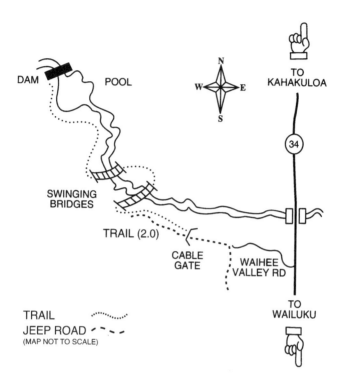

Waihee Valley Trail

(Hiking Area No. 24)

Rating: Hardy Family.

Features: Swimming, waterfalls, views, fruits.

Permission: Maui Agribusiness, Tel. 244-9570 for written permit.

Hiking Distance & Time: 2 miles, 1 1/2 hours.

Driving Instructions:

From Lahaina (31 miles, 1 1/4 hours) southeast on Route 30 to Wailuku, right on Route 32, left on Route 34 (Kahului Beach Road), right on Route 34 through Waihee, left on Waihee Road 0.7 mile from Waihee School, follow paved road for 0.5 mile to end, and bear right on unpaved road for 0.2 mile to cable gate. Park your car on the shoulder outside the gate even if the cable is unlocked when you arrive, it may not be when you return. DON'T LEAVE VALUABLES IN THE CAR.

From Wailuku (10 miles, 1/2 hour) east on Route 32, left on Route 34, then as above.

Introductory Notes: Waihee (lit., "slippery water") Valley is one of the easiest valley hikes on the island, and it is one of the prettiest valleys on the island, with narrow canyon and steep vertical walls from which water cascades and falls. The terrain is relatively level for the whole distance. Since it is a watershed area, hikers should not hike beyond the dam.

On the Trail: From your car, walk up the road and bear right. The first mile of the hike is on a maintenance road that follows the stream (right) and an irrigation channel (left). Look for guava trees and thimbleberries along the trail. Ginger is particularly abundant, and conspicuous by its fragrant aroma. There are torch ginger, with its long, bamboo-like stalk and red blossom, and yellow ginger, which is more fragrant.

Ti (Cordyline terminalis) plants are also abundant. They should be familiar to all visitors who have seen a hula show. The long, narrow leaves are used to make hula skirts, and have also been used by Hawaiians to make thatch, raincoats, sandals, plates to serve food, and wrappers for food.

As the trail levels, there are views into the valley and east to the ocean. The stream is usually dry up to the point of the water intake. After one mile, two successive swinging bridges cross the stream bed. After crossing the second bridge, be on the lookout for mountain apple trees (eugenia malaccensis) alongside the trail. I could find only a couple of these trees, which bear a small, deep-crimson fruit with a pure-white pulp and a large, round seed. It is much sought after by locals, who know the best places and best trees.

Be careful here, particularly with children, because after the bridges the trail climbs above the stream along the canyon wall. Below the ridge, an elaborate irrigation system is designed to catch the stream water and to channel it via a system of ditches. This is a good opportunity to examine the system up close. Upstream about 200 yards is a second dam and water-intake system. This is the end of the trail. From here, you are able to view the waterfalls in the back of the canyon as well as the steep vertical walls. Below the dam, large pools provide a cool swim or a refreshing splash.

It is possible to continue into the canyon by following the stream, but the going is rough and wet. If it is raining in the canyon, there is also the danger of flash flooding.

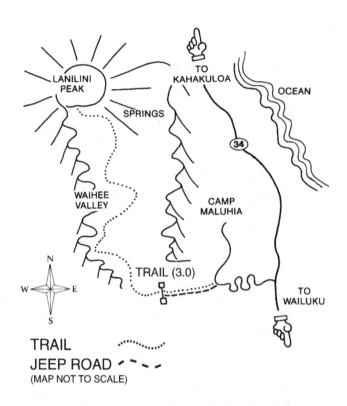

TRAIL ·········

JEEP ROAD ✓ ‒ ‿

(MAP NOT TO SCALE)

Waihee Ridge Trail

(Hiking Area No. 25)

Rating: Strenuous.

Features: Views of Waihee Canyon and Valley, Central Maui, the north side.

Permission: None.

Hiking Distance & Time: 3.0 miles, 2 hours, 1,500-feet gain.

Driving Instructions:

From Lahaina (32 miles, 1 1/4 hour) southeast on Route 30 to Wailuku, right on Route 32, left on Route 34, (Kahului Beach Road) through Waihee. Turn left on road posted "Camp Maluhia" and drive 0.8-mile to the trailhead a short distance before the camp.

From Wailuku (11 miles, 1/2 hour) east on Route 32, left on Route 34, then as above.

Introductory Notes: The Waihee (lit., "slippery water") Ridge trail and area are under the management of the Hawaii State Department of Land and Natural Resources and are regularly maintained.

On the Trail: From the parking area, pass through a turnstile and cross the pasture and ascend to the trees above. You may be surprised by grazing cattle in the heavy brush along the road. Relatively sweet common and strawberry guava abound along the trail. Shortly, a gate across the road marks the border of forest-reserve land. If the gate is locked, passage is provided a few feet to the right of the gate. In a few hundred feet the road ends and a foot trail begins. It turns right and climbs the ridge through an area of grass, ferns and trees.

The trail is marked every 1/4 mile. There are a number of overlooks into Waihee Canyon and to the north into Makamakaole (lit., "not without intimate friends") Gulch. At the 0.7-mile point and beyond for a distance, there are superb views of the valley. Thereafter, the trail switchbacks and ascends the narrow ridge that is heavily foliated, wet, muddy, and in places quite steep so that it is necessary to use the trees and bushes for support. After two miles, the trail reaches a flat, grassy tableland that may or may not be passable if it is too wet and boggy.

Be on the lookout for edible thimbleberries (Rubus rosaefolius), which grow profusely in this area. These red berries grow on a small bush with white flowers.

From the tableland, it is less than a mile to Lanilili (lit., "small heaven") Peak and breathtaking views of the north side of the island and of the surrounding valleys. Conveniently, a picnic table is on the summit.

Taro

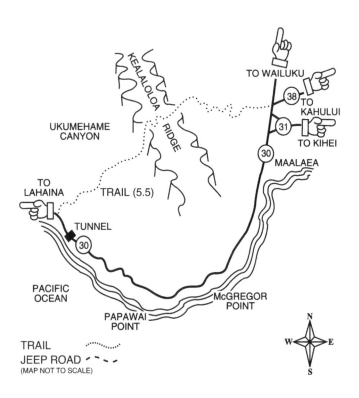

TRAIL ......
JEEP ROAD ʼ ˉ ˎ ˎ
(MAP NOT TO SCALE)

Lahaina Pali Trail
(Hiking Area No. 26)

Rating: Strenuous.
Features: Views of Central Maui, Kihei, Haleakala, Molokini, Kahoolawe, Lanai, Hawaii.
Permission: None
Hiking Distance & Time: 5.5 miles, 3 hours, 1,600-feet gain/loss.

Driving Instructions:

From Lahaina (11 miles, 1/2 hour to westside trailhead) southeast on Route 30 to 11-mile marker and parking lot on the left side of the road.

From Wailuku (6 miles, 1/4 hour to eastside trailhead) south on Route 30 to 5-mile marker just past junction with Route 38. Cross over a white bridge and turn right to posted trailhead.

Introductory Notes: Originally constructed in 1840, the Lahaina Pali Trail fell into disrepair with the construction of a carriage road and later the present highway along the coast. Then in 1992, Na Ala Hele, (Lit., "trails to go") a statewide organization under the State Department of Land and Natural Resources surveyed, cleared and brushed the trail aided by hundreds of volunteers. The trail was dedicated in June, 1993.

I recommend that you begin hiking from the Maalaea (east side) Trailhead. This is the steeper part of the trail, but, if you begin hiking in the morning, the sun will be at your back. If you have two vehicles, leave one at the opposite trailhead. This is a hot hike with infrequent shade. Two quarts of water per person and sound hiking boots are recommended. Rocks and exposed tree roots are underfoot and are a hazard throughout the trail.

On the Trail: From the trailhead, walk on the dirt road with your back to the highway directly toward the base of the mountain. The road turns left and goes about 150 yards to a posted parking area and a trail sign which directs you off the road and onto a footpath shaded by large kiawe (Prosopis pallida) trees, a common tree found on the islands whose thorns seem to find their way into feet and legs. Its branches are long, slender and flexible, while the flowers are pale yellow and tiny. The bark contains tannin and a gum that is valuable in making varnish and glue. The wood is a source not only of fuel and lumber but also of honey, medicine and fodder, which is produced from its bean like yellow pods containing 25% grape sugar.

The trail begins a steady climb up the east side toward Kealaloloa Ridge. Look on both sides of the trail for abandoned concrete water wells and for concrete platforms that held large guns. The site was a military post constructed during WW II as a part of the island's defense system. Several metal posts and rolls of barbed wire mark the military boundary at the half-mile mark.

Shortly thereafter, the trail emerges from the canopy provided by the kiawe trees and follows a steeper, serpentine course. You're likely to find glass fragments and even bottles scattered on the trail and trailside. You're asked to inspect them if you choose, but to leave them where found. They may be significant artifacts which may be collected and studied at some future date. The trail curbing throughout the hike is thought to be from the original trail construction. Some of it is in good condition and an example of dry wall construction still commonly employed in Hawaii.

After the first mile, the trail becomes increasingly steeper but the views improve with every step. To the east, Kahului, the airport, sugar and pineapple fields comprise the neck portion of Maui with Haleakala, the house of the sun, overlooking its creation in the distance.

Low scrub and ground cover dominate throughout the next few miles. Puakala (Argemone glauca) is a white, prickly poppy related to the common North American species. Lantana (Lantana camara) is a popular flower that blooms almost continuously. Its flowers vary in color from yellow to orange to pink or red. Another flower, the ilima

(Sida fallax) has bright flowers ranging in color from yellow to rich orange to dull red.

Several ironwood trees (Casuarina equisetifolia) are conspicuous on the ridge line to the west which is approximately the midpoint and the highest point (1,600 feet) on the trail. From this vista, you might be able to distinguish Hawaii, "the Big Island" to the right of Haleakala. To the south, lies Kihei, Maui's "Gold Coast," and offshore, the islands of Molokini, Kahoolawe and Lanai. As a bonus, between November and March, migratory humpback whales can be spotted in the waters below where they come to mate or to give birth.

From the ridge, the trail begins a gentle descent passing over a jeep road that goes north up the ridge and continuing on to the Olowalu Trailhead a few miles distant. More kiawe trees and vegetation provide some shade for the balance of the hike. State officials believe that abandoned house sites are scattered along this side of the ridge, but further studies need to be made. If you explore off the trail do not disturb or remove rocks. Look for letters chiseled on large rocks below the ridge. Most of them are letters in the paniolo (cowboy) style with bars at the bottom of the letter. Some of the writing may be decades old while others are more recent. It is believed that students passing through over the years may have used the rocks to practice their lettering.

The foot trail joins the old Lahaina carriage trail about 100 yards from the Olowalu Trailhead and the main highway. Follow the road a short distance to a foot path on the left that descends a stone stairway to the trailhead and a parking lot. A long, white sand beach and several shady picnic spots are just across the highway. It's also a good swimming and snorkeling beach.

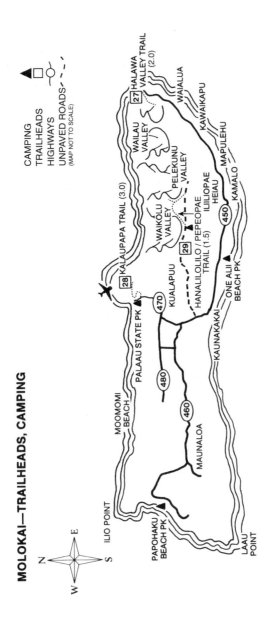

MOLOKAI—TRAILHEADS, CAMPING

CAMPING
TRAILHEADS
HIGHWAYS
UNPAVED ROADS
(MAP NOT TO SCALE)

Molokai
The Friendly Isle

The Island

Molokai is the island for a person who feels that Hawaii is overdeveloped and over commercialized and is looking for outdoor experiences. The fifth largest island in the Hawaiian chain - 37 miles long and 10 miles wide - Molokai was once known as the "Lonely Island" because the native sufferers of Hansen's disease (leprosy) were once banished here by the monarchy. Today, perhaps in response to an effort to change the island's image and to reflect more accurately its character, Molokai is known as the "Friendly Island." Locals still wave to passing motorists, shout greetings across the street to friends, and congregate in the few bars and restaurants in Kaunakakai, Molokai's town, to "talk story" with friends and visitors. The slow-paced, relaxed life style is infectious.

Politically a part of Maui County, Molokai was created by three volcanoes. Mauna Loa is a shield volcano on the west side rising to 1381 feet; Kamakou, on the east side, is the island's highest point at 4970 feet; and about 2 million years after most of the island was formed, Kauhako (405 feet) erupted and formed the Kalaupapa peninsula. It is along the range of mountains and valleys on the east and north sides of the island that the best hiking trails are to be found. Indeed, the four valleys on the north coast, Waikolu, Pelekunu, Wailau and Halawa, offer outstanding outdoor experiences. Practically speaking, only Halawa is accessible on foot. Pelekunu and Wailau can be reached on foot but only by skilled hikers and outdoors people who are able to deal with hardships particularly the descent into these valleys. I strongly recommend hiring a local guide for either trek. The others can be reached by boat in the summer during calmer seas.

Although Molokai has retained a "nontourist," "low-key" style, it still offers adequate accommodations. There are a couple of hotels and a couple of condominiums offering satisfactory-to-first-class rooms and apartments, a number of car-rental agencies offering a wide range of vehicles, and a few good restaurants. No public transportation is available on the island, but hitchhiking is legal.

Camping

State Campgounds

Palaau State Park Campground ($5 per person per night) is located nearly in the center of the island at 1600 feet elevation and eight miles from Kaunakakai. Restrooms, picnic tables, grills and water are available. The campground is located in a heavily wooded portion of the park where it is always cool and sometimes wet and damp. It is a short walk to the Kalaupapa trailhead.

County Campgrounds

The county offers two beach camping areas on Molokai. One campground is at One Alii County Beach, 3.3 miles east of Kaunakakai and the other is at Papohaku, 23 miles west of Kaunakakai. Each has the same amenities as Palaau State Park. Camping fees are $3 for adults and $.50 for children. Reservations may be made through the County of Maui (see Appendix). Of the two, only Papohaku located near the Sheraton Molokai Hotel on the west side has a good swimming beach.

State Forestry Campground

Wilderness camping is allowed in the Molokai Forest Reserve without a fee by permission of the Division of Forestry (tel. 553-5019). At Waikolu Lookout plans are underway (1999) to reconstruct and refurbish the cabin, pavilion, restrooms, and barbecue pits. It is located 13.4 miles from Kaunakakai, but 10 miles of this distance is on a rough forest road which is passable in a four-wheel drive vehicle. All addresses are in the Appendix.

Hiking

Molokai offers some particularly interesting hiking and backpacking experiences. With the exception of Halawa Valley, the trails included are infrequently traveled. Kalaupapa does entertain visitors daily, but few hike the trail. Most fly to the peninsula or ride in on mules.

The Wailau Valley on the north shore and the Wailau "trail" require special note. Wailau Valley is one of the few nearly pristine places in Hawaii that is accessible on foot - almost. The trailhead is 15 miles east of Kaunakakai behind Iliiliopae Heiau (look for highway marker), but the trail from the heiau up the valley to the pali (cliffs) is not clearly defined. The 3000-feet descent of the pali into Wailau Valley is very difficult. On it, the trail is where the hiker can manage. The Wailau Trail should not be attempted by anyone who is not experienced in Hawaiian terrain or does not possess considerable outdoor skills. I suggest that you join a hiking group, such as the Sierra Club, which usually make an annual trek into Wailau, or else hire the services of a local person who will guide you. There are a number of persons on the island who will serve as guides, particularly in Halawa Valley. Ask around. There are also a number of local boatmen who take people in and out of Wailau in the summer when the ocean allows safe passage. In any event, Wailau is an exciting experience. There are a number of camping spots along the beach and others on a 50-feet rise above the beach on the east side of the valley. The valley abounds with bananas, plums, mountain apples, guava, thimbleberries, and fresh-water prawns and shellfish.

Permits to camp in Wailau Valley are required and may be obtained from the Forestry & Wildlife Office, Department of Land & Natural Resources, on Molokai. The office has announced emphatically that permits will not be issued "to those whom the Ranger deems inexperienced or otherwise unfit to safely negotiate this difficult and dangerous trail."

Halawa Valley Trail

(Hiking Area No. 27)
(See map, p. 240)

(Halawa Valley Trail is presently closed. A dispute between residents, property owners and State officials is under negotiation. Please respect signage at the trailhead.)

Rating: Hardy family.
Features: Waterfalls, swimming, fruits.
Permission: None
Hiking Distance and Time: 2 miles one-way, 1 hour.
Driving Instructions:
   From Kaunakakai (28 miles, 1 1/2 hours) drive east on Route 450 to Halawa Valley. When the roads levels in the valley, locate a small church and a dirt road on the left. Park in the turnouts near the church or in the parking area at Halawa Beach Park, a short distance away. The trailhead is at the church.

Introductory Notes: Halawa (lit., "curve") Valley would most certainly be on anyone's list of the best places to visit in Hawaii. It contains all that a person expects in Hawaii - a good, pleasant hiking trail, fruits, and a generous pool in which to swim at the base of Moaula (lit., "red chicken") Falls. The valley is about 1/2 mile wide at the beachfront and about three miles deep. It was once heavily populated, but a tsunami in 1946 and almost annual flooding have discouraged permanent residents.

On the Trail: From the church, go left on the dirt road where you'll see a number of houses on both sides of the road. Do not turn right or left off the road, but follow it for 1/2 mile to its end. A foot trail continues past a couple of houses and alongside a stone wall on the left for about 150 yards. Then make a right turn directly to the stream. Scout around for the easiest and safest place to cross Halawa Stream.

The trail continues on the opposite bank of the stream in the shade of giant mango (Mangifera indica) trees, whose fruit when ripe - usually March to October - is absolutely delicious. The large, pear-shaped fruit with orange pulp is quite sweet and juicy. The wood from these large, beautiful trees has been used for craftswood, furniture and gun stocks. From the stream, the trail passes under mango trees and up a short rise to where it intersects a trail paralleling the stream. The fork to the right goes to the beach over private land. The fork to the left, our trail to the falls, passes more mango trees and countless noni (Morinda citrifolia), or indian mulberry, from whose roots and bark a yellow and a yellowish-red dye were produced. The small, warty-looking fruit was eaten in times of famine. It is a small evergreen with large, shiny, dark-green leaves.

From here to the next stream crossing, the trail parallels a water pipe. It also passes by and bisects the remains of numerous taro terraces which once yielded great quantities of taro, from which the Hawaiian staple, poi, is produced. After you cross the north fork of Halawa Stream, Moaula Falls is about one hundred yards distant. Before you swim at Moaula, you should know about the legend of the moo (lizard) who lives here. It is safe to swim only if moo is happy, which can be determined by placing a ti leaf in the pool. If it floats, all is well; but if it sinks, well, you're on your own!

About 75 yards from the north fork stream crossing and just before the falls, a spur trail bears off to the right and up the cliff. The trail levels and is soon lost in the brush. If you continue through the brush, Hipuapua (lit., "tail flowing") Falls is about one-fourth mile distant. Be extremely cautious here. The trail to Hipuapua is not clear, and a rockslide before reaching the falls makes passage difficult. The best route is to scramble down the pali to the stream and to rock hop to the falls. But be cautious, the rocks are wet and slippery. Look for mountain apples (Eugenia malaccensis) on your way to Hipuapua. These lemon-sized apples, when ripe, are deep-crimson with a pure white pulp and a large round seed. They make an ideal snack after a swim at Moaula.

Kalaupapa Trail

(Hiking Area No. 28)
(See map, p. 240)

Rating: Strenuous.

Features: Historical sites, views.

Permission: A permit is required to hike. The permit allows entry to the trail and includes a tour of the colony, since no one is allowed to travel unescorted on the peninsula. Persons under 16 years may not visit Kalaupapa. Arrangements are made through Damien Tours (567-6171). Advance reservations are recommended.

Hiking Distance and Time: 3 miles one-way, 2 hours, 1600-feet loss.

Driving Instructions:

From Kaunakakai (9.6 miles, 1/2 hour) drive west on Route 450, right on Route 470 to the entrance of Palaau State Park just beyond the Molokai mule barn. Walk right on a dirt road at the Park's entrance to the trailhead.

Introductory Notes:

"To see the infinite pity of this place,
The mangled limb, the devastated face,
The innocent sufferers smiling at the rod,
A fool were tempted to deny his God.
He sees, and shrinks; but if he look again,
Lo, beauty springing from the breast of pain!
He marks the sisters on the painful shores,
And even a fool is silent and adores."

After a week on the Kalaupapa peninsula in 1889, where he spent much of the time playing with leper children, Robert Louis Stevenson left this bit of verse with the sisters when he departed. I do not believe that anyone can visit Kalaupapa without being affected, some profoundly. Certainly these 4 1/2 square miles, which are bounded by vertical 2000-feet cliffs on the one hand and a rough sea on the other, have changed a great deal since that first day that Father Damien de Veuster set foot on shore in 1873. This first white resident of the peninsula was dedicated to aiding the forsaken souls who were banished to this leper colony. Many were tossed overboard from the ships that brought them and did not survive the swim to shore. Those who did survive found an inhospitable society where children, women and the seriously ill were exploited by other sufferers from leprosy and where survival of the fittest was clearly the rule. For 16 years, until leprosy took his life, Father Damien attended to the spiritual, medical, and material needs of the populace. He built a church, but he also built houses, a hospital, and, perhaps most importantly, a patient society where exploitation was replaced by cooperation. After Father Damien's death in 1889, Brother Joseph Dutton and many others carried on his work. Today, Hansen's disease is controlled with the use of sulfone drugs, so that it is not necessary to isolate sufferers. The peninsula is now under the authority of the National Park Service, and Kalaupapa is likely to become a national park soon. Meanwhile, the 80 (1999) patients who remain are guaranteed a home as long as they choose, but they are free to leave.

Years ago, the Catholic Church began considering the question of sainthood for Father Damien. Robert Louis Stevenson expressed the feeling that the patients had for Damien during his life, and many have had after discovering this remarkable man. In 1890 Stevenson concluded a letter to Rev. C. M. Hyde, who had been severely critical of Damien, by writing, "Well, the man who tried to do what Damien did, is my father, and the father of the man in the Apia bar, and the father of all who love goodness; and he was your father too, if God had given you grace to see it."

On the Trial: Before descending the trail, walk to the guard rail by the U. S. Navy facility for a fine view of Kalaupapa (lit., "the flat plain") below. The peninsula was built long after the rest of Molokai by Kauhako (lit., "the dragged large intestines"), a 405-feet shield volcano. It is best to begin your hike before 8:30 a.m., when it is cool and you won't be troubled by the tour mules. The trail, which was recently rebuilt, is wide and safe in spite of its abrupt descent and 26 hairpin turns. Throughout the day, shade trees and trade winds offer relief from the heat. There are numerous places along the trail to view Kalaupapa. This is not the trail used by Father Damien; it was farther east. The so-called Damien trail was dynamited after the priest's death by the people who owned a ranch in the flat country above the cliffs. It seems that some of the patients would ascend the trail and steal and slaughter cattle for food. After the trail reaches the beach, it is about 1/4 mile to the mule corral and a paved road which leads to Kalaupapa town. Your tour guide will meet you at the corral. You are not allowed to wander beyond this point. It is permissible to stroll along Puwahi (lit., "broken conch") Beach, before reaching the coral, where you are likely to encounter patients pole-fishing or throwing nets. The patients are very friendly and are quick to "talk story".

Hopefully, Richard Marks, the county sheriff, will be your guide. He is a patient, resident and all-around wonderful man whose reportoire will fascinate and cheer you in spite of the somber surroundings.

Hanalilolilo/Pepeopae Trail
(Hiking Area No. 29)
(See map, p. 240)

Rating: Strenuous.
Features: Mountain and coastal views, native flora, swamp, camping.

Permission: Camping permits from Department of Land & Natural Resources, Division of Forestry and Wildlife. No fee.

Hiking Distance and Time: 1.5 miles, 1 hour, 500-feet gain.

Driving Instructions:

From Kaunakakai (13.4 miles, 1 hour) FOUR WHEEL DRIVE VEHICLES ONLY. Drive west on Route 450 for 3.4 miles to a dirt road on the right just before a large white bridge and opposite the "Molokai Aggregate Co." Go right on the dirt road for 10 miles to Waikolu Lookout. Do not attempt this road in a conventional car. The road is not posted, so bear left whenever you meet another road. However, do not turn left into the fields. You will be ascending a ridge and heading in the direction of tall trees. If you do not reach the forest reserve (posted) after driving 5.6 miles on the dirt road or the Nature Conservancy Camp 0.2 mile beyond, you are on the wrong road. From the camp, it is 3.2 miles to the "sandalwood boat" and from there 1.0 to the lookout and picnic area.

Introductory Notes: The "sandalwood boat," or Lua Na Moku Iliahi (lit., "pit of the sandalwood ship"), which is alongside the road one mile before the lookout, deserves a note. It is believed that a chief had this pit constructed to the dimensions of the hold of a sailing ship. Sandalwood trees were then cut and the logs were placed in the pit and sold to traders by the pitful.

Waikolu (lit., "three waters") Lookout provides a dramatic view into narrow and steep Waikolu Valley from a 3700-feet perch. During wet periods countless waterfalls burst forth from the cliffs. A recently constructed water tunnel provides most of the water for the south side of the island. On a clear day, the view is breathtaking. However, on a cloudy day you may see your shadow on the clouds - the rare Spectre of the Brocken.

On the Trail: Hanalilolilo (lit., "disappearing place") gets its name from the illusion that some experience here. They say that as they approach Hanalilolilo (the area above Waikolu Valley) it seems always to be receding.

From Waikolu Lookout walk 0.2 mile (Waikolu Valley is on the left) on the road to the trailhead sign on the left side of the road. The entire hike is through a native forest of ohia lehua and a variety of ferns. Initially the trail climbs in the forest at the head of Waikolu Valley. Views of the valley are not good here because the ohia trees are so profuse. The ohia is a noble tree, a native tree and the most common tree in Hawaii. It has gray-green leaves and tassel-like red flowers that look like those of the bottlebrush plant. Legend holds that the flower is a favorite of Madame Pele, the goddess of volcanoes, and if it is picked without the proper incantation she will cause rain to fall. There are many varieties of ferns along the trail. The most common tree fern on the island is the Hawaiian tree fern, hapuu (Cibotium menziesii), whose trunks were used to make tikis, fences, pathways and orchid logs. In times of famine, the fleshy stems of the fern were eaten. The ulei (Osteomeles anthyllidifolia), or Hawaiian rose, is particularly abundant near the trailhead. It is a single, sweet-scented thornless rose usually found on a low shrub which sometimes grows to a height of 14 feet. Its hard wood, known for its pliability, has been used for bows, back scratchers, and javelins used in the Hawaiian game of pahee.

A short distance from the trailhead, you pass a water-works on the left side, from which you may get your last view of Waikolu Valley. About 1/2 mile beyond, be alert for a large lava-walled, fern-lined pit on the right. It is the type of formation that when combined with lush tropical folia-tion is one of the treasures of Hawaii. From this point to the tableland, the trail twists and turns through a heavily foli-ated native rain forest where the safest footing is on the roots of the trees. One false step and it's mud to the knee. Avoid the soft, damp mudholes in the middle of the trail.

You emerge on the tableland where you are greeted by a boardwalk constructed by the 1985 Alu Like Summer Youth Group commemorating the Hawaiian Bog Studies of 1938. The boardwalk allows for an easy walk to the cen-ter of the tableland.

At a junction turn left on the Pepeopae Trail and fol-low the boardwalk for 0.6 mile through a rain forest to sev-eral precipitous points overlooking Pelekunu (lit., "smelly from lack of sunshine") Valley. It is an extraordinary view into the valley and beyond to the sea.

After returning to the tableland, retrace your steps to the trailhead, or go in the opposite direction on the board-walk into the ohia forest on a 1/2-mile trail that will take you to a spur road off the main forest road. Continue a short distance on the spur road to where it joins the main road. Turn right and follow the road to the Hanalilolilo Trailhead and the Waikolu Lookout some 2.5 miles distant. The road to Wailoku Lookout twists, turns, and drops through two gulches. Bear to the right at all intersections.

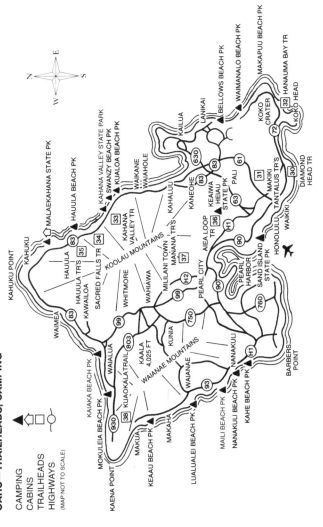

OAHU—TRAILHEADS, CAMPING

CAMPING
CABINS
TRAILHEADS
HIGHWAYS
(MAP NOT TO SCALE)

Oahu
The Gathering Place

The Island

Take a walk along Waikiki Beach any time of the day, any time of the year, and you will understand why this, the third largest of the Hawaiian Islands, is called Oahu, "the gathering place:" Everyone is here - Japanese, Chinese, Filipinos, Blacks, Samoans, Germans, Canadians, Australians, Americans and others.

What is it that brings people here from all over the world? Can it be the air temperature, which seldom varies by more than 10 degrees, with a year-round average of 75 degrees F? Can it be the 80 degree water temperature at Waikiki Beach? Can it be the enchantment of precipitous cliffs and heavily overgrown valleys existing as backdrops to a city covered with asphalt and high-rise buildings? Can it be the fascinating blend of the multi-ethnic population? Can it be the life style in which individuality reigns supreme, and muumuus and cutoffs, oxfords and bare feet, tuxedos and swimsuits intermingle in the restaurants and night clubs? Can it be the surf, the music, the suntanned bodies, the Aloha spirit, the wild fruits, the hiking, the camping, the slow pace of life, the....?

The truth is that Waikiki and Honolulu are all of these things. The truth is that long before the first-time visitor arrives, Hawaii has transmitted its message via the plaudits of happy visitors, the media, and the Hawaii Visitors Bureau. The truth is that the first-time visitor has been primed for pleasure long before his jumbo 747 flies over Diamond Head and lands in Honolulu. For most people, there are no disappointments, and they return again and again.

Indeed, the crowds are sometimes so great that people spill off the sidewalk onto Kalakaua Avenue in order to get by casual strollers. Combine the million of tourists who visit Oahu annually with the one million or so permanent residents (about 80% of the state's population) and you have a lot of people on a rather small island.

Honolulu was not an original Hawaiian city. It was established by the followers of Captain Cook who, in search of anchorage, discovered this protected deep-water bay. Honolulu (lit., "protected bay") grew rapidly and was soon recognized as the trading and business center of the islands by King Kamehameha III. The official capital of the Kingdom of Hawaii was moved from Lahaina, Maui, to Honolulu in 1850. For the next 85 years, the southeast end of the city remained a swamp where taro was cultivated and ducks and other marsh birds roamed freely. However, in the past 40 years Waikiki has been dramatically altered from its humble beginnings to become one of the most recognized beaches in the world.

The two mountain ranges and the island of Oahu were created by volcanic eruptions. Oahu took shape as subsequent lava flows filled the area between the ranges until the present 607 square miles remained. In time, the Koolau mountain range on the east side and the Waianae mountain range on the west side were further sculpted by natural forces, so that both have gently sloping parts and steep precipitous areas.

Camping and Cabins

The camper should keep in mind that most of the campsites on Oahu are in heavily populated areas or in areas accessible to population centers. Consequently, all of the ills of urban living are present - thievery, damage to equipment, drunkenness. Campers should not leave valuables and equipment unattended or unprotected.

Hiking can be an exciting way to see Oahu, and camping can make your visit an inexpensive one. Since camping is a popular activity with local people, make your plans in advance and obtain permits as soon as you arrive on the island. There are four state campgrounds on the island and numerous county beach parks where camping is permitted.

State Campgrounds

Camping is permitted at four campgrounds in the state park system on Oahu. Sand Island State Recreation Area, located in Honolulu Harbor, provides close to town camping. The campground at Keaiwa Heiau State Park in Honolulu is in a shaded, wooded area near the trailhead of the Aiea Loop Trail. The third state campgound is located at Kahana Valley State Park which offers beach camping and board and body surfing at one of Oahu's most beautiful bays and sandy beaches. A marvelous hiking trail loops through Kahana Valley (See pp. 282-285).It is located on Kamehameha Highway (#83) on the east coast. Malaekahana State Park, the fourth campgound, is located just north of Laie on a beautiful white sandy beach.

Permits are not issued earlier than two Fridays before the weekend of occupancy and are not issued for more than five (5) consecutive days. Camping begins at 8 a.m. Friday and ends at 8 a.m. on Wednesday. Campgrounds are closed Wednesday and Thursday. Reservations may be made no sooner that 30 days before the first day of camping by mail from the Department of State Parks (address in Appendix). Campers are charged a fee of $5 per person, per night (address in Appendix).

Private Campground/Cabins

In addition to the State Campground at Malaekahana (cited above) a portion of the park has been leased by the Friends of Malaekahana who offer 24 hour,7 days a week, thirty secured campsites with modern facilities and hot showers. Camping fees are $5 per person per night. Permits are available up to one year in advance.

They also rent tent cabins for clients who don't wish to sleep on the ground. Each is a large, screened structure with a private sleeping area, beds and a separate dining area with a roomy lanai.

Housekeeping cabins in the park are also under the Friends management. Their group cabin is priced at $275 per night for up to 20 persons. Six family beach houses (priced at $70 for 6-8 persons). are equipped with a full kitchen, comfortable beds and living room furniture. Bedding, eating and kitchen utensils are available for rent at a nominal fee. The concessionaire's office is in the park. (Mailing address is in the Appendix.)

County Campgrounds

The County of Honolulu operates over 450 recreational parks and sites located on the island. Camping is permitted at 14 beach parks.The number and location of the parks changes frequently due to heavy use. Permits are not issued earlier than two Fridays before the weekend of occupancy and are not issued for more than five (5) consecutive days. Camping begins at 8 a.m. Friday and ends at 8 a.m. on Wednesday. Campgrounds are closed Wednesday and Thursday. Camping permits can be obtained from the Departmentof Parks and Recreation in Honolulu or any of 10 satellite city halls located around the island. (All addresses are in the Appendix). All the campgrounds have cold-water showers, drinking water and restrooms. Most of the beach parks receive heavy use, so they are not always clean and the facilities are not always in good operating order. The campgrounds at Waimanalo, Mokuleia, Keaau, Lualualei, and Nanakuli are recommended, since they are usually clean and they have ample space for camping. Trailer camping is permitted at all of the parks where tents are allowed except Lualualei Beach Park. Trailers must be self-contained, since there are no electrical or sewer connections.

Hiking

There is more to Oahu than world-famous Waikiki, Diamond Head and Pearl Harbor. On the windward (east) side of the island are the Hawaiian communities of Hauula and Laie, where numerous valley hikes and beach camping, away from the crowds, await the outdoorsperson. The north shore of Oahu may well be the surfing capital of the world, with the Banzai Pipeline, Sunset Beach and Waimea Bay.

Although there are no hikes on Oahu to compare to the Kalalau Trail on Kauai or the trails in Haleakala Crater on Maui, there are trails to excite and to challenge the hiker. The hikes to Sacred Falls and into Makiki Valley are equal to any of the valley hikes on the other islands.

While most of the hikes on Oahu are short-distance, part-day hikes, I have included a wide selection of trips from short, easy family walks to long, difficult hikes. I have not included areas from which hikers are forbidden by law (protected watershed) or where the terrain is dangerous and unsafe even though local people may boast of their adventures into these places. Each year numerous injuries and some fatalities occur where people have hiked in spite of the prohibition. For example, a prominent sign at the end of the Manoa Falls Trail warns hikers not to climb above the falls, where the terrain is brittle and treacherous. Nevertheless, numerous injuries, rescues, and even deaths have been recorded there in recent years. However, good judgment and a regard for the time-tested rules of hiking are good protection.

The Bus

The fine public transportation system on Oahu deserves a special note. Many visitors make the mistake of renting a car when "The Bus" - yes, that's what it's called - is convenient, reliable, comfortable and inexpensive. The Bus makes regular stops at most places of interest on the island. Unquestionably, The Bus is the best bargain on Oahu. For one low fare you can ride nearly 100 miles around the island: From Honolulu, the Bus travels along the east coast, passes across the north shore and returns through the central part of Oahu to Honolulu. The system is so reliable that I have included instructions for taking The Bus to the trailheads.

Backpacks must be carried on the lap or stored under the seat. Call 848-5555 from 5:30 a.m. to 10 p.m. daily for information and schedules.

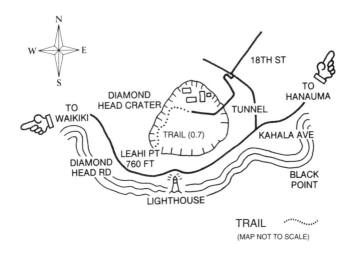

Diamond Head Trail

(Hiking Area No. 30)

Rating: Family.

Features: Panorama of greater Honolulu area, historical site, extinct volcanic crater.

Permission: Fee to enter.

Hiking Distance and Time: 0.7 miles, 1 hour, 550-feet gain.

Driving Instructions:

From Honolulu (4 miles, 1/4 hour) drive south on Kalakaua Ave., right on Diamond Head Road and around to east side of crater, left at sign marked "Civ-Alert USPFO" opposite 18th St. Follow road through tunnel into crater to parking area on left.

Bus Instructions:

From Waikiki on Kalakaua Ave., take bus #58 (Hawaii Kai/Sea Life Park) to 18th St. and Diamond Head Road at a sign marked "Civ-Alert USPFO." Follow this road into the crater.

Introductory Notes: Although the hike to the summit of Diamond Head is hot and dry, the panorama offered from the top and along the rim trail is striking. This is a "must" hike for the whole family. Although a large portion of the crater and the surrounding area are on a military reservation, the hiking trail is under the jurisdiction of the Division of State Parks.

Without question, Diamond Head is the most photographed and the most readily identifiable place in Hawaii. Before the arrival of Western man, the area was known as Leahi (lit., "casting point"). In the early 1800s British sailors found calcite crystals in the rocks on the slopes of the crater and thought they were diamonds. Following the discovery, the tuff crater was called Kaimana-Hila (lit., "Diamond Hill), and today the world-famous place is known as Diamond Head. Geologists estimate that the crater was formed some 100,000 years ago by violent steam explosions. During World War II Diamond Head was an important bastion for the protection of the island. Gun emplacements, lookout towers, and tunnels were concealed in and on the walls of the crater. Although abandoned in recent years, these places are interesting to investigate, particularly for children. It is helpful to carry a flashlight, since the trail passes through two short tunnels and up a spiral stairway.

On the Trail: The trailhead on the northwest side of the parking area is marked, and the trail is easy to follow to the summit. Kiawe (Prosopis pallida) trees abound on the floor of the crater. These valuable trees with fernlike leaves and thorny branches are the descendants of a single seed planted in 1828 by Father Bachelot, a priest, in his churchyard in Honolulu. The tree is a source not only of fuel and lumber but also of honey (produced from the flower), medicine, tannin and fodder, which is produced from its beanlike yellow pods containing 25% grape sugar.

As you continue along the gently rising trail to the first concrete landing and lookout, you should be able to identify a number of birds. Two species of doves, the barred dove (Geopelia striata) and the spotted dove (Streptopelia chinensis), are common and abundant on Oahu. The spotted dove, the larger of the two, has a band of black around the sides and back of the neck which is spotted with white. The barred dove is pale brown above, gray below, and barred with black. You should also see the beautiful, bright red, male cardinal (Richmondena cardinalis) with its orange beak and black face.

The concrete landing is the first of many lookout points along the trail. You have a good view of the crater and are able to distinguish some of the bunkers and gun emplacements on the slopes and on the crest of the crater. Follow the steps and the pipe railing to the first tunnel. You cannot see daylight at the end of the tunnel because it turns to the left at midpoint. A flashlight is not necessary to pass through the tunnel safely, but it is a comfort to small children since it is dark. As you leave the tunnel, investigate the rooms in the concrete building opposite the exit. They contained supplies and a power unit. Look for the bunker behind the building and hike to the left to a viewpoint over-looking the crater. A steep staircase - 99 steps - leads the hiker into a short tunnel at the end of which is an observation room and the first view of Waikiki and the greater Honolulu area. Look for the room containing a spiral stairway. Climb the stairway and then the ladder which takes you to the top and to the summit of Diamond Head. The concrete building at the summit is situated on top of Leahi Point at an elevation of 760 feet. Keep a watchful eye on children, for the summit's flanks are precipitous. The observation point at the summit provides a shady and comfortable picnic spot as well as a panoramic view.

It is possible to hike completely around the rim of the crater and to return to the parking lot by cutting through the brush, but the trail is steep and dangerous due to loose volcanic rock and ash. Do not attempt this alternative route to the parking area. You will find numerous observation points and gun emplacements around the rim similar to those at the summit.

Honolulu from Diamond Head

Honolulu Mauka Trail System (Makiki/Tantalus)

(Hiking Area No. 31)

Rating: See individual hikes.

Features: Waterfall, views of Honolulu, wild fruit, Job's tears, native and introduced flora, valley views.

Permission: None. Stop in at the Hawaii Nature Center in Makiki Valley for a map of the Honolulu Mauka Trail System. It is free and larger than the map provided in this book.

Hiking Distance and Time: See individual hikes.

Driving Instructions:

To Makiki Valley trailheads

From Ala Moana Shopping Center, drive north on Keeaumoku St to Makiki Heights Dr. and continue straight on paved drive in Forestry Baseyard (2135 Makiki Heights Dr.). Park on the right side behind the Nature Center.

To Tantalus trailheads

From Ala Moana Shopping Center, drive north on Keeaumoku St to Makiki Heights Dr. then go right on Tantalus Dr. (Trailheads are posted roadside).

To Moana Flats trailhead

From Waikiki, drive north on Manoa Road to road's end at Lyon Arboretum and trailhead.

To Judd Memorial trailhead
From Waikiki take H-1, turn right on Route 61 (Pali Highway), turn right on Old Pali Highway, right on Nuuanu Pali Drive for 0.7-mile to Reservoir No. 2 spillway just before bridge marked "1931."

Bus Instructions:

To Makiki Valley trailheads
From Waikiki/Kuhio Ave, take bus #2 ("School-Middle St") or bus #13 ("Liliha-Puunui") to Beretania/Keeaumoku Streets. Transfer to bus #17 ("Makiki") to Keeaumoku/Nehoa Streets. Walk up Keeaumoku to Makiki Heights Dr. and Forestry Baseyard and trailheads by Nature Center.

To Tantalus trailheads - No bus service.

To Moana Falls trailhead
From Ala Moana Center take bus #5 ("Moana") to end of the line (Kumuone St) and walk up Moana Road several blocks past Lyon Arboretum to trailhead.

To Judd Memorial Trail
From Waikiki take bus #4 (Nuuanu-Dowsett) to Nuuanu Pali Drive/Kimo Drive. Walk up Nuuanu Pali Drive to the Trailhead.

Introductory Notes: Oahu's Makiki Valley/Tantalus, a stones throw from Waikiki, offers more than a dozen short, easy-to-moderate rated trails for the family and several longer, more challenging treks for the outdoorsperson. Trails are posted and maintained by Na Ala Hele, Hawaii's Statewide Trail and Access Program.

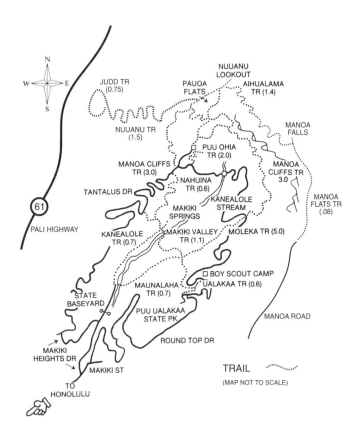

N

W E

S

JUDD TR
(0.75)

NUUANU
LOOKOUT

PAUOA
FLATS

AIHUALAMA
TR (1.4)

NUUANU TR
(1.5)

MANOA
FALLS

PUU OHIA
TR (2.0)

MANOA CLIFFS
TR (3.0)

MANOA
CLIFFS TR
3.0

NAHUINA
TR (0.6)

TANTALUS DR

KANEALOLE
STREAM

MANOA
FLATS TR
(.08)

MAKIKI
SPRINGS

61

PALI HIGHWAY

KANEALOLE
TR (0.7)

MAKIKI VALLEY
TR (1.1)

MOLEKA TR (5.0)

BOY SCOUT CAMP

MAUNALAHA
TR (0.7)

UALAKAA TR (0.6)

STATE
BASEYARD

PUU UALAKAA
STATE PK

MANOA ROAD

ROUND TOP DR

MAKIKI
HEIGHTS DR

MAKIKI ST

TO
HONOLULU

TRAIL

(MAP NOT TO SCALE)

To plan an outing, consult the map and trail descriptions below. Each trail narrative contains the distance, elevation gain/loss if 500 feet or more, a brief description of trail highlights and mention of some of the flora and fauna found trailside. There are six trails in Makiki Valley, three trails in the Tantalus area and two connecting trails (Nuuanu, p. 276 and

Aihualama, p. 277) from the Tantalus area to the two trails to which they lead (Judd Trail, p. 277 and Manoa Flats Trail, p. 278). If this is confusing, choices are simple by consulting the trail map and the accompanying trial narratives. You can readily plan several loop hikes.

Tantalus and Round Top Drives combine to make a popular auto tour above Honolulu. The many turnouts, which provide panoramas of Honolulu, are favorites of visitors and locals in the daytime and lovers in the evening. Local students named this area "Tantalus" after the mythical Greek king. Tantalus Mountain (2,013 feet) was so named, it is suggested, because as the students hiked, the peak seemed to recede. (You may recall that Tantalus was punished by being made to stand in a pool of water that receded each time he tried to drink).

You have a choice of numerous trailheads. Consult the map and the trail discription. Most of the trails are short and suitible for families with small children.

Makiki Valley Trails

Kanealole Trail, 0.7 mile, 1/2 hour, 500-feet gain (trail rating: family).

This trail on the west side of the Hawaii Nature Center and Kanealole Stream is usually wet and muddy, but it is a gentler ascent than the Maunalaha Trail on the east side. The trail follows an old road that was once used by work crews to control the growth in the valley. Although the hike is uphill, there is abundant shade along the trail, which makes for a fairly cool and enjoyable hike for the whole family. Look on the left side of the trail as you ascend for surinam cherries (Eugenia uniflora) which, when bright red, are quite sweet. This small, ovate cherry from Brazil is a local favorite for making jelly. The Kanealole Trail ends at a junction with the Makiki Valley Trail, that goes across the valley to the right. Go left a short distance on the Makiki Valley Trail to join the Nahuina Trail, which will take you to Tantalus.

Maunalaha Trail, 0.7 mile, 1/2 hour, 555-feet gain (trail rating: family).

From the east side of the Nature Center, the trail crosses a footbridge over Maunalaha Stream and begins an ascent that passes through avocado, juniper, eucalyptus and bamboo in the lower parts. Periodically, a break in the forest allows views of Honolulu and of Manoa Valley. You'll surely be able to identify the octopus, or umbrella tree,(Brassaia actinophylla) whose peculiar blossoms look like the long, spreading arms of an octopus. The new blossoms are first greenish-yellow, then light pink and finally deep red. At trail's end at the intersection with the Makiki Valley Trail, several trail choices are possible.

Makiki Valley Trail, 1.1 miles, 1 hour (trail rating: family).

This east-west trail traverses Makiki Valley. (The valley was named after a type of stone found here that was used as a weight for an octopus lure.) The trail-head on the west side is about 2 miles up Tantalus Drive from Makiki Heights Drive, north of a eucalyptus grove where the road makes a sharp turn. The trail-head on the east side is about at the midpoint of the Ualakaa Trail (p. 273).

From the Tantalus Drive trailhead, the trail descends eastward through a forest into Makiki Valley, passing the Nahuina Trail on the left (north) and, shortly, the Kanealole Trail on the right (south). At this second junction, pause to look for springs in the brush to the left of the junction. The grass and brush should be matted where other hikers have made their way to the springs, 30 feet north of the junction. It is an enchanting place to pause to enjoy the beauty and the solitude. It is also a place to pick Job's tears (Coix lacrymajobi), which are abundant. The black, blue-gray and white, pea-sized beans of this plant are favorites with local people, who string them into attractive necklaces, leis and rosaries. Ranging from one foot to six feet high, the plant is a coarse, branched grass with long, pointed leaves. The beans are easy for children to string with a needle and heavy thread.

From the junction, the trail turns in and out of small gulches and crosses a couple of small streams, passing through a richly foliated, forested valley. One of the many delights along this trail is the mountain apple (Eugenia malaccensis), which is abundant and within easy reach. What a treat! The apples are found on both sides of a stream in a very peaceful setting in which to pause and enjoy this succulent red fruit. Up the hill from the stream at an unmarked junction, the Moleka Trail goes to the left to meet the Manoa Cliffs Trail at Round Top Drive, the Makiki Valley Trail goes straight about 1/4 mile more to end where it meets the Ualakaa Trail, and the Maunalaha Trail to the right goes to Makiki Valley and the baseyard.

Nahuina Trail, 0.75 mile, 1/2 hour, 600-feet gain (trail rating: hardy family).

Nahuina was constructed by the Sierra Club's Hawaii Chapter, which organized volunteers in 1979 to link the Tantalus and Makiki Valley hiking areas (see map). The idea was good because there is a lot of hiking pleasure to be gained from the loop hikes now possible. From the Manoa Cliffs trailhead on Tantalus Drive, the Nahuina Trail is easy to find. It is about 150 yards down the road on the left side (east), at the end of a white guard rail. From the junction with the Makiki Valley Trail, the Nahuina Trail heads north to Tantalus Road.

On the trail, look for the common amakihi, a tiny, endemic, yellowish-green forest bird found on leafy braches in search for insects, nectar and fruit.

Moleka Trail, 0.75 mile, 1/2 hour (trail rating: hardy family).

Joining the Makiki Valley and Tantalus-Round Top, the Moleka Trail, like the Nahuina, was constructed in

1979 by volunteers organized under the leadership of the Sierra Club's Hawaii Chapter. Of the two trails, the Moleka is in good condition and is easy to locate and to follow. The trailhead on Round Top Drive is opposite the Manoa Cliffs trailhead, southeast of the turnout and parking area.

Ascending from Makiki Valley Trail, look for edible red thimbleberries growing on a small thorny bush with white flowers. The trail gently contours along the valley slope, providing numerous views into Makiki Valley. Before reaching Round Top Drive, you step into a natural garden of ti, ginger (both white and yellow), bamboo and the delightfully beautiful Heliconia (Heliconia humilis), or "lobster claw," so named because the bright red bracts are similar to boiled lobster claws.

Ualakaa Trail, 0.53 mile, 1/2 hour (trail rating: family).

Ualakaa (lit., "rolling sweet potato"), was constructed in 1980 by volunteers organized by the Sierra Club's Hawaii Chapter. The purpose was to connect Puu Ualakaa State Park with the Makiki/Tantalus hiking area.

The trailhead is 0.1 mile from inside the entrance of Ualakaa State Park at telephone pole #9 on the right side just as the road makes a sharp turn. From here, the trail ascends, paralleling Round Top Drive for a short distance until it meets, entering from the left, the Makiki Valley Trail. The Ualakaa Trail ends shortly on Round Top Drive just opposite Camp Ehrhorn, a Boy Scout camp.

Tantalus Trails

Manoa Cliffs Trail, 3.4 miles, 2 hours, 500-feet gain (trail rating: hardy family).

Just 3 miles up Tantalus Drive, a sign identifying the trail and a spur road that leads to a Hawaiian Telephone Co. facility mark the trailhead for the Manoa (lit., "vast") Cliffs Trail. The trail is well-maintained and easy to follow. You are likely to share the trail with students from the University of Hawaii, since the area is used as an outdoor classroom.

The initial, forested portion of this wide, well-maintained trail contours the hillside. A number of native and introduced plants, some of which are identified by markers, are found along the trail. According to the Division of Forestry, 33 native species of flora have been identified. You should not have any trouble finding guava and thimbleberry, two introduced plants whose fruit is edible. Guava (Psidium guajava) trees are particularly abundant throughout the area. The yellow, lemon-sized fruit is a tasty treat high in Vitamin C. Red thimbleberries (Rubus rosaefalius), which are also profuse, grow on a small, thorny bush with white flowers.

About 1 mile from the trailhead, you reach a junction. The trail to the left (north) is unnamed. At the junction with the unnamed trail, the Manoa Cliffs Trail makes a sharp right and follows switchbacks up a hill for 0.2 mile to the Manoa Cliffs/Puu Ohia trail junction (actually, a pair of junctions 30 feet apart). Puu Ohia leads north (left) down the hill and south (right) up the hill while the cliffs trail continues east.

The remaining part of the Manoa Cliffs Trail hike contours the hillside above Manoa Valley. Spectacular views of the valley are possible from a number of viewpoints. Keep a sharp eye on small children, however, for parts of the hillside along the trail are steep. There are a number of overgrown trails leading off both sides of the trail which should be avoided. One spur trail, a short distance east from the Manoa Cliffs/Puu Ohia junction, switchbacks up the hill to meet the Puu Ohia Trail. The Manoa Cliffs Trail turns south and emerges on Round Top Drive at the other trailhead for this hike, from where it is 1.4 miles west (right) to your car via the road or 0.9 mile west to the Puu Ohia trailhead.

Puu Ohia Trail, 0.75-mile 1/2 hours, 500-feet gain (trail rating: family).

The Puu Ohia (lit., "ohia tree hill") trailhead is easy to find. It is 0.5 mile from the Manoa Cliffs Trailhead near the uppermost point of Round Top and Tantalus Drives, where you will find a large parking area opposite the trailhead (the nearest street number is 4050).

The first 0.5 mile of the trail follows a circuitous route up a hill. The trail then straightens and goes along the side of the ridge a short distance to where a number of trails lead off down to the right. Bear left and follow the trail to where it meets a paved road, then follow the road to its end at a Hawaiian Telephone Co. facility. With luck you may spot the apapane, a deep-crimson bird with black wings and tail and a slightly curved bill. The population on Oahu of this endemic bird has been declining. The trail continues north from behind and to the left of the telephone building and descends to meet the Manoa Cliffs Trail.

Pauoa Flats Trail, 0.75 mile (trail rating: family).

Pauoa Flats is replete with Eucalyptus (Eucalyptus robusta) and paper-bark (Melaleuca leucandendra) trees. The eucalyptus has thick, pointed leaves with a capsule type fruit, while the distinguishing feature of the paper-bark tree is bark that can be peeled in sheets. This tree has been planted on the islands for conservation purposes in wet, boggy areas. Although the flats is level, it is usually wet and slippery and it has exposed roots which are hazardous and potential ankle-busters.

At trail's end you'll have a glorious view of Nuuanu Valley below.

Nuuanu Trail, 1.5 miles, 1,000-feet loss (trail rating: strenuous).

This is a steep, 1000-foot descent following 20-plus switchbacks to Nuuanu Stream and Nuuanu Drive from where bus transportation is available.

Be cautious as you descend, particularly if the trail is wet, and pause to enjoy periodic breaks in the forest to view Nuuanu Valley below. Norfolk Island trees dominate the lower portion of the trail. These majestic, perfectly symmetrical giants are not pines. They have tiny, overlapping leaves that have the appearance of a needle. The strong, straight trunks were once widely used for masts on ships. Today, many local artisans produce attractive bowls, which are very popular with locals and visitors.

Judd Trail, 0.75 mile (trail rating: family).

(see pp.266-267 for driving and bus instructions to trailhead.)

Dedicated the Charles S. Judd Memorial Grove in 1953, this forest in Nuuanu Valley was named in honor of the first "localboy" Territorial Forester.

The loop-trail follows the forest-reserve boundary near a residential area and then turns downhill toward Nuuanu Stream where you'll find numerous pools in which to cool-off, particularly if you have hiked from the Tantalus trails.

Above the stream, you'll find places where locals participate in mud sliding, an ancient Hawaiian sport popular with Hawaiian royalty. Participants would slide down the hill on pili grass or on ti leaves — today on a plastic sheet — to the pool below. The stream parallels Nuuanu Road where bus transportation is available.

Aihualama Trail, 1.3 miles (trail rating: hardy family).

From Pauoa Flats, the Aihualama trails descends through a bamboo forest, which offers some interesting sights and sounds as the wind passes through the bamboo. Views of Diamond Head and Waikiki are possible from a couple of vistas. The trail can be wet and muddy due to frequent showers throughout the year, but the rewards are great. Huge koa trees, with their crescent-shaped leaves, and interesting banyan trees with their aerial roots growing earthward from horizontal branches, combine with aromatic and delightfully beautiful ginger to excite the senses. At trail's end, Manoa Falls come into sight.

Manoa Flats Trail, 0.8 mile
(trail rating: family).

(See pp. 266-267 for driving and bus instructions to trailhead.)

The trail to Manoa (lit., "vast") Falls is easily accessible from downtown Honolulu, which probably accounts for its popularity. You can expect to share the trail and the pool with local people as well as visitors. Nevertheless, pack a lunch and make the trip to the falls, for it is worth the time.

A chain gate and a foot bridge at the end of the road mark the trailhead for the hike into Manoa Valley along Waihi (lit., "trickling water") Stream. Most of the trail is muddy and a bit slippery because heavy rains have washed away soil around trees and exposed their roots. The heavy rains also sustain a heavily foliated area where vegetation common to damp areas is abundant. The trail is easy to follow through the forest reserve. There are some fruit trees along the trail, but the likelihood of finding fruit is slim because of the popularity of the hike. The yellow, lemon-sized guava may be found as well as the popular mountain apple. This succulent apple is small and red, has a thin, waxy skin, and is usually ripe in June.

At midpoint, the canyon narrows and the footing becomes wetter. There are a number of larger pools where you may see hikers or residents swimming . You should be able to see the falls from a number of points along the trail. The junglelike setting at the falls makes for an enchanting place to swim and picnic if it is not too crowded.

The Division of Forestry prohibits entry into the closed watershed beyond the falls. Furthermore, numerous injuries and a few fatalities have been recorded as a result of people hiking in this prohibited area.

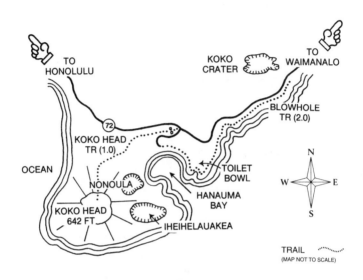

Hanauma Bay Trail

(Hiking Area No. 32)

Rating: Hardy Family.

Features: Swimming, snorkeling, tidepools, historical
sites, blowhole, views of coastal area.

Permission: Entrance fee.

Hiking Distance and Time: 2 miles, 1 1/2 hours.

Driving Instructions:

From Honolulu (12 miles, 1/2 hour) drive southeast on
H-1, which becomes Route 72, then right on Hanauma
Bay Road to parking lot.

Bus Instructions:
   From Waikiki at Kuhio, take the "Beach Bus" to Hanauma Bay.

Introductory Notes: To visit Oahu but fail to hike and swim at Hanauma is a mistake. Hanauma Bay is not only a strikingly beautiful place, but it also offers outstanding snorkeling.

On the Trail: In 1967 Hanauma Bay was declared a marine-life conservation district, which meant that no marine life could be caught here or injured in any manner. Consequently, it is a delightful experience to investigate tidepools or to snorkel and to observe the variety of sea life under water. Hanauma Bay was once a crater, until the sea broke through the southeast crater wall.

   From the beach, hike (left) along the shelf above the water on the east side of the bay. Be alert not only for interesting tidepools but also for waves which may splash onto the shelf. While the danger of being overcome by a wave is slight, it is wise to keep a watchful eye on the water. Be certain to visit the popular "toilet bowl" just beyond the far end of the bay. This interesting feature is a hole about 30 feet in circumference and 10 feet deep which is alternately filled and emptied from beneath as waves come in and recede. Bathers jump or slide into the bowl as it fills. Then, to escape, they scramble out when the water rises to the top of the bowl.

   From the "toilet bowl" you can climb to the ridge overlooking the bay or follow the coastline around Palea (lit., "brushed aside") Point. From here to the blowhole you are likely to find many local people fishing so pause to examine their catches and to exchange pleasantries.

You will find that a smile and an inquisitive attitude will usually make a friend.

After the first mile, you may choose to hike to the road and to follow it to the blowhole, since the ledge above the water is narrow, and one needs some agility to climb, crawl and jump over the lava while trying to avoid the crashing surf. However, by timing the waves and by using good judgment, you can make it to the blowhole at Halona (lit., "peering place") Point. A blowhole is a narrow vent in the lava through which water is forced by the charging surf. The blowhole at Halona Point "blows" water geysers 30-50 feet into the air, depending on surf conditions. It is a happy terminus to a delightful hike.

Toilet Bowl

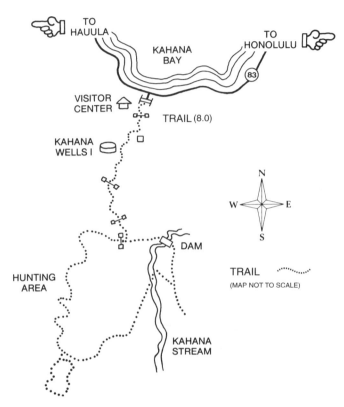

Kahana Valley Trail

(Hiking Area No. 33)

Rating: Hardy family.

Features: Mountain apples, rose apple, swimming, "living park."

Permission: None. Check at visitor center for current trail conditions.

Hiking Distance and Time: 8 mile loop, 5-6 hours.
Driving Instructions:

From Honolulu (26 miles, 1 hour) drive northwest on H-1, then right on Route 63 (Likelike Highway), then left on Route 83 to Kahana Valley State Park.

Bus Instructions:

From Ala Moana Center take bus #55 (Kaneohe / Circle Island) to Kahana Valley State Park.

Introductory Notes: Kahana (lit., "cutting") Valley State Park has been designated by the state legislature as a "living park." By definition, such a park is intended "to nurture and foster native Hawaiian culture and spread knowledge of its values and ways. ...This goal is to be achieved by the individuals living there, who will educate the public."

In July 1980 a committee composed of state-park officials and valley residents was formed to develop a program which will be offered to visitors. In the late summer of that year, the state completed a visitor center and a pavilion where some of the 140 valley residents and others will exhibit their skills so that visitors may learn about the traditional Hawaiian way of life in Kahana Valley. Inquire at the visitor center for current programs.

Kahana was once a much larger, thriving self-contained community where the people practiced the traditional concept of "ohana" - family units related by blood, marriage and adoption. Ample annual rainfall (average of 75 inches along the coast to 300 inches in the back of the valley) sustained the farms, and the ocean provided seafood for the residents. To date, the Bishop Museum has identified 120 small wet terraces and 12 irrigation canals constructed to grow taro.

The Kahana Valley hike is an enjoyable walk for the entire family.

On the Trail: From the visitor center, a jeep road leads into the valley for a little over a mile, to a fourth and last gate and the beginning of a hunting area and of a loop trail into the valley. Along this first mile, you pass some demonstration pavilions and public restrooms. Shortly, you pass the "Kahana Well" facility on the right, then a couple of hunter checking stations, and, just before the beginning of the loop trail, a papaya grove.

At the last gate, a large sign on the right side inside the gate identifies the entrance to the hunting area. From this junction one jeep road goes left for a couple of hundred yards and ends at the stream and a dam. The road to the right, bordered by hala trees, ends in about 1/4 mile at a large water tank. A foot trail continues beyond and leads into the valley. After crossing a small stream, the trail passes through a mountain-apple orchard. In season - usually between June and August - these succulent red apples are the highlight of the trip.

Beyond a second small stream crossing, the trail descends to a small clearing surrounded by hala trees.The trail to a short loop trail goes right and shortly reaches a junction where the trail goes right and left. The trail to the left descends to Kahana Stream. It's a pleasant, easy but very wet hike to

Kahana Stream. It is necessary to make several stream crossings throughout the loop, but you'll find several generous pools in which to swim. One large pool is under the shade of a giant mango tree.

Just before the stream, avoid a number of spur trails that go in different directions. The trails were probably made by hunters, by hikers looking for a place to cross the stream when the water is high, and by people looking for rose apple (Eugenia jambos), an edible, egg-shaped golden fruit with rosewater taste and odor. Related to the mountain apple, the rose-apple tree is an evergreen with narrow, pointed leaves and large, greenish-white pompon flowers.

Returning to the main loop trail, go right. The trail descends to the stream opposite a concrete water intake that is under a tangle of hau branches. Cross the stream here and crawl under the limbs to the trail, which becomes clear a short distance beyond the hau trees. The trail ascends out of this small gulch for 0.2-mile to where it makes a sharp left and descends 1/2 mile to the stream and the dam.

Because of the heavy rainfall in the valley, it is not always easy to make the stream crossing. If you make it, be alert for the trail-marking tape on trees, which will direct you to the dam and the gauging station. Be cautious when walking on the dam. It can be very slippery. Once across the dam, a jeep road ascends to the junction with the main trail. Go right at the junction to return to the trailhead.

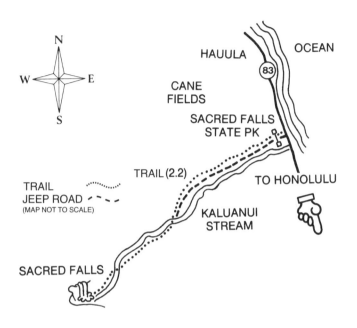

Sacred Falls Trail

(Hiking Area No. 34)

Rating: Hardy family.

Features: Waterfall, swimming, fruits.

Permission: None, but DO NOT hike if the trail is closed. There is a danger of flash floods during rainy periods.

Hiking Distance and Time: 2.2 miles one way, 1 1/2 hours.

Driving Instructions:

From Honolulu (28 miles, 1 1/4 hours) drive northwest on H-1, turn right on Route 61 (Pali Highway), then left on Route 83 to the sign "Sacred Falls State Park" on the

left.
Bus Instructions:
From Ala Moana Center take bus #52 (Kaneohe / Circle
Island) to Sacred Falls State Park.
Introductory Notes: Kaliuwaa (lit., "canoe hold" or "canoe leak") is the Hawaiian name for Sacred Falls. Probably the name was changed because "Kaliuwaa" is difficult
to pronounce and because "Sacred Falls" sounds more
romantic to most tourists. In truth, ancient Hawaiian belief
regards the entire valley as sacred to the gods. Legend
holds that the pool at the base of the falls is bottomless and
leads to another world where a demon lives. The waves in
the pool are thought to represent the struggle between the
demon and the thrust of the falls, which prevents him from
entering this world. Interestingly, another Hawaiian name
for the falls and pool is Kaliuwaa, which literally means
"the big pit." To pacify the gods thought to live in the area,
believers wrap a stone in a ti leaf and place it along the
trail. They believe this act will protect them from falling
rocks. Don't miss this hike. Although the trail is usually
muddy, it is a fairly easy stroll for the family and offers
fruits, picnicking and swimming.

On the Trail: From the trailhead it is 1.2 miles on a cane
road to the valley trail. Ahead, you can see the narrow
canyon that contains the falls. The road terminates at a
large, flat, grassy area that once served as a parking lot. On
the left side of this open place, the road becomes a trail,
which then crosses a dry stream bed and ascends gently
into the canyon. Shortly, the trail reaches Kaliuwaa
Stream, where it is necessary to rock-hop or wade.

In addition to the legends mentioned above, this enchanting lush island paradise is said to be the home of

Trail to Sacred Falls

Kamapuaa (lit., "child of a hog"), who is half human and half swine. Near the end of the valley to the left of the trail, you will cross at the base of a dry fall. This is the site, legend recounts, where Kamapuaa turned himself into a giant hog so that his followers could escape a pursuing army by climbing up his back to safety on the ledge above. The deep impression where water only occasionally falls is said to have been made by the weight and size of his body. Mountain apple trees abound here and when ripe, this succulent, red, pear-shaped fruit is a treat.

The falls can be heard crashing to the valley floor and can be seen around the next turn in the trail after a stream crossing. The valley walls rise to 1600 feet, but the falls drop only 87 feet. The generous pool at the base is usually muddy and very cold. You might wish to swim or splash in the stream just below the pool. In any event, there is plenty of room for a picnic on the large rocks in this cool, shaded canyon.

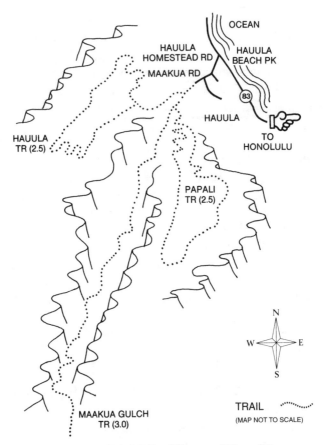

Hauula Valley Trails

(Hiking Area No. 35)

Rating: See individual hikes.

Features: Views of valley and coastal area, swimming, waterfall, fruits, native and introduced flora.

Permission: None.

Hiking Distance and Time: See individual hikes.

Driving Instructions:

From Honolulu (30 miles, 1 1/4 hours) drive northwest on H-1, right on Route 61 (Pali Highway), left on Route 83 to Hauula, left on Hauula Homestead Road opposite the north end of Hauula Beach Park for 0.2 mile and park at the intersection with Maakua Road.

Bus Instructions:

From Ala Moana Center take bus #52 (Kaneohe / Circle Island) to Hauula Beach Park. Cross the highway and walk up Hauula Homestead Road to the trailhead.

Introductory Notes: Three good hikes, camping and swimming await the outdoorsperson in this Hawaiian community. In Hauula (lit., "abundant hau") you will find old Hawaii mixed with the new. You will find local people surf fishing, throwing a net, "talking story" and having 3-4 generation ohana ("family") picnics on the beach. There are not many tourists who hike these trails, but you are likely to encounter local school children with their teacher or Boy Scouts with their leader.

Hauula Trail, 2.5 miles loop, 1 1/2 hours, 600-feet gain/loss (trail rating: hardy family).

Walk straight into the woods between the houses on Maakua Road. A paved driveway bears right to a private residence and our trail swings left on a dirt road which leads to a trail register. A short distance beyond, the Hauula Trail goes right, the Maakua Gulch Trail goes straight ahead and the Papali (Maakua Ridge) Trail goes left.

The Hauula Trail passes through some heavy brush and then follows switchbacks up a ridge to where Norfolk Island pines dominate. The fallen needles provide a soft underfooting and make the air aromatic. At midpoint along the ridge, do not take the trail entering on the right but bear left up the ridge. The trail switchbacks up the ridge, traverses Waipilopilo (lit., "smelly water") Gulch, and then ascends along another ridge overlooking Kaipapau (lit., "shallow sea") Valley, from which you have good views of the Koolau Mountain Range and of the east-side coastline and of Hauula. The route then gently slopes and descends to join the initial portion of the trail, on which you retrace your steps.

Maakua Gulch Trail, 3 miles one-way, 3 hours, 1,100-feet gain (trail rating: strenuous).

Walk straight into the woods between the houses on Maakua Road. A paved driveway bears right to a private residence and our trail swings left on a dirt road which leads to a trail register. A short distance beyond, the Hauula Trail goes right, the Maakua Gulch Trail goes straight ahead and the Papali (Maakua Ridge) Trail goes left.

If it is raining or the stream water is high, do not hike into the valley. Flash flooding is possible.

Maakua Gulch becomes narrower and narrower, and the trail twists and turns along a route which crisscrosses the stream countless times. Be prepared to get wet and to rock-hop throughout the last half of the hike, since the trail is in the stream bed there. The narrow canyon and its high, steep walls make this an enchanting hike. Another compensation is the frequent clusters of red mountain apple trees and a good supply of guava trees. The beautiful kukui (Aleurites moluccana) tree is common in the gulch. Nicknamed the "candlenut tree," the kukui tree was a valuable resource until the 20th century. Kukui-nut oil was burned for light, the trunk was used to make canoes if the more durable koa tree was not available, and beautiful and popuular leis were made of the nuts. To make a lei, each nut must be sanded, filed and polished to a brilliant luster that is acquired from its own oil. Kukui is also the Hawaii State tree. The hike ends at the base of a small cascade - or, if you're an expert scrambler, the base of a small waterfall just above. At the bottom of the waterfall and the bottom of the cascade are pools large enough for a cooling dip.

Papali Trail, 2.5 mile loop, 2 hours, 800-feet gain/loss (trail rating: hardy family).

Walk straight into the woods between the houses on Maakua Road. A paved driveway bears right to a private residence and our trail swings left on a dirt road which leads to a trail register. A short distance beyond, the Hauula Trail goes right, the Maakua Gulch Trail goes straight ahead and the Papali (Maakua Ridge) Trail goes left.

The Papali (lit., "small cliff or slope") Trail enters a grove of hau (Hibiscus tiliaceus) trees at the trailhead. In the wild, this yellow-flowered hibiscus grows twisting and branching along the ground, forming an impenetrable mass of tangled branches. The lightweight hau wood was used for canoe outriggers, fish floats, adze handles and fence posts. Maakua Stream slowly trickles through the hau grove and must be crossed. The trail then climbs sharply along switchbacks, passing concrete slabs that once supported water tanks. The trail heads toward the mountains for about a mile and then turns east and descends into Papali Gulch and crosses tiny Papali Stream. Although you'll share the scenic stream crossing with mosquitoes, pause in this serene place. Civilization seems a long way off. From here, the trail ascends along the ridge, until it rejoins the earlier trail segment near the concrete slabs. In the last mile of the hike you have outstanding views of Hauula town and north to Laie Point.

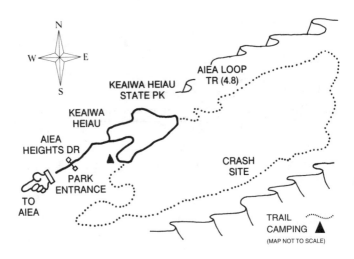

Aiea Loop Trail

(Hiking Area No. 36)

Rating: Hardy family.

Features: Views of Pearl Harbor, fruits, camping, Keaiwa Heiau.

Permission: Camping fee. Permits from Division of State
Parks (see Appendix).

Hiking Distance and Time: 4.8 miles loop, 3 hours.

Driving Instructions:

From Honolulu (12 miles, 1/2 hour) drive northwest on
H-1, bear left at sign "Aiea #78," go right at "Aiea"
turnoff and follow Moanalua Road downhill to a right
turn on Aiea Heights Drive, and go to its end. After
entering the park, follow the one-way road to the northeast end of the park and a sign marking the upper Aiea
Loop trailhead.

Bus Instructions:
From Ala Moana Center take bus #11 (Honolulu\Aiea Heights) to Aiea and to the Kaamilo/Aiea Heights Drive junction. Walk up Aiea Heights Drive to Keaiwa Heiau State Park and to the trailhead.

Introductory Notes: Take time to visit the remains of the heiau (a pre-Christian place of worship) by the park entrance. Keaiwa (lit., "the mystery") Heiau was an ancient healing temple where a priest by the same name was said to have had mysterious healing powers. Keaiwa used the plants grown in the area for medicinal purposes, and instructed novitiates in the art of healing. As is true at so many heiaus in the Islands, little remains of the structures, since they were made mainly of wood and grass. Keaiwa Heiau State Park offers a good family hiking trail, first-class picnic grounds in the forested setting, and a comfortable campground. The Aiea (lit., "Nothocestrum tree") Loop Trail is likely to be crowded on weekends when local people come to enjoy the park and to hike.

On the Trail: The first part of the trail snakes along the ridge on a wide and well-maintained path where you can identify thin-barked eucalyptus, symmetrical Norfolk Island pine and ironwood (Casuarina equisetifolia), with its long, thin, drooping, dull green needles. Many of these trees are the result of a reforestation program begun by Thomas McGuire in 1928. The shade from the big trees and the trade winds make this part of the hike both cool and pleasurable.

The trail makes a sharp right turn at 1.6 miles, where a trail to Koolau Ridge departs eastward, and then follows the ridge above North Halawa (lit., "curve") Stream, from which views of the Koolau Mountains and North Halawa

Valley are good. The loop trail descends through a forest of trees where you will find some native trees, including koa and ohia lehua. At the 3-mile point, look to the right of the trail for the remains of a C-47 cargo plane that crashed in 1943. Just beyond the crash site, a bridle path leads off to the left to Camp Smith and then the loop trail swings to the right and downhill to cross Aiea Stream. Before crossing the stream, you may choose to stroll along a trail to the left which follows the stream. The Aiea Loop trail crosses the stream and then climbs up to the campground and the lower Aiea Loop trailhead, which is just across the grass below the only toilet building in the camping area.

Sugar cane - Hawaiian candy bars

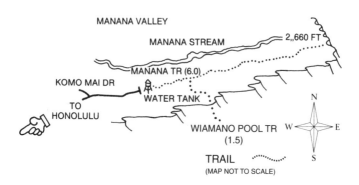

Manana Trails

(Hiking Area No.37)

Rating: See individual hikes.

Features: Views from the Koolau Mountain Range, native and introduced flora, swimming, waterfalls.

Permission: None.

Hiking Distance and Time: See individual hikes.

Driving Instructions:

From Honolulu (15 miles, 1/2 hour) drive northwest on H-1 to Pearl City (Exit 10), bear right on Moanalua Road to its end, then right on Waimano Home Road (0.7-mile), and finally left on Komo Mai Drive to the end.

Bus Instructions:

From Ala Moana Center take bus #53 (Honolulu/Pacific Palisades) to Pearl City Shopping Center (Kamehameha Highway and Waimano Home Road intersection). Transfer to Pearlridge-Pearl City Shuttle bus and take to Komo Mai Drive. Walk up Komo Mai Drive to trailhead.

Introductory Notes: The trail to Waimano Pool is a relatively easy hike except for a steep portion from the ridge into the valley. Local hiking clubs periodically perform maintenance on the trail, but it can become overgrown in a short period of time.

The Manana Trail is one of a number of trails which take you to peaks atop the Koolau Mountain Range. This trail is little traveled and is overgrown in places, and should be attempted only by skilled hikers. (It is possible to connect with the Waimano Trail by following the cliffs to the south, but the connecting route is very dangerous and not advised). Rain and mud are frequently encountered in this relatively pristine place. If you are looking for solitude and for the joys as well as the trials present in a rain forest, then Manana will satisfy you.

Waimano Pool Trail, 1.5 miles, 1 1/2 hours, (trail rating: hardy family).

On the Trail: A paved pedestrian passageway leads 0.4-mile to a water tank.Shortly thereafter, you'll pass a powerline tower on the left. Strawberry guava is abundant along this portion of the trail. The wide, well-defined trail dips and then begins to ascend a rise. Here, the Manana Trail goes left and the pool trail, which isn't posted, goes right. The trail may be obscured by eucalyptus leaves. Be cautious and alert as you descend into the valley. Portions of the trail may be overgrown before reaching the stream. Watch for rocks and exposed tree roots eucalyptus, guava and koa trees are abundant along the lower part of the trail. When the trail levels, the falls and the stream should come into view. You'll find numerous places to swim, particularly during the rainy season. It's a delightful place to picnic.

Manana Trail, 6 miles, 4 hours, 1700-feet gain (trail rating: strenuous)

On the Trail: A paved pedestrian passageway leads 0.4-mile to a water tank. Shortly thereafter, you´íll pass a powerline tower on the left. Strawberry guava found trailside, when in season, provide a tasty treat. The wide, well-defined trail dips and then ascends to reach a junction where your trail goes left and the Waimano Pool Trail goes right. The Manana Trail climbs 1700 feet to a peak atop the Koolau Range. For your protection, stay on the ridgeline and avoid the side trails, most of which lead to Manana Stream to the north (left) or Waimano Stream to the south. Time permitting, you may wish to hike to Manana Stream for a swim.

The trail passes under a canopy of eucalyptus trees and some koa trees, which are struggling to overcome the revages of a severe fire in 1972. Sandalwood trees (Santalum freycinetianum), once flourished here and throughout Hawaii. An important source of income in earlier times for the islands, the wood was exported for use in furniture and for its oil and perfume. In fact, China imported so much sandalwood that the Chinese once called Hawaii the "Sandalwood Islands."

The trail is rough and is overgrown in portions of the last three miles so be alert. The trail traverses a series of saddles along the ridge. A variety of ferns and low scrub dominate the upper part of the trail and seem to reach out to scratch and cut the legs and arms, so protective clothing is well-advised.Strong winds greet the hiker at the summit, and on a cloud free day,views into Kaalaea (lit., "the ocherous earth") Valley and beyond to Kaneohe Bay and the Makapu Peninsula are possible.

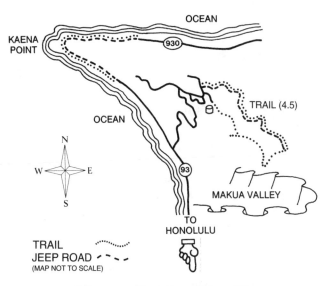

Kuaokala Trail

(Hiking Area No. 38)

Rating: Strenuous.

Features: Views of mountain and coastal area, fruits, camping.

Permission: Permit to hike and camp from the Division of Forestry (see Appendix).

Hiking Distance and Time: 4.5-mile loop, 3 hours, 800-feet gain/loss.

Driving Instructions:

From Honolulu (41 miles, 2 hours) drive northwest on H-1, which becomes Route 93 when the freeway ends. Drive past Makua town to a military road and a guard shack on the right just before the end of the paved road. Go right on the military road and check in at the guard shack. Drive 2.6 miles on the military road to the designated parking area.

Bus Instructions:

From Ala Moana Center take bus #51 (Honolulu-Makaha) to the end of the line near the surfing beach north of Makaha. Walk or hitchhike to the military road and guard shack.

Introductory Notes: A good hike, solitude and magnificent views are what you will find in the Kuaokala (lit., "back of the sun") Forest Reserve. The access road is under military jurisdiction, so permits are a must.

On the Trail: The trailhead and the designated parking place are one and the same. If you look back about 100 yards along the road you drove on and then to the left to a water tank, you will see the point at which you will emerge from the loop hike. The route descends on the paved road next to the parking area and continues on a dirt jeep road for 2.8 miles. The paved part of the road is lined with guava trees whose fruit is some of the sweetest I have ever eaten. These lemon-sized fruits are yellow and soft when ripe.

The trail makes a number of dips and turns in and out of small gulches which are heavily shaded by eucalyptus, pine, and cypress trees. After about one mile the trail ascends a ridge over open country and then reaches a number of points from which panoramas are possible of the saddle area between the two mountain ranges of Oahu, of the Koolau Mountains to the east and of the north shore. These viewpoints are pleasant places to pause. From the second vista point, at a gate and cattle guard, look to the front across a gulch to the ridge at the head of the gulch.

You will be hiking along that ridge overlooking Makua Valley. From the second vista point, the trail makes a steep descent and snakes over the gulch's floor before ascending to the ridgeline. Just before the ridge, at the 2.6-mile point at a turnout on the left, the remains of the Kuaokala shack are partly visible through the tall grass. From here, the foot trail is just 0.2 mile. A short distance from the abandoned shack, you reach a four-road junction. Follow the road to the front-right a short distance to a turnout which was once the start of a jeep road and which leads uphill to a group of eucalyptus trees. At this point you have your first view of Makua (lit., "parents") Valley.

The footpath part of the Kuaokala Trail begins to the right from the viewpoint overlooking Makua Valley and descends west along the north ridge above Makua Valley. After a descent, the trail ascends to a perch 1800 feet above the Makua Valley floor, where views of the valley and the west coast of Oahu are outstanding. Then the trail makes another descent and begins to turn north through open forest. The "golf ball" at the Kaena Point Satellite Tracking Station at the trailhead is now visible. The trail continues a circuitous path through the forest until it reaches a trail junction at the 4.0-mile point. The spur trail straight ahead ascends a short distance to a viewpoint, and the main trail turns to the right. Take the spur trail and enjoy the views. It is a good lunch spot. Return to the main trail and follow it to the water tank. Then walk down the paved road from the tank to the main road and turn right to reach the trailhead.

Appendix

For Maui, Lanai, and Molokai

Superintendent, Haleakala National Park (write)

P.O. Box 369,
Makawao, HI 96768

• park information
• crater cabin reservations

Haleakala National Park Headquarters (in person)

Crater Road
☎ (808) 572-4400

• park information
• crater camping permits
• crater cabin keys

Online: http://www.nps.gov/hale/index.htm

Division of State Parks

54 So. High Street
State Office Building
Wailuku, HI 96793
☎ (808) 984-8109

• camping permits
• cabin rental reservations
• camping permits for Molokai

Online: http://hawaii.gov/dlnr/dsp/index.html

Maui County Department of Parks & Recreation

War Memorial Gym
Kaahumanu Avenue
Wailuku, HI 96793
☎ (808)270-7389

• camping permits

Online: http://www.co.maui.hi.us/ (search - "camping")

Maui County Dept. of Parks and Recreation (Molokai)

P.O. Box 1055
Kaunakakai, HI 96748
☎ (808) 553-3204

• camping permits
  for One Alii (Molokai)

Online: (same as above)

Lanai Company (Private)

Lanai City, HI 96763
☎ (808) 565-3000

• camping permits for
  Hulopoe Beach

Camp Pecusa (Private)

800 Olowalu Village
Lahaina, HI 96761
☎ (808) 661-4303

• camping and cabin permits

For Oahu

Division of State Parks
1151 Punchbowl Street   • camping permits
Room 310
Honolulu, HI 96813
☎ (808) 587-0300
   Online: http://www.hawaii.gov/dlnr/dsp/index.html

State Division of Forestry
1151 Punchbowl Street   • hiking permits
Room 325   • camping & shelter use permits
Honolulu, HI 96813
☎ (808) 587-0166
   Online: (same as above)

Honolulu County Department of Parks & Recreation
Honolulu Municipal Building
650 So. King Street   • camping permits
Honolulu, HI 96813
☎ (808) 523-4525 or 27
   Online: http://www.co.honolulu.hi.us/parks/permits.htm

Friends of Malaekahana (Private)
56-335 Kamehameha Hwy   • Cabin and camping permits
Kahuku, HI 96731   for Makaekahana State Park
☎ (808) 293-1736

For Hawaii

Superintendent, Hawaii Volcanoes National Park
Hawaii 96718   • park information
☎ (808) 985-6000   • hiking permits
                               • camping permits
   Online: http://www.nps.gov/havo/visitor/visit..htm

Volcano House, Hawaii Volcanoes National Park
P.O. Box 53   • rental camper cabins
Hawaii 96718   for Namakani Paio
(808) 967-7321   • hotel rooms at Volcano
                                 House
   Online: (same as above)

Hawaii County Department of Parks & Recreation
25 Aupuni Street   • camping permits
Hilo, HI 96720
☎ (808) 961-8311
    Online: http://www.hawaii-county.com/parks/permit.htm

Hawaii County Transit System
25 Aupuni Street   • bus information and schedules
Hilo, HI 96720
☎ (808) 961-8744

Division of State Parks
P.O. Box 936   • camping permits
75 Aupuni Street   • rental cabin information &permits
Hilo, HI 96720   • hunting and fishing requirements
☎ (808) 974-6200
    Online: http://www.hawaii.gov/dlnr/dsp/index.html

For Kauai

Division of State Parks
State Building, Room 306   • camping permits for
3060 Eiwa Street   state parks and for Kalalau Trail
P.O. Box 1671   • hiking information
Lihue, HI 96766
☎ (808) 274-3444
    Online: http://www.hawaii.gov/dlnr/dsp/index.html

State Division of Forestry
State Building, Room 306   • hiking information
3060 Eiwa Street
P.O. Box 1671
Lihue, HI 96766
☎ (808) 274-3433
    Online: (same as above)

Kauai County Department of Parks & Recreation
4444 Rice St.   • camping permits
Lihue, HI 96766
☎ (808) 241-6660
    Online: http://www.kauaigov.org/parks.htm

Kokee Lodge Ventures, Inc • Kokee cabin information
P.O. Box 819   and reservations
Waimea, Hawaii 96796
☎ (808) 335-6061
          Online: http://www.alternative-hawaii.com/accom/kccspp.htm

Index

Index